GLOBALIZATION AND THE HARMONIZATION OF LAW

JARROD WIENER

PINTER
London and New York

PINTER

A Cassell Imprint
Wellington House, 125 Strand, London WC2R 0BB
370 Lexington Avenue, New York, NY 10017-6550

First published 1999

British Library Cataloguing in Publication Data
A catalogue record for this book is available from the British Library.

ISBN 1 85567 576 5 (Hardback)
1 85567 577 3 (Paperback)

Library of Congress Cataloging-in-Publication Data
Wiener, Jarrod.
Globalization and the harmonization of law / Jarrod Wiener.
p. cm.
Includes bibliographical references and index.
ISBN 1-85567-576-5 (hardback)
ISBN 1-85567-577-3 (paperback)
1. Law—International unification. 2. Commercial law. I. Title.
K605 .W54 1999
341.7'53—dc21 98-52850
CIP

Typeset by BookEns Ltd, Royston, Herts.
Printed and bound in Great Britain by Biddles Ltd, Guildford and King's Lynn

CONTENTS

	Preface	vii
	Abbreviations	xiii
1	Introduction: on governing a permeable society	1
2	From public to private international governance	20
3	Harmonizing the regulation and supervision of international banks	41
4	Harmonizing the control of money laundering	82
5	Harmonizing copyrights on the Internet	100
6	The efficacy of harmonization and pressures for 'harmonization spread'	134
7	The harmonization of private international commercial law: the *Lex Mercatoria*	151
8	Conclusion: Re-establishing protective jurisdiction in the era of globalization – empire of law?	184
	Select Bibliography	199
	Index	220

To Sarah

PREFACE

The idea for this book came to me one bitter cold, grey morning in February 1995 while I hurried across the campus of the University of Kent at Canterbury – though, as usual, I took a few seconds to look down the hill and admire the mist encircling the Cathedral. I was returning to my study from a lecture on the harmonization of private international trade law by Dr A. M. F. Maniruzzaman of the Kent Law School. Appropriately, this book began on a campus overlooking a medieval trading city as I pondered the revival and codification, in the 'globalized' international political economy, of anational rules, the *Lex Mercatoria,* developed by traders in Europe long before the Westphalian system emerged. What struck me in particular was that the high degree of interconnectedness among international traders in the post-Second World War era had led them – and many lawyers and international organizations – to demand an internationally harmonized system of law akin to that which existed before Europe was carved up into distinct sovereign states. After a period in which the *Carta Mercatoria* and other documents, and the repeated practice and custom of the traders themselves, established a rules-based system for the conduct of trade, sovereign states emerged and exercised their powers to make their own laws according to national, cultural, and religious peculiarities, or worse, for prestige or for the sake of being different. Regulatory differences created risk. Could it be that 'globalization' had rendered the world of international trade so small that for practical purposes 'progress' meant going back to a system of harmonized regulation that pre-dated the exercise of carving up territory into sovereign-controlled regulatory spaces?

The question of whether 'progress' in international trade law really meant going back to the norms and rules common to most of Europe before the Dark Ages remains an unresolved question. To be sure, there is great debate among international lawyers about whether there is much similarity between the thirteenth-century *Carta Mercatoria* and, say, the ICC's INCOTERMS. While I had become bemused by this debate in which I had immersed myself perhaps far too deeply, I was relieved to see that disciplines other than International Relations also engage in fairly serious navel-gazing. But the theoretical question remained: is the hyper-interconnectedness that is (sometimes) referred to as 'globalization' leading to an erosion of state sovereignty – autonomy, difference – over national (municipal) legislation in favour of some common international standard?

This question was precisely what I had been hoping to answer when I decided, in the autumn of 1994, to read for an LLM in International, Commercial, and European Law. My 'home' discipline of International Relations had only just begun to debate the political, economic and social consequences of globalization. What about the legal consequences? And, if there are any, what political, social and economic implications follow from an end of difference? Having had little exposure to the discipline of law – perhaps lawyers already knew the answer – gaining formal training seemed like a good place to start. I am grateful to my Head of Department, Professor A. J. R. Groom, for permitting me to indulge this interest by reading for the law degree, and to Anne Rushworth and others in the Staff Development office at the University of Kent for helping me to finance it.

Having read widely in this sister discipline, I found that lawyers and regulators were most certainly grappling with the effects of globalization on the law, and the questions they were grappling with were fascinating. For instance, the technology of the Internet affords a person in State A the means through which to commit a crime in State B without actually going, in person, to State B. A person in State A can break into a computer network of a bank in State B and transfer the money to State C. Where does the crime occur? Which state's law applies? Another example could be that a person in State A defames a person in State B, but the defamatory statements are read in numerous states, say from a bulletin board located in State C. Where does the act of defamation take place, in the state where the statements are written, in the state where they are read, or where the injury to the other person is manifest? Clearly, technology had connected societies and individuals located in different parts of the globe to such an extent that the potential for a myriad of social relations had advanced much faster than the social institutions to govern those relations. Individuals had become global actors, yet the frameworks establishing rules, rights, and duties remained tied to a territory, and tied to a pre-information age conception of society.

The most interesting issue, it seemed to me, was what would happen if State B had legislation to outlaw electronic theft and electronic defamation but State A did not? Consider copyrights for information on the Internet. If State A had legislation to protect rights-holders, but State B did not, the intellectual property of those in State A would be at risk from those in State B reaching into State A with a computer and a modem, and indeed, this would make a mockery of State A's legislation due to its inability to enforce its domestic laws outside of its territory. In this connection, lawyers were conceiving ways to 'harmonize' the laws and regulations of different states, i.e., to make them more alike. Harmonization in itself might not stop a person performing illegal acts, but if the acts were defined as illegal in both State A and State B, a person could more easily enforce his or her rights.

It began to strike me that, just as the highly interconnected world of international trade was demanding common standards, norms and laws to mitigate differences in national systems of regulation, so lawyers and regulators were suggesting that issues that arise due to the interconnectedness of societies through communication technologies could be far more easily dealt with if states were to adopt similar laws.

While the debates surrounding these issues as the discipline of law came to terms with globalization certainly were interesting, there was no overall conceptual framework in that discipline that would help me to marry the concerns at the micro-level, with which lawyers mostly were interested, and international governance, in which I primarily was interested. Similarly, there was little in International Relations theory, the majority of which concentrates on the macro-organization of policy – mechanisms through which states navigate the constraints of an anarchical system through public policy coordination. International Relations has appreciated for a very long time the interface between domestic policy and foreign policy – that some foreign policy is domestic policy and, conversely, that some domestic policy is foreign policy. It has also appreciated for a long time the interface between policy, both domestic and foreign, with the codification of standards of conduct in public international law, and in yet 'softer' standards of conduct such as those embodied in 'international regimes'. However, apart from a few theories of integration, such as functionalism, and parallel national action, few theoretical frameworks existed to conceptualize how the small – the incremental, functional, issue-oriented, and therefore diffuse – changes to states' laws through harmonization impacted on the larger picture i.e., the 'steering mechanisms' of governance in the international system.

What I was interested in, effectively, was the interface not of public *policy* – the authoritative articulation of interest – with mechanisms of international governance, but between domestic (municipal) *law* and international governance. To what extent does parallel national action within municipal legal frameworks act as a mechanism of international governance? The thought that struck me as I hurried through the cold that February morning in Canterbury, expressed far more succinctly here with the benefit of a few hundred pages of practice, was that pressures of globalization could be prompting the harmonization of the municipal laws of states in functionally specific areas, and that this is resulting in diffuse but uniform systems of international governance. This initial thought could have been overshadowed by a myriad others on that morning, the most likely being to warm freezing cold fingers, were it not for Dominic Powell's comments of encouragement when I shared it with him, and I am naturally grateful for this.

I chose to investigate in depth certain case studies while I pondered the larger theoretical questions. My choice of case studies – the protection of copyrights on the Internet, the regulation of international banks, and the control of money laundering – all shared certain key characteristics. They were all elements of 'globalization', meaning that the problems of state control arose as a result of deregulation and liberalization, of technological advances in communication and transport, and of the highly integrated nature of international practices among organic communities in international civil society. Each of these areas presented risks to states through the actions of individuals, i.e., Net-surfers, international bankers, or criminals. Each area defied regulation by a state acting singly, because these individuals, or the consequences of their actions, crossed borders while state laws did not. This book does not elaborate a theory in any rigorous way, but it does point to key issues and questions that need to be addressed in building one.

I would like to thank an anonymous reviewer for Cassell for very helpful comments and suggestions, both in a lengthy referee's report and in the margins of an original draft of the text. I have not satisfied all of the comments, and surely others will find fault with other aspects of this book. I can anticipate at least the more obvious of these.

One concerns the inter-disciplinary nature of the research. By combining research in municipal law and International Relations theory there is a danger of falling between two stools, so to speak, and satisfying neither the lawyers for whom my treatment of complex legal issues may be too cursory, nor my colleagues in International Relations who may frown on my unorthodox, even eclectic, methodology. Indeed, I have attempted an inter-disciplinary analysis by examining law and extrapolating to international politics, rather than, more conventionally, the other way around. I was interested in the measures that states were taking internally (inside) within their municipal systems of law and looking for consequences in international governance (outside). I was interested in governance, which I defined in my own mind in terms of state action and state regulation, albeit at a 'low' level of analysis, and I seemed to be agreeing with the assumption implicit in the law literature that there *should* be regulation and that *states* ought to do it. This more statist bent nevertheless coexisted with the fact that the pressures on governance were emanating from individuals, or civil society actors, suggesting a pluralist perspective.

There are other points which may raise eyebrows. The empirical work was done between 1994 and 1997, and the theoretical aspects written later. The case studies that I chose are rapidly moving targets, and although I kept an eye on recent developments, I did not incorporate up-to-the-minute commentary, the rationale being that end-points must be declared somewhere. Notwithstanding, as the reader will recognize, these end-points are not arbitrary.

I also hope that my critics will see this book as an opening salvo on a question to be studied in an ongoing project for research, which it is, rather than my last words. If this book raises more questions than it answers and stimulates further research, particularly by getting the lawyers and the International Relations community more deeply engaged with each other, then I will derive some satisfaction from annoying them both.

ACKNOWLEDGEMENTS

At this juncture, I wish to thank those who helped me to see my failings, some of which I was able to correct, with the usual disclaimer than any errors remaining are my responsibility. Chris Brown, Mervyn Frost, and A. J. R. Groom commented encouragingly on various drafts of the work; Geoffrey Underhill provided extensive comments on an early paper in which I set out some initial theoretical propositions; and Ronen Palan provided helpful comments on the chapter on international banking. An early draft of the chapter on Internet copyright was presented to a planning session on the 'International Relations of the Internet' at a conference of the European Consortium for Political Research in Oslo in April 1996. I would like to thank the participants for their helpful comments, and particularly Keith Webb for presenting the paper in my absence.

The faculty of the Kent Law School were inspiring, in particular

Abdul Maniruzzaman and Robin MacKenzie, the latter especially for encouraging me to publish a term paper in a new journal devoted to the subject of money laundering. For kind permission to reproduce the article, 'Money Laundering: Transnational Criminals, Globalisation, and the Forces of "Redomestication"', that was published originally in the *Journal of Money Laundering Control* (Vol. 1, No. 1, June 1997, pp. 51–62) largely unaltered here, I would like to thank Henry Stewart Publications, London. I would also like to thank Uma Suthersanen at Queen Mary, London, for encouragement and helpful advice regarding sources on the impact of technology on intellectual property law.

The research for this book benefited from the assistance of a bright student of mine at Kent, Carolina Winters, who volunteered her time to search painstakingly through the library and the Internet for obscure material, for which I am grateful. I am also grateful to the Faculty of Social Science at the University of Kent which made available a small grant for the use of Lexis/Nexis. I would like to thank Anja Sablon, the secretary of the Brussels School of International Studies, for her assistance with the preparation of the bibliography and the final drafts. Finally, thanks to Petra Recter at Cassell for taking an early interest in the project and for showing patience and understanding as I completed the manuscript.

It is perhaps appropriate that as this book began overlooking the mists of a medieval city, that it should conclude with my current vistas being the buildings of the European Commission in the 'Capital of Europe', the seat of one of the most ambitious projects of harmonization. No doubt, Februaries here will be colder than those in Canterbury.

Jarrod Wiener
Brussels School of International Studies
of the University of Kent at Canterbury

ABBREVIATIONS

AALCC	Asian-African Legal Consultative Committee
BSA	Bank Secrecy Act
CCC	Copyright Clearance Center
CFTA	Currency and Foreign Transaction Reporting Act
CHAPS	Clearing House Automated Payments System
CHIPS	Clearing House Interbank Payments System
CJA	Criminal Justice Act
CTR	Currency Transaction Report
EIS	European Information Society
EFT	electronic fund transfer
FATF	Financial Action Task Force
FBSEA	Foreign Bank Supervision Enhancement Act
FCC	Federal Communication Commission
GATS	General Agreement on Trade in Services
GATT	General Agreement on Tariffs and Trade
GDP	Gross Domestic Product
G-IMS	Government-led International Monetary System
IACAC	Inter-American Commercial Arbitration Commission
IBA	International Banking Act
IBF	International Banking Facilities
IBRD	International Bank for Reconstruction and Development
ICC	International Chamber of Commerce
ICSID	International Center for the Settlement of Investment Disputes
IITF	Information Infrastructure Task Force
IMF	International Monetary Fund
INCOTERM	Standard trade terms of the International Chamber of Commerce
LAB	Legal Advisory Board
LAFB	Libyan Arab Foreign Bank
LCA	London Court of Arbitration
LDC	Less Developed Country
LLM	Master of Laws

MFN	most favoured nation
M-IMS	market-led international monetary system
MTN	multilateral trade negotiations
NAFTA	North American Free Trade Agreement
NII	National Information Infrastructure
NTB	non-tariff barrier
OECD	Organization for Economic Cooperation and Development
OFC	offshore financial centre
OPEC	Organization of the Petroleum Exporting Countries
OTC	over-the-counter
PLR	Public Lending Right
RAROC	Risk-Adjusted Return on Capital
RFPA	Right to Financial Privacy Act
SDR	Special Drawing Rights
TRIPS	Trade-Related Aspects of Intellectual Property Rights
UCP	uniform customs and practice
UNCTAD	United Nations Conference on Trade and Development
UNCITRAL	United Nations Commission for International Trade Law
WIPO	World Intellectual Property Rights Organization

CHAPTER 1

INTRODUCTION
On Governing a Permeable Society

THE PROBLEM: THE WESTPHALIAN SYSTEM AND CIVIL SOCIETY ACTORS

How do states that are highly integrated into transnational networks ensure that their laws and regulations apply to transnational criminals? How do states protect their economic security from shocks from outside, such as the collapse of imprudently supervised banks? How do states protect their societal security from undesirable transnational forces that puncture their borders by means of computer networks? These are serious questions, which have been asked by Susan Strange, among others, who have argued that the state is 'retreating', 'receding', or otherwise 'hollowing out'.[1] It is indeed an important challenge to reconcile the Westphalian system of compartmentalized and differentiated legal jurisdictions with transnationally mobile civil society actors who exploit communication technologies, hide behind the laxity of some sovereign regimes, and present other states with security risks.[2]

Some of these civil society actors are thieves, or dealers in drugs, body parts, and people who exploit the fact that some states guard their sovereign right to enact bank secrecy laws and launder their profits through the international financial system by means of electronic fund transfers. The efforts of law enforcement officials, on the other hand, are bound by administrative processes in obtaining evidence and constructing paper trails. As Barry Rider noted, 'there is really no international capability at present to deal with serious organised crime at its own level of operations'. He continued, 'Much of

---

[1] Susan Strange, *Retreat of the State*, Cambridge: Cambridge University Press, 1996.

[2] The term 'security' is used here in a broad sense to include societal and economic security. See Ole Waever, Barry Buzan, Morten Kelstrup, and Pierre Lemaitre, *Identity, Migration and the New Security Agenda in Europe*, London: Pinter, 1993.

our criminal law is tied to notions of physical property that were no doubt meaningful in the seventeenth century but which hardly accommodate developments in communications technology.'[3]

Other actors are international banks, such as the Bank of Credit and Commerce International, that have been able to evade government oversight by exploiting loop-holes in regulatory frameworks to operate without adequate reserves, let alone engage in all manner of fraudulent activity.[4] Shocks to the financial system of a state can emanate by contagion from an imprudent decision taken by a bank elsewhere, especially one which is improperly supervised. Witness the unfolding financial crisis in East Asia, and particularly in Japan in the spring of 1998, which is worrying many in the United States and Western Europe, for example.

Yet others are Internet users who are able to reach into a state from outside to commit a crime without physically breaching the borders of that state. For instance, from June to July 1994, individuals in St Petersburg breached the security of Citibank's network, the Citibank Cash Management system, and conducted several unauthorized transfers of funds totalling approximately US$3 million from the Philippine National Bank to a bank in Finland, and from Djakarta and Buenos Aires to San Francisco and Israel.[5] And, while a state may pass a law to protect copyrights for information on the Internet, Internet users outside the state may not be bound by such laws. While those subject to the jurisdiction of that state will be bound under pain of legal sanction not to copy and distribute a text obtained over the Internet, this would not apply to a person situated in another state,

---

[3] Barry Rider, 'The financial world at risk: the dangers of organised crime, money laundering and corruption', *Managerial Auditing Journal*, vol. 8, no. 7, pp. 3–14, at p. 11.

[4] The Bank of Credit and Commerce International was incorporated as a holding company in Luxemburg and the Cayman Islands. Not only did these states maintain strict bank secrecy legislation, but the status of holding companies was left ambiguous in Luxemburg law, and hence it was not considered by regulators to be a bank that would fall under their remit for supervision. See Duncan E. Alford, 'Basle Committee Minimum Standards: international regulatory response to the failure of BCCI', *George Washington Journal of International Law and Economics*, vol. 26, 1992.

[5] Radio National Transcripts, Background Briefing, Australian Broadcasting Corporation, 9 June 1996. Available at URL: http://www.abc.net.au/rn/talks/bbing/bb960609.htm; and 'Taking the bite out of fraud', *The Virginian Pilot*, 2 October 1995, p. 10. See also Hearing of the House Banking and Financial Services Committee: Organised Crime and Banking, Chaired by Representative Jim Leach, *Federal News Wire*, 28 February 1996.

whose government has not signed an international copyright treaty, who reaches into that state with a computer and modem.[6]

Concerns about the evasion of laws and regulations are by no means new, though perhaps recent discussions have 'securitized' the threat of transnational forces to a greater extent.[7] The same sorts of concerns that have been raised about international banks, transnational criminals, and individual Internet users have been raised at one point or another about foreign currency traders, transnational corporations, and even international travellers carrying infectious diseases.[8] In longer historical perspective, international banking establishments' avoidance of state controls is as old as the Rothschilds' sophisticated evasion of Napoleon's Continental Blockade.[9] The essential problems of the international protection for copyrights were revealed as early as 1886,[10] and fears of technological advances permitting large-scale infringements were raised with the advent of the photocopier, if not the printing-press.[11] As for money laundering, a noted scholar in the area, Barry Rider, has commented that 'the laundering and hiding of money is as old as the notion of wealth'.[12]

Recent securitization of these issues could be due in some measure to sociological phenomena, for instance alienation due to a realization of the growing boundaries of global society, or a fetishizing of postmodern

---

[6] The early response in the United States was to place responsibility on the system operators, as in *Playboy v. Frena, Sega Enterprises Ltd. v. MAPHIA, Frank Music Corp v. Compuserve,* and *Religious Technology Center v. NETCOM.* See Dan Burk, 'Patents in cyberspace: territoriality and infringement on global computer networks', *Tulane Law Review,* vol. 68, no. 1, 1993; and William Galkin, 'Jumping the gun on sysop liability', *The Computer Law Report,* no. 13, 6 November 1995, distributed by Galkin@aol.com.

[7] On securitization and speech-acts, see Ole Weaver, 'Securitization and desecuritization', in Ronnie D. Lipschutz (ed.), *On Security,* New York: Columbia University Press, 1995, pp. 46–86.

[8] Indeed, I have done so. See 'Editor's note', *Global Society: Journal of Interdisciplinary International Relations,* vol. 1, no. 1, 1996, pp. 7–10.

[9] See Karl Erich Born, *International Banking in the 19th and 20th Centuries,* Warwickshire: Berg Publishers Ltd, 1977.

[10] See W. R. Cornish, *Intellectual Property: Patents, Copyright, Trade Marks and Allied Rights,* 2nd edn, London: Sweet & Maxwell, 1989, Chapter 10.

[11] Henry H. Perritt, Jr., 'President Clinton's National Information Infrastructure initiative: community regained?', *IIT Chicago-Kent Law Review,* vol. 69, 1994, pp. 991–1013, at p. 1012.

[12] Barry Rider, 'Editorial', *Journal of Money Laundering Control,* vol. 1, no. 1, 1997, p. 4.

society.[13] To whatever extent this may be so, the fact remains that contagion risks from shocks in the international financial system are greater since the deregulation of international finance in the 1970s and the advent of electronic clearing systems. Indeed, it is difficult to argue that the international financial system has not become globalized, if globalization is defined stipulatively as the increased speed and volume of transactions made possible by deregulation and liberalization, and by technological advances, the parameters of which are dictated by those in possession of the technology rather than by geographical demarcations.[14]

The speed at which vast sums of money flow through the global financial system has increased dramatically in the wake of the technological revolution, the most important elements of which are 24-hour electronic trading in money markets, electronic fund transfers and electronic data interchange in the interbank clearing systems. Money no longer occupies a physical space, rather, it is merely electronic impulses containing information about wealth. In the foreign currency market, where approximately US$1.2 trillion is traded daily,[15] there are examples of traders pressuring the central banks of states, ranging from the selling short of the money supply of New Zealand by Andy Krieger to the pressure exerted on the European Monetary System in 1992 by the trading activities of George Soros and others, and, of course, the turmoil in East Asia in the latter part of 1997.

Similarly, the highly interdependent payments systems among international banks is such that a state's borders no longer act as fire-walls for contagion risks, due for instance to large-scale defaults or a 'run' on a bank in another state. In the United Kingdom, the Clearing House Automated Payments System (CHAPS) handled an average of

---

[13] See Anthony Giddens, *The Consequences of Modernity*, Stanford: Stanford University Press, 1990; John Gerrard Ruggie, 'International structure and international transformation: space, time and method', in Ernst-Otto Czempiel and James Rosenau (eds), *Global Changes and Theoretical Challenges: Approaches to World Politics for the 1990s*, New York: Lexington Books, 1989.

[14] This definition avoids the criticisms that globalization is not truly a global, even, or new process. See Paul Hirst and Grahame Thompson, *Globalisation in Question*, Cambridge: Polity Press, 1996. For a succinct, yet comprehensive review of the literature on globalization, see Anthony McGrew, 'The globalisation debate: putting the advanced capitalist state in its place', *Global Society: Journal of Interdisciplinary International Relations*, vol. 13, no. 3, September, 1998, 299–322.

[15] See Gregory J. Millman, *Around the World on a Trillion Dollars a Day: How Rebel Currency Traders Destroy Banks and Defy Governments*, London: Bantam Press, 1995, p. xvii.

32,000 transfers a day in 1991, with an average daily value of £75 billion.[16] In the United States, the Clearing House Interbank Payments System (CHIPS) handled an average of 148,801 transfers a day in 1990, with an average daily value of US$885 billion, while FedWire processed 67 million transfers with an aggregate value of US$199 trillion.[17] In 1995, the number of FedWire transactions increased to 76 million, involving US$223 trillion.[18] It has been estimated that the payments systems in the United States, Germany, and Japan turn over the equivalent of their annual GDP every few days.[19] At present, an estimated US$6 trillion passes daily through international interbank payment and settlement networks.[20] For economist Richard O'Brien, such movements of vast amounts of money with such speed represents the 'end of geography'.[21]

Transnational money laundering through electronic fund transfers also increased following financial deregulation to launder the estimated annual US$1 trillion global profits from organized crime.[22] With the background noise of the activity in the interbank payments system, it is difficult to trace, let alone stop, the transfers of funds from illicit origin.

The Internet and communications technologies similarly involve the compression of territory through the increase in speed. As Immanuel Wallerstein observed, 'The size of the world-economy is a function of the state of technology, and in particular the possibilities of transport

---

[16] Anu Arora, *Electronic Banking and the Law*, 2nd edn, Banking Technology Ltd, 1993, p. 52.

[17] Sarah Jane Hughes, 'Policing money laundering through funds transfers: a critique of the regulation under the Bank Secrecy Act', *Indiana Law Journal*, vol. 67, Winter 1992, p. 283.

[18] Testimony of Edward Kelly, Governor of the Federal Reserve Board, Hearing of the House Banking and Financial Services Committee: Organised Crime and Banking, Chaired by Representative Jim Leach, *Federal News Wire*, 28 February 1996.

[19] 'International banking: coping with the ups and downs', *The Economist*, Survey, 27 April 1996, p. 15.

[20] *Ibid.*

[21] Richard O'Brien, *Global Financial Deregulation: The End of Geography*, London: Pinter, 1990.

[22] This estimate is by M. B. Comstock, 'GATT and GATS: a public morals attack on money laundering', *Journal of International Law and Business*, vol. 15, Fall 1994, pp. 139–177. Of course, all estimates of things that cannot be seen must be recognized as such.

and communication within its bounds.'[23] Whereas it took two days in 1870 for market information from London to reach New York by telegraph,[24] it became nearly instantaneous one hundred years later. Such advances have been most remarkable in the latter decade of this century. In fact, it has been said that the 1990s were 'the decade of telecoms and other forms of electronic communication'.[25] Indeed, the amount of full-text information available on the World Wide Web is increasing daily as libraries, research organizations, and other information providers up-load documents to the Internet. The 'virtual library' envisioned by the US Congress as a massive storage system for 'hundreds of trillions of bits of data ... giving thousands of users simultaneous and nearly instantaneous access to that data'[26] is an emerging reality. So is the potential for infringements of copyright on an unprecedented scale. In the words of the US Congress Office of Technology Assessment:

> Although Congress has always had to reckon with technological change, the new information and communications technologies available today are challenging the intellectual property system in ways that may only be resolvable with substantial changes in the system or with new mechanisms to allocate both rights and rewards.[27]

At the heart of most concerns that state authority, defined as the ability to exercise control over a well-defined territorial space, is being challenged is the fact that the security threats are not easily defined within territorial terms of reference. The strong thesis has been put forth by Paul Virilio that 'space is no longer in geography – it's in

---

[23] Immanuel Wallerstein, *The Modern World-System: Capitalist Agriculture and the Origins of the European World-Economy in the Sixteenth Century*, New York and London: Academic Press, 1974, p. 349.

[24] See Jorma Ahvenainen, 'Telegraphs, trade and policy: the role of the international telegraph in the years 1870–1914', in Wolfram Fischer, R. Marvin McInnis, and Jurgen Schneider (eds), *The Emergence of a World Economy, 1500–1914*, Part II: 1850–1914, Papers of the IX International Conference of Economic History, in Komission bei Frank Steiner Verlag Weisbaden GmbH, 1986, esp. table on p. 507.

[25] Susan Strange and John Stopford, *Rival States, Rival Firms: Competition for World Market Shares*, Cambridge: Cambridge University Press, 1991, p. 5.

[26] P.L 102–94: 'The High Performance Computing Act of 1991', and the proposed amendment in US Congress H.R. 1757, 'High Performance Computing and High Speed Networking Applications Act of 1993' of 21 April 1993. Section 310 (b)(1) and (2): Applications for Libraries, Washington, DC: USC, Government Printing Office, 1993.

[27] US Congress, Office of Technology Assessment, *Intellectual Property Rights in an Age of Electronic Information*, Washington, DC: USC, Government Printing Office, 1986.

electronics ... There is a movement from geo- to chrono-politics: the distribution of territory becomes the distribution of time.'[28] At root, it can be said that with every innovation in civilization there are concerns about the applicability and adaptability of the traditional methods by which societies protect themselves. As territory becomes compressed, as sovereign borders no longer represent fire-walls to destabilizing risks emanating outside of a state, concerns arise about the effectiveness of the fundamental mechanisms that have evolved for organizing a society: its laws. At issue is nothing less than the ability of the state to exercise sovereignty, in the sense of protective jurisdiction.

Perhaps it is the problem of regulating the activities of individuals who can be in many states at once, of responding to challenges that cannot be seen, and of stabbing with inadequate laws at shadows in cyberspace that has led some to throw in the towel on behalf of the sovereign state. Indeed, there have been in various contexts a symphony among many scholars about the devil of anarchy, the loss of state control, challenges to governance, and the erosion of sovereignty.[29] For instance, Kenichi Ohmae, writing about multinational firms, has touted a borderless world, in which 'the nation–state has become an unnatural, even dysfunctional unit for organising human activity'.[30] In the context of international finance, Malcolm Waters has referred to a 'postmodernising effect' in the international economy such that 'the entire system has become more difficult to control. States are placed at the mercy of financial markets.'[31] And, following a review of a range of transnational challenges, Susan Strange concluded that the state is 'hollowing out', because sovereignty has leaked away, upwards by leave of the state through international treaties, and downwards to civil society actors.[32]

From the vantage point of these writers, the twilight before the dawning of the new millennium, there indeed may be nothing more contemporary in International Relations than the end of world politics

---

[28] Paul Virilio, *Pure War*, New York: Semiotext(e), 1983, p. 88.

[29] See generally, Barrie Axford, *The Global System: Economics, Politics and Culture*, Cambridge: Polity Press, 1995; and Dani Rodrik, *Has Globalization Gone Too Far?*, Washington, DC: Institute for International Economics, 1997.

[30] Kenichi Ohmae, *The Borderless World: Power and Strategy in the Interlinked Economy*, London: Collins, 1990. See also Ohmae, *The End of the Nation-State*, London: HarperCollins, 1995.

[31] Malcolm Waters, *Globalisation*, London: Routledge, 1995, p. 88.

[32] Strange, *The Retreat of the State*, op. cit.

as we know it. Sovereignty is, after all, the concept which allows us to recognize the source of legitimate power and authority over the affairs that occur within a well-defined territorial space. Although our understanding of the concept of sovereignty has changed over time,[33] since the Peace of Westphalia[34] states have defended jealously their claims to exercise supreme authority over a territory carved on the physical map of the world through every means from diplomatic accommodation to military confrontation. While certainly this discussion does not intend to prioritize the territorial aspects of sovereignty to the exclusion of others, such as constitutional independence,[35] and loyalty,[36] nor to confuse its internal/external dimensions,[37] nor even to skirt over the objections of pre-positivist international lawyers and postmodernists to the contrary,[38] the fact remains that the effective control over a well-defined territorial space remains a central feature of state sovereignty. As Chris Brown put it, 'To be a sovereign state always implies to be in effective control of a territory ... Being in effective control in late 20th century sovereign states means being in a position to manage the domestic economy and to preserve law and order.'[39]

---

[33] See Jens Bartelson, *A Genealogy of Sovereignty*, Cambridge: Cambridge University Press, 1995.

[34] The cacophony of dissent is anticipated here, and the reader is referred to Martin Wight, *Systems of States*, London: Leicester University Press, 1977.

[35] See Alan James, *Sovereign Statehood: The Basis of International Society*, London: Allen & Unwin, 1986.

[36] For instance, Gidon Gottlieb, *Nation Against State*, New York: Council on Foreign Relations, 1993.

[37] This is meant in both senses of the usage. See R. B. J. Walker, *Inside/Outside: International Relations as Political Theory*, Cambridge: Cambridge University Press, 1993; and Robert Jackson, *Quasi States: Sovereignty, International Relations and the Third World*, Cambridge: Cambridge University Press, 1994.

[38] By pre-positivist, I am referring to Hugo Grotius, *Prolegomena to the Law of War and Peace* (1625), New York: Bobbs-Merill, 1957; and certain ways in which Samuel Pufendorf carried on this tradition in *The Law of Nature and of Nations* (1672), London: R. Sare, 1717. For a very interesting postmodern critique of sovereignty, see Cynthia Weber, *Simulating Sovereignty: Intervention, the State and Symbolic Exchange*, Cambridge: Cambridge University Press, 1995. See also John Gerrard Ruggie, 'Territoriality and beyond: problematizing modernity in international relations', *International Organization*, vol. 47, no. 1, Winter 1993, pp. 139–74.

[39] Chris Brown, 'Back to normal? Some reflections on sovereignty and self-determination after the cold war', *Global Society: Journal of Interdisciplinary International Relations*, vol. 10, no. 1, 1996, pp. 11–23, at p. 15. See also Cynthia Weber, op. cit; and John Gerrard Ruggie, 'Territoriality and Beyond: Problematizing Modernity in International Relations', op. cit.

Territory generally denotes the boundaries of political authority. Thus, the point of lamentations about the loss of state sovereignty, whether these are framed as postmodern critiques of modern social organization or raised in debates about globalization (and the preceding debates about interdependence),[40] is that the sovereign prerogative to enforce municipal law in a territory is frustrated, even attenuated, because transnational risks permeate its borders.

Is the Westphalian system up to the task of permitting political authorities whose states are subject to risks by civil society actors to discipline them if the latter are out of the reach of the state's legal jurisdiction? So long as the system of states is one of differentiated regulatory regimes bounded by the borders of sovereign territory while civil society actors are transnationally mobile, or the repercussions from whose actions are felt transnationally, the compartmentalized system of legal jurisdictions could continue to force states into a defensive posture, reacting to threats and risks emanating from global society rather than applying effective political authority on them.

THE ARGUMENT OF THIS BOOK

It could be that proponents of the 'lost sovereignty' thesis have rushed to answer questions that we do not yet know how to ask. This book is therefore an attempt to reframe the question not of 'how much' sovereignty has been lost, but of 'how' sovereign control has changed and adapted by adopting an inter-disciplinary and multi-levelled approach. Does a borderless world need to be an orderless one? To be sure, there are many ways in which states cooperate on a range of issues, from public-policy coordination through international treaties, international organizations, institutions, regimes, and a range of less formal contacts. This book is about one mechanism of international governance at the level of municipal law that has been more or less neglected in International Relations. The devil is in the detail, and this book examines legal intricacies.[41] This study is not an attempt to build

---

[40] As brought into mainstream discourse by Robert Keohane and Joseph Nye, *Power and Interdependence: World Politics in Transition*, Boston: Little, Brown, 1977, although I have in mind interdependence from at least a century before.

[41] On the relationship between 'globalization' and law, see Martin Shapiro, 'The globalisation of law'; and Benjamin R. Barber, 'Global democracy or global law: which comes first?', both in *Indiana Journal of Global Legal Studies*, vol. 1, no. 1, 1993. Available at URL: http://www.law.indiana.edu/glsj/vol11/.

a rigorous theory; rather, it is an attempt to refine questions by introducing an aspect of governance at the level of municipal law, orient future work in more empirically grounded analyses, and raise issues relating to the significance of investigating 'low-level' international governance. The argument proceeds as follows.

Private international governance

The central thesis of this book is that a convergence of practices among important international civil society actors has led to a rational uniformity of governance by the United States and the European Union. By convergence of practices is meant a similarity in the performance of a particular act in different states, such as international banking, money laundering, international trade, or communicating via the Internet. By rational uniformity of governance is meant that the discipline of the actors performing these practices is being performed in similar ways by different states. In other words, since the practices of international banking, international trade, and communicating on the Internet are similar in different states, the mechanism of governance of these practices has become similar.

This study concentrates on the United States and the Member States of the European Union, to whom it has been important to liberalize and deregulate private finance, trade, and computer-mediated communications for a host of public-policy reasons. However, it has also become important to re-regulate the activities of private individuals who present risks to the state. This chapter outlines in general terms the manner in which this has been done. The first process is that of 'domesticating' control through the passage of municipal law which localizes control of the actors on sovereign jurisdiction. In some cases, this has been accompanied by a 'privatization' of the function of policing international practices, such as by placing the onus on banks to detect and report money laundering, or by placing the onus on Internet systems operators to stop copyright infringements. The related process has been the functional harmonization of municipal laws in these areas to mitigate differences and to create functionally assimilated regulatory spaces which transcend state borders. Chapter 2 argues that because of this functional similarity of municipal law spilling over state borders, municipal law has become an aspect of international governance.

The regulation and supervision of international banks

Chapter 3 begins the empirical investigation with international banking regulation and supervision. This chapter is concerned with the measures that the United States and the European Union have agreed in the Basle Committee on Banking Regulation and Supervisory Practices[42] for the supervision of foreign banking establishments to control the risks inherent in international banking. The Basle Committee is not a formal international organization, but rather a forum to discuss issues. It does not enunciate law, but rather 'concordats', and its agreements are non-binding. Chapter 3 examines how transatlantic agreement in this forum has led to the harmonization of municipal laws, namely the United States Foreign Bank Supervision Enhancement Act of 1991 and the European Union's Directive on the Supervision of Credit Institutions on a Consolidated Basis.[43]

Chapter 3 begins with the assumption that the increased volume of liquidity and international lending and the increased interdependence among banks due to the speed of transfers in the intricate nexus of interbank payments systems has increased the threat of contagion and systemic risk. That is, the potential risk to the entire system due to credit and solvency risks in one part of the system has increased. This has placed the onus on states to formulate regulations for prudential and sound banking, particularly given central banks' role as lender of last resort in the event of a crisis.

It is argued that international regulation historically has not kept pace with the internationalization of banking. The regulation of banking has been national, whereas banking has become increasingly internationalized, particularly in the OECD countries that have become more permeated by foreign banking establishments. Measures that have been taken in the past at the international level have been taken mainly in response to crises. Whereas the function of a national lender of last resort has been accompanied by national measures to ensure

---

[42] Known as the 'Basle Committee', this is an informal consultative group under the auspices of the Bank for International Settlements at Basle, Switzerland, comprised of representatives of the central banks of Belgium, Canada, France, Germany, Great Britain, Italy, Japan, The Netherlands, Switzerland, the United States, Luxemburg, and Sweden.

[43] US Foreign Bank Supervision Enhancement Act of 1991 (FBSEA, Pub. L. No. 101–242, sections 201–215, 105 Stat. 2236–305) and the Second Council Directive 92/30 of 6 April 1992 on the Supervision of Credit Institutions on a Consolidated Basis, *Official Journal of the European Communities*, 1992 (L110), p. 52.

safety and soundness, such as reserve requirements and depositor's insurance, the internationalization of banking has put pressure on such national measures.

Thus, the focus of the exposition is on the manner in which agreement in the transatlantic community has been devised to reconcile the practice of international banking with national expectations of stability. The investigation finds that, whereas the desire to liberalize international banking could be accompanied by a 'race to the bottom' in regulatory regimes, prudence has been a foremost concern. The United States and the European Union have attempted to reconcile the principle of sound and prudential supervision of banking while they have driven the process of further global financial liberalization. Moreover, unlike previous attempts to supervise international banks, the Basle Committee Minimum Standards for the Supervision of International Banking Groups and their Cross-Border Establishments[44] is proactive in that it empowers states to 'lock out' from their territory banks that do not meet the new minimum standards.

While the United States and the European Union are at the forefront of efforts to negotiate a more liberal market-access regime for banking, they have reserved the right through their municipal laws enacted in conformity with the Minimum Standards to recognize the power of foreign supervisory authorities prior to permitting the establishment of a foreign financial institution in their territory. Thus, it is argued that finance is no doubt becoming more globalized, but that the regulatory measures point to a 'domestication' of regulatory powers – to localize risk and to control it through municipal law – and thereby rein in the risks inherent in international banking. Chapter 3 finds that the municipal legislation in the United States and the European Union in this area has become harmonized.

The control of money laundering

Continuing the focus on international finance, Chapter 4 investigates the measures that the United States and the European Union have implemented to control the growing problem of money laundering. If the international financial system may be likened to the metaphorical

---

[44] Committee on Banking Regulation and Supervisory Practices, *Minimum Standards for the Supervision of Banking Groups and their Cross-Border Establishments*, 1992.

'cobweb' of World Society,[45] it has become evident that this cobweb is conducive to spreading security threats emanating from nearly all parts of the globe, as well as being rather effective at hiding the spiders that lurk within it. Indeed, the *Strategic Survey, 1994/95* stated that 'transnational crime inescapably violates national borders, thus challenging one of the most fundamental attributes of sovereignty'.[46] It proceeded to characterize as a 'security threat' the activities of criminals who take advantage of bank secrecy laws, 24-hour global money markets and electronic fund transfer facilities to disguise the source of, and thereby to launder, the profits from other illicit activities. In an address to the United Nations General Assembly, US President Clinton stated that, 'criminal enterprises now move large sums through the international financial system that dwarf the gross national product of some nations'[47] and called upon the international community to formulate a collective response to organized crime, which an earlier Presidential Decision Directive (PDD-42) had called a 'threat to US national security'.[48] Former United Nations Secretary-General, Dr Boutros Boutros-Ghali, echoed this sentiment in an article in *Foreign Affairs* where he drew attention to the 'alarming' elements of globalization, namely the growth of transnational criminal activities.[49]

Chapter 4 finds that the United States and the European Union have attempted to 'domesticate' control over money laundering by enacting municipal legislation, and moreover to 'privatize' the policing of the international financial system by placing the onus on banks to detect and report suspected money laundering. Banks now face criminal charges if they do not report 'suspicious' transactions. A corollary to

---

45 John Burton, *World Society*, Cambridge: Cambridge University Press, 1972.

46 'Transnational crime: a new security threat?', *Strategic Survey, 1994/95*, London: Institute for Strategic Studies, 1995, pp. 25–33.

47 'UN must declare a war on drugs and crime, says Clinton', *The Times*, 23 October 1995; 'Clinton's war on "new perils"', *The Independent*, 23 October 1995, p. 10; 'New US foreign policy concept evolving', *Reuters Newswire*, 23 October 1995.

48 For the foreign policy implications, see the testimony of Robert Sims, Special Advisor on International Criminal Justice to the Assistant Secretary on International Narcotics and Law Enforcement Affairs, Department of State, to the Hearing of the House Banking and Financial Services Committee on Organised Crime and Banking (Rep. Jim Leach, Chair), in *Federal News Service*, 28 February 1996. In relevant part, he stated: 'Transnational organized crime threatens America's national security and foreign policy interests in a number of regions of the world, undermining legitimate economies and threatening emerging democracies.'

49 Boutros Boutros-Ghali, 'Global leadership after the cold war', *Foreign Affairs*, March/April 1996, esp. pp. 86–98.

this domestication has been a process of harmonization across the Atlantic. The legislation in the United States comprises the Money Laundering Act of 1986, the Anti-Drug Abuse Act of 1990, the Annunzio–Wiley Anti-Money Laundering Act of 1992, and the Money Laundering Suppression Act of 1994.[50] In the European Union, Member States have enacted legislation in conformity with the Council Directive on Prevention of the Use of the Financial System for the Purposes of Money Laundering,[51] such as the United Kingdom's Criminal Justice Act 1993.[52] Such measures have been taken in conformity with agreed principles in the Basle Committee, such as the 'Know Your Customer' rule, which requires financial institutions to ensure the 'cleanliness' of deposits made in the state's territory. This is another example of the transatlantic community being presented with a security threat from the process of globalization, and their attempts to 'domesticate' and localize control, in this case through privatization. Accompanying this domestication has been harmonization.

Copyrights on the Internet

On 15 September 1993 the Clinton–Gore administration launched the National Information Infrastructure (NII) in the United States.[53] In December of that year, former European Commission President Jacques

---

[50] See J. J. Rusch, 'Hue and cry in the counting-house: some observations on the Bank Secrecy Act', *Catholic University Law Review*, vol. 37, Winter 1988, pp. 465–88; and F. C. Razzano, 'American money laundering statutes: the case for a worldwide system of banking compliance programs', *Detroit College of Law Journal of International Law and Practice*, vol. 3, 1994, pp. 277–307.

[51] European Directive on the Prevention of the Use of the Financial System for the Purposes of Money Laundering. Council Directive 91/308, *Official Journal of the European Communities*, (L166) 1991, at p. 77.

[52] There have been others in the United Kingdom, such as the Drug Trafficking Offences Act 1986, the Drug Trafficking Act 1994, and the Northern Ireland (Emergency Provisions) Act of 1991. See R. Finney, 'UK money laundering law after the reports of 1993', *Butterworths Journal of International Banking and Finance Law*, December 1993, pp. 530–7.

[53] For the Clinton administration's plans, see: Executive Office of the President, 'The National Information Infrastructure: agenda for action'. Available through gopher.-wiretap.spies.com. For a synopsis of developments of the National Information Infrastructure and the global information infrastructure, see Ralph J. Andreotta, 'The National Information Infrastructure: its implications, opportunities, and challenges', *Wake Forest Law Review*, vol. 30, Spring 1995, pp. 221–40.

Delors outlined similar measures for a European Information Society (EIS).[54] Both plans envisioned national (in the case of the United States) or regional (in the European Union) computer networks to create a variety of innovative entertainment and information services, including 'digital libraries'. The regulation of copyrights in these 'libraries', and the protection of copyrighted material on the Internet, were resolved, more or less, at a diplomatic conference at the World Intellectual Property Organization in December 1996 where a new treaty was adopted.[55] Chapter 5 examines proposals that were under consideration in the United States and the European Union, and finds that the issues that were raised, and the means that were considered to adapt national legislation to the new digital environment were very similar. Again, in this case there has been an attempt to 'domesticate' by localizing control on the territory of the state and to 'privatize' policing the Internet for copyright infringements by placing the onus on systems operators to do so. Moreover, the legislation to enact the WIPO treaty in the United States, and the draft Directive in the European Union, while still at the drafting and consultation stage, shows a remarkable similarity.

A caveat

The strategy of domestication and harmonization of municipal law must be problematized, and Chapter 6 does this. While there is harmonization in these areas among states that are highly integrated into international networks, as in the transatlantic community, it is because these states have incentives to do so. However, for harmonization to be truly effective will require a truly global approach, lest some states' lax laws remain a haven for illicit and destabilizing activity. No doubt proponents of the strong globalization thesis would question whether the governance mechanism explained in this book – or indeed, any form of governance – that is confined to the few states

---

[54] This has also been called an Information Services Market. For the EU programmes relevant to its information technology programme, see in particular: Commission of the European Communities, 'Proposal for a council decision setting up a programme for an information services market', COM (570) final, 23 January 1991. Available at www.echo.lu/programmes/en/DELTA_2.html.

[55] WIPO Copyright Treaty, Adopted by the Diplomatic Conference on Certain Copyright and Neighbouring Rights Questions, 20 December 1996.

of the transatlantic area is effective at meeting challenges that are global in nature.

The safety and soundness of the international banking system cannot be guaranteed simply because a few states will lock out from their territory banks that are not adequately supervised by their home regulatory authorities. The intricate system of obligations among banks crosses numerous borders, and the collapse of a large bank in a state not participating in consolidated supervision can affect the system as a whole. Similarly, the attempt to stop money laundering by policing the deposits in a few states cannot guarantee that dirty and hot money will not be introduced into the system in another state that maintains strict bank secrecy laws. Finally, the harmonization of the copyright laws of a few states for material on the Internet, even if accompanied by such technological measures as encryption and digital signatures, cannot be enforced in other states, nor can it overcome the problems of tracing infringements of copyright and gaining adequate compensation. There are indeed limitations to the harmonization of municipal laws as an approach to counter the challenges to regulation presented by globalization.

The suggestion that all states adopt the same laws stretches concepts of imperialism and raises to new heights problems of relativism on a par with those raised by current debates about an emerging global culture.[56] For instance, the criminalization of money laundering extends deeper into what states define as a 'crime'. To criminalize the movement of money derived from illegal activities requires that all states criminalize the same things, or legally regulate the same activities, otherwise definitions of what constitutes 'dirty' and 'hot' money will also vary. Even in the area of drug trafficking, which has received the most attention in discussions about money laundering – perhaps unduly, to the exclusion of economic crime – one need only look to The Netherlands to see the very different views that are taken on this issue.

The central concern of this book is not with the efficacy of harmonization on a global scale, although pressures for 'harmonization spread' are discussed. Among these are market forces, such as the desire of banks in other states to gain access to the large banking markets of the United States and the European Union. Another is

---

[56] For instance, Mike Featherstone (ed.), *Global Culture: Nationalism, Globalisation and the World System*, London: Macmillan, 1991; and Ronald Robertson, *Globalisation: Social Theory and Global Change*, London: Sage, 1992.

diplomatic pressure which the United States is exerting on states to enact similar anti-money-laundering legislation.

However, the examination of private international trade law in Chapter 7 shows that states with very diverse legal, administrative and commercial traditions have accepted the principles, customs and usages of the cosmopolitan commercial community because of their high degree of integration into the trade system. It is suggested that it is not inconceivable that high degrees of integration into other systems could prompt states to undertake similar harmonization more widely.

The unification of international trade law: The *Lex Mercatoria*

A market economy requires a supportive legal framework, and international trade is the oldest activity in the international economy to have been promoted by assurances of legal stability. Commercial states have adopted systems of law to guarantee and enforce such essentials as the sanctity of contract and private property rights. National systems of commercial law still differ in many respects, such that there are likely always to be legal risks in international commercial transactions. Nevertheless, the development of a highly integrated system of international commerce would have been impossible without the legal frameworks of commercial states sharing sufficient commonality to provide at least the necessary confidence for the business community to undertake contracts and some guarantee against crime.

As international trade has become more complex, many states have harmonized such things as contract terms, usages and customs to provide a greater degree of predictability in international commerce. In fact, it has been said that states are permitting the rebirth of an ancient system of law that pre-dated national law, called the *Lex Mercatoria*.[57] In the pre-national era in Europe, the community of traders resolved disputes according to a cosmopolitan system of rules. The consolidation of the states system promoted differences in national laws, rules and administrative procedures. However, the process may have come full circle in that states have incentives to promote the streamlining of the global trade system, and many are carrying out in their municipal

---

[57] Trakman, 'The evolution of the law merchant: our commercial heritage', *Journal of Maritime Law of Commerce*, vol. 153, 1981, pp. 179–96; B. M. Cremades and S. L. Plehn, 'The next Lex Mercatoria and the harmonisation of the laws of international commercial transactions', *Boston University International Law Journal*, 1984, p. 317.

laws the cosmopolitan rules, customs, and usages of the commercial community. Private international commercial law may be entering postmodernity by reverting to cosmopolitan principles while riding on the coercive force of the Westphalian system.

What Chapter 7 shows is that it is not only the risks of globalization that are promoting harmonization, but its positive aspects as well. States benefit from trade, and harmonization in this area is designed to streamline the integration of their commercial communities into the international trade system.

Chapter 7 also suggests that the advanced form of harmonization characteristic in the usages, customs and standard form contracts that are found today in international trade may foreshadow the developments in the other areas under consideration in this book. International trade pre-dates the modern states system while that of deregulated finance (in its present form) is only twenty years old, and electronic communication mediated by the Internet is still in its infancy.

EMPIRE OF LAW?

The thesis of this book about a convergence of municipal laws across the Atlantic following the activities of civil society actors has implications for the debate over globalization, and is of relevance to international governance. The cases chosen for this study are archetypal of the ease with which the borders of states are permeated, and the speed with which the domestic realm is affected by events that occur outside of them. That states are evolving mechanisms of governance argues against the strong thesis of globalization that 'lost sovereignty' accompanies permeation by transnational activities.

But the main point also speaks to processes of homogenization identified in some political theory; that international pressures and processes lead to an assimilation or homogenization of societies in terms of their basic authority structures, organization and institutions. For instance, Karl Marx envisioned that the spread of capitalism would lead to the assimilation of domestic social and political structures as well as to class antagonisms in capitalist states. More recently, Francis Fukuyama noted that technological rationalism and economic modernization lead to an assimilation of basic societal structures.[58]

[58] For a brief comparison of Edmund Burke, Karl Marx, and Francis Fukuyama, see Fred Halliday, 'International society as homogeneity: Burke, Marx, Fukuyama', *Millennium: Journal of International Studies*, vol. 21, no. 3, 1993, pp. 435–61.

Other writers have noted that the adoption of neoliberalism is promoting a convergence of states at the level of their policy priorities, which determines the level and kinds of state involvement in the economy and in the provision of social services, which Stephen Gill has called a 'disciplinary neoliberalism'.[59]

The implications of this study are that the activities of international civil society actors are similarly leading to a convergence, but of the municipal legal systems of states that are highly integrated into transnational practices. An important development of this is for International Relations to develop a theoretical understanding of where the functional harmonization of municipal law following the practices of international civil society actors is leading, in terms of our conceptions of sovereignty and governance, and most especially in terms of the sum total of a series of incremental mitigations of difference. Could it be that, just as disciplinary neoliberalism is foreclosing public policy options and forcing a similarity of domestic structures, the pressures of civil society actors are leading to homogenized regulatory spaces that transcend state boundaries, an 'Empire' of municipal law?

---

[59] See Stephen Gill, 'Globalisation, market civilisation, and disciplinary neoliberalism', *Millennium: Journal of International Studies*, vol. 24, no. 3, 1995, pp. 399–423. See also Edward Broadbent, 'The rise and fall of economic and social rights: thoughts on justice and stability in the North Atlantic world', and Christopher Pierson, 'Globalisation and the changing governance of welfare states: superannuation reform in Australia', both in *Global Society: Journal of Interdisciplinary International Relations*, vol. 12, no. 2, January 1998, pp. 15–31, and 31–49, respectively.

CHAPTER 2

FROM PUBLIC TO PRIVATE INTERNATIONAL GOVERNANCE

The purpose of this chapter is to outline a conceptual framework for examining 'low-level' international governance, that is, international governance arising from the level of private law in the municipal systems of sovereign states.[1] That this is necessary is due to a hegemony in International Relations of prioritizing mechanisms for international governance at the level of public authority or the coordination of public policy, whether this be in the form of a world government, public international law, international organizations and institutions, or international regimes. The idea that international governance can arise from systems of municipal law may be counter to much theorizing in International Relations that has imposed conceptual dichotomies of inside/outside, where municipal law is confined to governance within the state.

Mechanisms of international order have advanced more or less in reaction to the problems that have given rise to disorder, and the emphasis on the public policy of governments is due to the fact that many of the most pressing problems of international order have come, and arguably continue to come, from the action of governments. To make absolutely clear, the argument advanced here is by no means meant to suggest that this problematic of international governance has shifted, or is losing relevance, in the era of globalization. However, it does suggest that, as outlined in the previous chapter, there is a

---

[1] 'Private law', as discussed in this book, means the laws that govern private individuals or natural persons as opposed to 'public law', which is meant to refer to international law that governs the conduct of states and arises out of the coordination of public policies. The use of 'public' and 'private' here therefore differs from the normal usage in most normative and critical International Relations theory: the reference to 'private' law does not mean that this law is not 'public', as all law, by definition, must be public. In most instances, the term 'municipal law' will be used to avoid any confusion, so long as it is recognized that it is intended to refer to the laws that govern individuals.

growing realization in the globalization literature and in the media of an emerging pressure on governance coming from the activities of private individuals. Following from this is an idea in some of the literature of an inability to control, to manage effectively, or to govern. Perhaps this lamentation of a lack of alternatives to the slow death of the sovereign state is due less to an inability in practice of the state to govern and more to an inability of scribblers to conceptualize alternative mechanisms of international governance.

'PUBLIC' GLOBAL GOVERNANCE I: THE WORLD STATE

Ideas of world government can be traced to antiquity. Dante, writing before the emergence of the Westphalian system during the struggles between papal supremacy and political independence in the early 1300s, idealized a unity of mankind under an all-powerful public authority.[2] Immanuel Kant, although pessimistic of the possibility of a super-state in 1795, and settling for a second-best 'pacific union', nevertheless believed a world state to be the optimal solution to the scourge of international disorder.[3] The First World War provoked similar ideas,[4] and the failure of the League of Nations to stop the events that led to the outbreak of the Second World War led the World Federalists, among whom were Clarence Streit, to revive Kant's ideas and to call for 'a Union now of the democracies [of] the North Atlantic ... in a great federal republic ... to create by its constitution a nucleus world government capable of growing into universal world government peacefully'.[5] The cause of establishing a 'world government' gained even greater urgency following the Second World War, when Norman Cousins, Gerard J. Mangone, and Frederick Shuman, among others, either mused or idealized detailed plans.[6] Others, such

---

2 Dante Alighieri, *De Monarchia*, E. Moore (ed.), London: Clarendon Press, 1916.

3 Immanuel Kant, 'Perpetual peace, a philosophical sketch', in Hans Rees, *Kant's Political Writings*, Cambridge: Cambridge University Press, 1970 (1988), pp. 93–130, esp. p. 105. Rees had noted of Kant's Pacific Union that 'on the analogy of individuals uniting to form a state, all states might be compelled to unite into a world state governed by law', p. 34.

4 Among whom were Arnold J. Toynbee, *Nationality and the War*, London, 1915.

5 Clarence K. Streit, *Union Now: Proposal for a Federal Union of the Democracies of the North Atlantic*, London: Jonathan Cape, 1939, p. 18.

6 See, for instance: Norman Cousins, *In Place of Folly*, New York: Harper, 1961; Gerard J. Mangone, *The Idea and Practice of World Government*, New York: Columbia University Press, 1951; Frederick Shuman, *The Commonwealth of Man*, New York:

as Grenville Clark and Louis B. Sohn, argued for more specific steps, such as the establishment of a world police force.[7] Even ardent realists such as Hans Morgenthau acknowledged the idea that a world state was indispensable for the survival of the world, although, not surprisingly, he believed that this was 'unattainable in our world'.[8]

The ensuing debate between cosmopolitan theorists pressing the cause of world government, on one side, and realists and other communitarian theorists, on the other, engaged questions that centred principally around the 'domestic analogy', including the extension to the international sphere of social contract theory and the power of public opinion; the prospect of governments surrendering sovereignty to a centralized system of allocating values; the difficulties of maintaining an international monopoly of organized violence; and the difficulties of transferring national allegiances and building political and ethical communities.[9] Indeed, these were questions that occupied later integration theorists, such as Karl Deutsch, whose project also concerned the construction of larger structures of political authority, though over a more limited geographical area.[10]

An important reason for the cosmopolitans' emphasis on public authority in creating order – of trying to make international governance through international government – is due to the fact that the principal offenders of international order had been public authorities. This was no less true in the days of Dante or Kant than it was of Clarence Streit and the World Federalists, although the urgency of the latter's project was born out of a fear that states would pursue through nuclear war the cause of 'protecting' the states system from those with hegemonial designs. The project of constructing international governance by means of 'building up' – building upon national government to greater forms of the same kind of governance – also

---

contd.
Alfred Knopf, 1952. For a summary of these and other approaches, see George A. Codding Jr., 'World federalism: the conceptual setting', in A. J. R. Groom and Paul Taylor, *Frameworks for International Cooperation*, London: Pinter, 1990, pp. 217–33.

7 Grenville Clark and Louis B. Sohn, *World Peace Through World Law: Two Alternative Plans*, Cambridge, MA: Harvard University Press, 1966.

8 Hans Morgenthau, *Political Among Nations: The Struggle for Power and Peace*, 6th edn, New York: Alfred Knopf, 1985 (1948), p. 563.

9 See Innis L. Claude Jr., *Swords into Ploughshares: The Problems and Progress of International Organization*, 3rd edn, New York: Random House, 1956; and Kenneth Waltz, *Theory of International Politics*, London: Addison-Wesley, 1979, pp. 112–13.

10 See Karl W. Deutsch, *Political Community and the North Atlantic Area*, New York: Doubleday, 1954.

stemmed from a particular conception of progress in the ordering of human affairs. Illustrative of this concept of progress is de Hevesy, who declared:

> In spite of successive reverses, a broad historical tendency towards the unification of the world is discernible throughout the centuries. This tendency has proceeded stage by stage: the family, the tribe, and the nation; the village, the town and the province; the State, the confederation, and – still to come – universal union.'[11]

Moral cosmopolitanism was thus wedded to an Enlightenment mould of linear progress in building upon known structures of governance, that being public authority.

The project of world government has become moribund. As Chris Brown observed: ' "Moral" cosmopolitanism has replaced the advocacy of world government as the cutting edge of cosmopolitan thought – thus bowing to the continued strength of the sovereign national state, and attempting to work around its more undesirable consequences.'[12] The project of promoting international order continued, though through more conservative means of policy coordination – treaties, international organizations and institutions, and international regimes – much as it had done since the mid-1800s.

'PUBLIC' GLOBAL GOVERNANCE II: INTERNATIONAL ORGANIZATION

From the mid-1800s, international organizations became, in the words of A. J. R. Groom, 'the principal tools for managing international relations', which stemmed from 'two watershed events in nineteenth-century Europe: the consolidation of the modern state system and the Industrial Revolution'.[13] This marriage of state authority with the increased transnational mobility of people, goods, money, post and

---

[11] Paul de Hevesy, *The Unification of the World: Proposals of a Diplomatist*, London: Pergamon Press, 1966, p. 219.

[12] Chris Brown, 'Back to normal? Some reflections on sovereignty and self-determination after the cold war', *Global Society: Journal of Interdisciplinary International Relations*, vol. 10, no. 1, 1996, p. 22. He went on to say, 'Possibly this emphasis has been mistaken.'

[13] See A. J. R. Groom, 'The advent of international organisation', in Paul Taylor and A. J. R. Groom (eds), *International Institutions at Work*, London: Pinter, 1988, pp. 3–19, esp. pp. 8–10. See also Paul Reuter, *International Institutions*, London: George Allen and Unwin, 1958.

ships, among other things, produced the coordination of public policy as the principal tool for international governance. Groom continued, 'The purpose of international organisation was to promote freedom under a set of rules which were negotiated by governments ... States were gatekeepers in the movements of goods, services, people, and ideas.'[14]

The state had become the highest form of political organization; the state as gatekeeper meant that progress in international governance was channelled into the coordination of states' public policies. Progress in ordering the international system became one of reconciling the policies favoured by distinct public authorities, which sometimes were complementary, and sometimes not. Following the First World War, and especially the Second World War, this project of international organization was prosecuted with a greater zeal, due, of course, to the fact that the main challenge to international order was the maintenance of international peace, which oriented analyses towards 'high politics'.

Yet, this project following the Second World War merely built upon the same thinking that governance is an activity for government public policy, and of international governance as the coordination of that public policy. Peace would be achieved through public international law and international organization. Liberal internationalists believed progress in the ordering of the international system to be a process of 'building upon' public policy through institutions signed under international law, such as the Charter of the United Nations.[15] The economy would be regulated by the same means: finance and trade would be subject to the same convergence of policy at the public level and the creation of interstate institutions, because the failure of governments to coordinate their policies in the inter-war years had led to a vacuum of governance.[16] The idea was to nationalize at the public level control of the international economy, according to internationally agreed normative frameworks, and to create interstate mechanisms for coordination. Lord Keynes and Harry Dexter White were therefore as much children of the Enlightenment as was Woodrow Wilson: the

---

[14] Groom, ibid.

[15] For a new historical account, see Andrew J. Williams, *Failed Imagination: New World Orders of the Twentieth Century in Historical Perspective*, Manchester: Manchester University Press, 1999.

[16] See Richard N. Gardner, *Sterling-Dollar Diplomacy in Current Perspective: The Origins and Prospects of Our International Economic Order*, New York: Columbia University Press, 1980; Charles Kindleberger, *The World in Depression, 1929–1939*, London: Allen Lane and Penguin Press, 1973.

failures of international governance of the economy stemmed from the fact that there was no mechanism for coordinating and managing internationally among governments in a way that promoted stability in the domestic context.

Theories of international institutions and international cooperation, such as neo-liberal and neo-realist institutionalism, while differing in their approach, help to explain the modern project of public policy coordination that has been the principal mechanism of international governance since the mid-1800s.[17] However, the emphasis of International Relations on public policy coordination as governance – to the exclusion of international governance at other 'levels' – risks reifying a belief that a practice that is over 100 years old is the only suitable, or best suited, mechanism for international governance. Some recent work, such as that of Mihaly Simai, continues to focus on the development of multilateralism within international institutions as the future of global governance.[18]

However, there are at least two problems with keeping the attention of International Relations on questions of 'global governance' wedded to the mould of public policy coordination. The first is that there are numerous forms of governance in international society that simply do not fit with conventional moulds. Following from this, and of more concern here, the second problem with a continued emphasis on international public policy coordination as international governance is that states no longer can nationalize control of international civil society actors through public policy. Are states still the gatekeepers in the movements of goods, people and ideas? The transnational mobility of some important civil society actors, such as international bankers, was curtailed following the Second World War. Governing international finance became a matter of coordinating public policy, for instance through the International Monetary Fund, not of disciplining private international bankers. However, the deregulation and privatization of the economy, as well as of international communications, have necessitated a shift in the governance of important aspects of international society away from measures of public policy to means of municipal law.

The question of preserving international 'order' in many issue areas has, quite rightly, concentrated on high politics, as it should when the

---

[17] The 'debate' between neo-liberalism and neo-realism, in grand terms, is not a theoretical debate at all, but a haggling over descriptions of processes.

[18] Mihaly Simai, *The Future of Global Governance: Managing Risk and Change in the International System*, Washington, DC: US Institute of Peace, 1994.

threats to order are amenable to, and effectively regulated by, the coordination of public policies. However, the question of 'order' in aspects of the present deregulated and liberalized international system is now one of disciplining private actors. In a global society whose borders are fast dissolving for civil society actors, International Relations requires a reconceptualization of 'order' at a lower level of analysis.

LIBERALISM AND PRIVATE GOVERNANCE

With some exceptions, there are few terms of reference in International Relations for investigating how 'lower levels' can contribute to governing international society. By low levels is meant here the domestic laws, regulations, and administrative structures of states that relate to private individuals. Early pluralist models of international society acknowledged the influence of non-state actors, but on the whole merely described an international system where multiple actors diffuse power and authority.[19] There is certainly now an appreciation of the fact that non-state actors who are transnationally mobile impact on the character of international governance.[20] James Rosenau's broad conception of 'steering mechanisms',[21] as well as work on international

---

[19] Such early pluralist accounts of international society were concerned mainly with breaking the state-centred mould of the realists. John Burton, and even Keohane and Nye – though surely less 'pluralist' – appreciated that some non-state actors could hold 'power', but did not provide a clear explanation of how mechanisms of international governance adapt because of their activities. See John Burton, *World Society*, Cambridge: Cambridge University Press, 1972; R. Keohane and J. Nye, *Power and Interdependence: World Politics in Transition*, Boston: Little, Brown, 1977.

[20] See, for instance the work of the Commission on Global Governance and the commentaries by Richard Falk, 'Liberalism at the global level: the last of the independent commissions', *Millennium: Journal of International Studies*, vol. 24, no. 3, 1995, pp. 563–76; and Lee-Anne Broadhead, 'Commissioning consent: globalization and global governance', *International Journal*, LI, vol. 4, Autumn 1996, pp. 651–88. Work in International Political Economy seems to be more sensitive to this question, for instance in the relationship between states and multinational corporations. See, for example, Susan Strange and John Stopford, *Rival States, Rival Firms: Competition for World Market Shares*, Cambridge: Cambridge University Press, 1991.

[21] James Rosenau, 'Governance in the twenty-first century', *Global Governance: Review of Multilateral and International Organization*, vol. 1, no. 1, Winter 1995, p. 18. See also Craig N. Murphy, *International Organization and Industrial Change Since 1850*, Cambridge: Polity Press, 1994; and Martin Shaw, 'The global revolution and the twenty-first century: from international relations to global politics', in Stephen Chan

civil society,[22] take a broader view of 'politics' on the international plane as interest aggregation and agitation which helps to shift the focus from purely public policy considerations.

However, while International Relations – as the study of the sociological processes of world society – has made advances in appreciating the role of transnational civil society actors in a number of areas, International Relations – as the study of international governance – has not, on the whole, engaged the enterprise of examining 'low level' governance in a systematic way.[23] In even fewer cases is international governance defined in terms of assimilated systems of municipal law that transcend sovereign states, although this question is particularly pertinent since current theorizing about the transformation of sovereignty is grappling with changing 'political spaces', or in John Gerrard Ruggie's terminology, 'multiperspectival institutional forms'.[24]

If anything, there are biases against the idea that low level governance can contribute to ordering international society. On a theoretical level, for instance, the ideas of functionalists of ordering international society through non-political, functional, technical, incremental steps has been dismissed. Robert Cox remarked of functionalists, 'they thought of those persons who were interested in effective performance of ... technical tasks as useful if often

---

contd.
and Jarrod Wiener (eds), *Twentieth Century International History: A Reader*, London: I. B Taurus, 1998.

22 See Justin Rosenberg, *Empire of Civil Society: A Critique of the Realist Theory of International Relations*, London: Verso, 1994; Ronnie D. Lipschutz, 'Reconstructing world politics: the emergence of global civil society', *Millennium: Journal of International Studies*, vol. 1, no. 3, 1992, pp. 389–420; and Alejandro Colas, 'The promises of international civil society', *Global Society: Journal of Interdisciplinary International Relations*, vol. 11, no. 3, 1997.

23 Of course, theories of functionalism have recognized that cooperation at lower levels of analysis could affect the shape of larger structures. See David Mitrany, *A Working Peace System*, Chicago: Quadrangle Books, 1966; and Ernst Hass, *Beyond the Nation State*, Stanford: Stanford University Press, 1964. However, studies of functional integration also have been concerned largely with matters of policy, in the sense that traditional spheres of national policy would be handed over to technical experts to be handled transnationally. Functional integration theories did not engage seriously the assimilation of national laws, especially outside of the European project with which they became closely associated.

24 John Gerrard Ruggie, 'Territoriality and beyond: problematizing modernity in international relations', *International Organization*, vol. 47, no. 1, Winter 1993, pp. 139–74.

unconscious builders of world government'.[25] As Donald Puchala stated, this was 'not really politics at all but technocratic dealings of little political consequence'.[26]

On another, philosophical, level, the difficulty in conceiving of international governance arising from systems of private regulation can be due to liberal 'myths' that perpetuate a conceptual separation of public/private.[27] Claire Cutler has identified four liberal myths that form the 'foundation for the separation of economic and political processes, giving rise to the association of economics with the private sphere and politics with the public sphere and rationalising their differential treatment'.[28] These 'myths' are that economic activity is natural, neutral and apolitical, consensual and non-coercive and efficient. Thus, the task of government regulation through 'public' law (which expresses public policy) is to ensure that no anti-competitive or deviant behaviour interrupts the natural flow of economic activity, and through private law (laws governing the relations between private individuals) to ensure fairness between contracting parties. Liberalism perpetuates the belief that the 'private' is not political, and therefore is not regulation, or power.

It is ironic that writers opining the demise of the sovereign state arising from the transnational activities of private individuals accept certain aspects of liberalism as given – privatization, deregulation – but an uncritical acceptance of the nature of government regulation in relation to these liberal 'myths' leads to the conclusion that regulation is futile. Much of the globalization literature seems to have accepted uncritically the liberal myth that public policy regulation *is* regulation and that private law is not, hence the conclusion that there is no way for states to control transnational civil society actors who present risks to the state. The strong thesis of globalization seems to restate, though less eloquently and with less theoretical rigour, the premise that a liberal market system tends to destroy the political foundations on which it

---

[25] Robert W. Cox, 'Introduction: perspectives and problems', in Cox (ed.), *International Organisation: World Politics*, London: Macmillan, 1969, p. 23.

[26] Donald J. Puchala, 'Integration theory and the study of international relations', in Richard L. Merritt and Bruce M. Russett, *From National Development to Global Community: Essays in Honor of Karl W. Deutsch*, London: George Allen & Unwin, 1981, p. 150.

[27] On these dichotomies, see Justin Rosenberg, *Empire of Civil Society*, op. cit.

[28] Claire Cutler, 'Global capitalism and liberal myths: dispute settlement in private international trade relations', *Millennium: Journal of International Studies*, vol. 24, no. 3, 1995, pp. 377–97.

depends, without realizing that a market system depends just as much on a 'private' regulation function as it does on public policy.[29] Indeed, it is doubtful whether capitalism would have emerged as a viable system without the private laws to guarantee at least the sanctity of private property and contract and to prevent crime. The suggestion that 'private', or municipal, laws do not provide a governance system in a deregulated and liberalized international system would be akin to suggesting that 'private' laws did not develop as aspects of governance in the domestic realm during the birth of capitalism.

While this public/private distinction contributes to a perceived lack of alternatives, it also does not touch centrally on the thesis of this book. With the exception of private international trade law, the laws that are investigated are public in the sense that they are designed to advance aspects of government public policy; they are not 'private' in the sense that they are not designed, like contract law, to regulate conduct between private individuals. The main blurring that occurs in considering municipal laws to be mechanisms of international governance comes in the conceptual separation of inside/outside – the function of municipal law, on the one hand, and the mechanisms of international governance, on the other. Indeed, a conceptual separation exists between *municipal* law that is regarded as falling *within* the domain of the state and *international* governance, which is regarded as an outgrowth of public policy. Occasionally, proponents of 'global civil society' make reference to the fact that some aspects of public international law apply to private individuals.[30] However, the municipal laws of states used to regulate civil society generally have not been thought to be mechanisms of international governance because they remained confined to the 'inside'.

While International Relations has been slow, particularly in the context of globalization, to appreciate the international governance aspects of the municipal laws of states, legal scholars have been attuned to the effects of globalization on the law. For instance, Alfred C. Aman Jr. has noted that:

> Domestic law – local, state or federal – may ... be affected significantly by a variety of forces outside the control of any of the local decision-makers involved. Global forces may encourage new forms of economic and legal harmonisation across legal and economic systems.

---

[29] See Karl Polanyi, *The Great Transformation*, London: Beacon Press, 1980.

[30] For instance, as relate to war crimes, or to mixed international commercial arbitration between states and aliens.

He goes on to argue for a focus 'directly on globalization as involving not only a shift in the *scale* of law, but also (and especially) the *dynamics* of legal processes'.[31] Also, there appears to be in the discipline of law an appreciation that regionalization and globalization are more complementary than opposing processes, and affect municipal laws similarly.[32] However, while lawyers are grappling with the 'globalization of law', none seem able to agree on what precisely this is. Does it mean harmonization of municipal law, or does it mean approximation of law through international treaty? Does it involve a denationalization of public authority and domestic legal orders, or does it increase the sovereignty of the state?[33] Yet, this is a debate which International Relations has yet even to engage seriously.

Several factors combine to make the domestic laws of distinct sovereign states instruments of international governance. The first, at the structural level, is political and economic liberalism. 'Structure' here refers to a neo-Gramscian superstructure of power and ideas and state-society

---

[31] Alfred C. Aman Jr., 'Indiana Journal of Global Legal Studies: an introduction', *Indiana Journal of Global Legal Studies*, vol. 1, no. 1, 1993, available: http://www.law.indiana.edu/glsj/vol11/aman.html.

[32] Stephen Zamora, 'Nafta and the harmonization of domestic legal systems: the side effects of free trade', *Arizona Journal of International and Comparative Law*, vol. 12, no. 1, pp. 401–27; Frederick M. Abbott, 'Regional integration mechanisms in the law of the United States: starting over', *Indiana Journal of Global Legal Studies*, vol. 1, no. 1, 1993. Available at www.law.indiana.edu/glsj/vol1/abbott.html. There is also an appreciation in some quarters of International Political Economy that regionalization and globalization are complementary. For a good summary, see Richard Higgott, '*De facto* and *de jure* regionalism: the double discourse of regionalism in the Asia Pacific', *Global Society: Journal of Interdisciplinary International Relations*, vol. 11, no. 2, 1997.

[33] For a small sample that illustrates the confusion, see: Benjamin R. Barber, 'Global democracy or global law: Which comes first?', *Indiana Journal of Global Legal Studies*, vol. 1, no. 1, 1993. Available at www.law.indiana.edu/glsj/vol1/; Jost Delbruck, 'Globalisation of law, politics, and markets - implications for domestic law: a European perspective', *Indiana Journal of Global Legal Studies*, vol. 1, no. 1, 1993. Available www.law.indiana.edu/glsj/vol1/delbruck.html; Martin Shapiro, 'The globalisation of law', *Indiana Journal of Global Legal Studies*, vol. 1, no. 1, 1993. Available: www.law.indiana.edu/glsj/vol1/shapiro.html; Elizabeth Zoller, 'Institutional aspects of international governance', *Indiana Journal of Global Legal Studies*, vol. 3, no. 1, 1995. Available: www.law.indiana.edu/glsj/vol3/no1/zoller.html; Gordon R. Walker and Mark A. Fox, 'Globalisation: an analytical framework', *Indiana Journal of Global Legal Studies*, vol. 3, no. 2, 1996. Available: www.law.indiana.edu/glsj/vol3/no2/walker/html. Fortunately, the approach of this book is not one of borrowing method from the lawyers, since there appears not to be one.

complex that legitimate certain modes of governance.[34] The structure under which the practices under investigation in this book have evolved, such as private international finance and computer-mediated communications, is due to the desire on the part of governments to liberalize and to privatize these practices. In the words of Ronnie D. Lipschutz, 'The principles of economic and political liberalism ... come to represent something like the *jus civile* of the civilized community, existing above the laws of individual states.'[35] By reference to 'above', Lipschutz is referring to a kind of ideational structure. Lipschutz recognizes that there is a vagueness to this 'operating system' of liberalism due to its broad parameters. Like an operating system on a computer, liberalism describes parameters for certain executable codes, and determines the manner in which individual computer users will write programmes, but it does not specify the programmes that will emerge. Similarly, while liberalism, for instance in international finance, requires lesser state involvement in managing flows of international capital, it offers little guidance beyond that.

The second factor that has made municipal laws mechanisms of international governance follows from this, and that is conflicting objectives of states' public policies. Certain practices – like finance and computer-mediated communications – have been liberalized and deregulated, yet while one goal of public policy may be liberalizing a particular area of activity, this can frustrate other aspects of government public policy. For instance, the liberalization of finance has promoted one aspect of public policy, to increase the circulation of private capital, but this has presented challenges to other aspects of states' public policy, such as by increasing the risk of pressure on the social safety nets for depositors maintained by many governments. If a state no longer controls the flows of capital internationally, but it does pick up the tab when things go wrong, there are incentives to re-regulate. That deregulation and liberalization have retained importance while presenting risks to other aspects of public policy in large measure explains re-regulation. And municipal law can be an effective method through which to discipline private individuals. If, as Lipschutz says, liberalism operates 'above' the laws of states, then an adaptation

---

[34] See Stephen Gill, *American Hegemony and the Trilateral Commission*, Cambridge: Cambridge University Press, 1990; Stephen Gill (ed.), *Gramsci, Historical Materialism and International Relations*, Cambridge: Cambridge University Press, 1993.

[35] Ronnie D. Lipschutz, 'Reconstructing world politics'. *Millennium: Journal of International Relations*, pp. 389–420.

process is required to hone the laws of states to fit within the broader goals. To continue the analogy, to govern a practice that is liberalized and privatized at the level of the 'operating system' requires honing the individual codes of the 'computer program'; that is, honing the laws and regulations that govern individuals, and individuals are the subjects of municipal law.

Indeed, the use of municipal law to discipline private individuals is by no means new. Since the time that modern states were consolidated, and indeed much earlier, public authorities, in the widest sense of the term, have always used law to control civil society actors and to regulate the economy.[36] As Michel Foucault observed, 'with government it is a question not of imposing law on men, but of disposing things; that is to say, of employing tactics rather than laws, and even of using laws themselves as tactics'.[37] Foucault continued, 'laws, decrees [and] regulations [are] the traditional weapons of sovereignty'.[38] While this method of control is not new, the orientation of the law to transnational risks may be new.

This is not to suggest that the laws investigated in this book have been handed down by fiat. If anything, the debates, for instance over the protection of copyright on the Internet, show that pluralist democratic processes are alive and well. The debate illustrates that the frames of reference about how to adapt the laws and coercive apparatuses of the state concern the balance between individual freedom, opportunities and social costs. For example, while there are competitive advantages for a bank to be able to operate with minimum capital reserves in a deregulated international banking market, and advantages to the economy in the form of increased liquidity, the social costs could be financial instability and pressure on government-maintained safety nets for depositors in the event of a bank failure. Similarly, while there are numerous economic, technological, educational and cultural advantages for the state and society to develop high-speed digital communications, there is a need to balance the rights of individuals to use the technology and to use and share

---

36 See, for instance, Gaines Post, *Studies in Medieval Legal Thought*, Princeton, NJ: Princeton University Press, 1964; and Sir Henry Sumner Maine, *Ancient Law: Its Connection with the Early History of Society and its Relation to Modern Times*, 5th edn, London: John Murray, 1874.

37 Michel Foucault, 'Governmentality', in Graham Burchell, Colin Gordon, and Peter Miller (eds), *The Foucault Effect: Studies in Governmentality*, London: Harvester Wheatsheaf, 1991, p. 95.

38 Ibid.

information with the rights of copyright holders to ensure that individuals will not lose an incentive for creativity.

Political debate in a free society encounters such dilemmas and engages in such debates almost daily, as they should. Debates centre around the extent to which the state, as the guarantor of rights and the arbiter of social and political conflicts, should intervene to limit freedoms for the wider good of the society, which at a basic level is the maintenance of an effective system of law. However, the debate also illustrates that the groundwork upon which such considerations takes place shifts fundamentally once an individual's will (to move money, to obtain information) translates into actions that are able to traverse space irrespective of sovereign borders without this also entailing the physical movement of the individual.

Political debate contained within a particular political community cannot resolve the dilemma of balancing rights when part of the equation is an unknown quantity residing outside. To take a simplified example, while State A can enforce legislation to ensure the soundness of banks located on its territory, it is very difficult, if not impossible, to govern the activities of other banks located in State B. If a bank in State B fails while owing large sums of money to a bank in State A, this can force the bank in State A to fail as well, leaving insecurity in the banking system and leaving the government of State A to reimburse its depositors. Thus, the difficult question arises whether one state's law, which on the whole is bound territorially (with certain notable exceptions for extraterritorial application), is sufficient to regulate the activities of civil society actors who are transnationally mobile, or whose actions are felt transnationally. As the recognized boundaries drawn by public officials on a physical map of the world become challenged, difficult questions arise in the search for consonance between threats to 'societal security' and the law. And, as the borders of a political community become permeable to the will and actions of individuals outside of them, the risks to the laws and regulations (and values) of that political community become transnationalized. Commensurately, the ability of the state, defined as public authority, to act as arbiter between the rights and freedoms of its constituent members and the social costs that emanate from outside its jurisdiction is called into question. Therefore, the ground upon which political authority is able to be exerted is most certainly shifting.

The use of municipal laws as instruments of international governance takes the form of two related processes. The first is domestication, by which is meant the adoption of municipal law to control the activities of individuals. The level of municipal law is precisely the level which governs the realm which the actors – bankers, criminals, traders, Internet users – inhabit. Domestication is meant in both literal senses of the word: to domesticate, as one does a wild animal; and to exercise domestic control through the passage of municipal laws. Domestication reins in, nationalizes, or localizes control of transnational civil society actors to the jurisdiction of the state as municipal laws, on the whole, are enforceable in a particular jurisdiction.[39] The process of domestication in some cases also involves the 'privatization of governance', as will be shown, such as by making banks responsible for recognizing money laundering and by making systems operators responsible for ensuring that no copyright infringements occur on the Internet.

The process of domesticating control has, as its corollary, the harmonization of those municipal laws. Deregulation and privatization place the onus on states to re-regulate through municipal law, yet the municipal law of one state is insufficient to regulate effectively transnational activities. The borders of a state are permeable to the actions of individuals outside, thus risks to the values of that state become transnationalized, and municipal law in one state may do little to stop risks generated by transnational actors. Clearly, so long as laws relating to civil society actors remain tied to territory while the risks increasingly are not, such threats could continue. The important caveat is that such threats will continue so long as the laws of sovereign states remain different. If all states were to supervise international banks to the same extent, or to control money laundering by the same means, transnational threats would be mitigated. Thus, it follows that states, acting singly, cannot assert control over transnational actors, at least as long as independent action promotes difference. The functional harmonization of laws among different states widens the regulatory space over which the laws preside.

Harmonization is a concept common to International Relations and comparative law. In the latter, it most commonly refers to 'conscious governmental efforts at legal reform to achieve some level of concordance with other legal systems'.[40] This study employs the term 'harmonization' as it is understood by A. J. R. Groom and Alexis Heraclides. For them, it involves 'institutionalised policy adjustments

---

[39] With notable exceptions for the extraterritorialization of laws. See M.N. Shaw, *International Law*, 2nd edn, Cambridge: Grotius Publications Limited, 1986, pp. 367–71.

[40] Stephen Zamora, op. cit., p. 404.

and alignments, often on the basis of some superordinate norm or standard ... [and] compatible parallel legislation or practices are separately instituted by different actors in order to reduce the impact of boundaries'.[41] Indeed, the effectiveness of the national laws adopted in the attempt to domesticate risk depends largely on harmonizing those laws across borders.

Groom and Heraclides continue, 'The scope [of harmonization] can be considerable and although there is little formal institutionalization, there may be much informal contact and consultation.'[42] The harmonization of laws between the United States and the European Union is occurring through informal international concordats and agreements that are not legally binding – they express broad statements of principle and agreement on the manner in which to proceed with domestic legislation – but lead to the adoption of essentially similar municipal legislation that remains legally enforceable within each state's jurisdiction. Harmonization is undertaken in many international organizations which oblige states to transpose international legal obligations into domestic law. However, it is important to stress that treaties normally impose obligations of *result* rather than an obligation of means.[43] What this study finds is that the United States and the European Union have pursued a strategy of harmonizing the *means* of controlling civil society actors who present risks to their public policies, sometimes to the letter of the law.

---

41 A. J. R. Groom and Alexis Heraclides, 'Integration and disintegration', in Margot Light and A. J. R. Groom (eds), *International Relations: A Handbook of Current Theory*, London: Pinter, 1985, p. 177. There are other definitions. As defined by R. J. Harrison and Stuart Mungall, harmonization involves 'creating standards implemented as policy by the individual states in their own ways'. R. J. Harrison and Stuart Mungall, 'Harmonization', in A. J. R. Groom and Paul Taylor, *Frameworks for International Co-operation*, London: Pinter, 1990, p. 58. Robert Cox defines harmonization as 'a process of close intergovernmental consultation where each government maintains the autonomy of its own decision-making process but attempts to meet the preoccupations of other co-operating governments', but this may give the misleading impression of a forced enterprise. See Cox, op. cit., p. 41.

42 Groom and Heraclides, op. cit.

43 International lawyers, such as Jost Delbruck, have described the effects of the 'globalisation of laws on domestic law' with reference to the law-making ability of international institutions. For instance, the General Agreement on Tariffs and Trade (GATT) and the OECD 'rely on the globalization, i.e., harmonization and denationalization of the domestic legal orders through international agreements that oblige the states to transpose the international legal obligations into domestic law'. See Jost Delbruck, 'Globalisation of law, politics, and markets', op. cit. Available at URL: http://www.law.indiana.edu/glsj/vol1/delbruck.html.

The functional harmonization of national laws is associated most closely perhaps with the project of regional integration among the Member States of the European Union. Beginning with Article 100 of the Treaty of Rome in 1958, Member States of the EU harmonized nearly 200 of their laws, regulations and administrative provisions in such diverse areas as taxation, social policy, transportation and the environment to eliminate obstacles to the establishment of a Common Market.[44] Harmonization here refers, as in the context of the European Union, to the process of assimilating national legislation over which each state retains jurisdiction. However, it does not imply the creation of super-national legislation or supra-national authority, nor does it entail a centralized system of drafting legislation. Just as harmonization is distinct from the development of Community law in the European Union,[45] the term is employed here to denote a process of national convergence by adopting similar municipal legislation that remains separately enforceable by each state.

While as much as 60 per cent of the national legislation of EU Member States originates in Brussels, the functional harmonization investigated here is far less 'wide' and 'deep'. This is a function of the differing impetus to the harmonization. That impetus in the European Union is politically determined by a conscious decision to build a Common Market and, to that end, to empower the European Commission to issue Directives which Member States enact in their national legislation. While harmonization in the European Union has accompanied a politically determined constructive process, in the sense that it is designed to build a region, the functional harmonization of concern here is a much looser, *ad hoc* process that is driven by shared interests to preserve public policies in the face of transnational challenges. In the European Union, sceptics of integration tout that a loss of state sovereignty has been a corollary to harmonization, such that it is now apposite in some quarters to speak of 'residual sovereignty' remaining in the Member States. On the other hand is the view that the European Union strengthens the state by pooling

---

[44] Other Articles relevant to harmonization are Article 100a, Article 100b, and Article 101. This discussion does not dwell on the mechanisms of harmonization in the European Union. For further information, the reader may consult a concise explanation in Daniel Vignes, 'The harmonisation of the national legislation of the EEC', *European Law Review*, 1990, pp. 358–74.

[45] Although it is recognized that Article 8A of the Single Act, 1992 establishes a more complex interface between Community and national law whereby the former may be substituted for the latter. See Vignes, ibid.

sovereignty.[46] This study finds that harmonization is intended to, and has the effect of, reasserting state sovereignty, though without the institutional outcomes that have been produced by the integration project in the European Union. As R. J. Harrison and Stuart Mungall have noted, 'the major advantage of harmonization in achieving policy congruence among various national actors is that it explicitly avoids intruding on national sovereignty'.[47]

The case studies in banking, money laundering and the Internet concentrate on the harmonization that has taken place across the Atlantic. This is because both the United States and the European Union are highly integrated into the international financial system and electronic communications networks, and they are permeated by the risks emanating from international banking establishments, transnational criminals, and by individuals copying materials on the Internet. The increased speed of transnational transactions and the intensification of the volume of such transactions due to technological developments, be they related to the flow of money – both legitimate and illegitimate – or to the dissemination of copyrighted material through digital communications networks, have challenged the ability of both the United States and the Member States of the European Union to regulate and to control.

The United States and the Member States of the European Union share similar interests in asserting control in these areas. Their interests in the regulation and supervision of banking are predicated upon the fact that they both maintain socially motivated central bank-administered schemes to promote the stability of their banking systems because their economies are highly dependent on preventing contagion and systemic risks in the financial system. Their interests in arresting money laundering stems from the fact that such activity enables criminals to reap the benefits of all manner of crime (and, of course, to evade taxation). Finally, their interests in controlling the copying of copyrighted material on the Internet is predicated upon their interests in advancing electronic communication to enhance the efficiency of their information-dependent economies in such a way that safeguards, and adapts, their existing regimes to protect intellectual property.

As Harrison and Mungall noted, 'harmonization suggests itself where discussion between national policy-makers may discover an

---

[46] See Robert Keohane and Stanley Hoffman, *The New European Community: Decision Making and Institutional Change*, Colorado: Westview, 1991.

[47] Harrison and Mungall, op. cit., p. 63.

existing value consensus which can be the ground for a wide range of agreements'. They continue:

> Interdependence ... provides conditions in which the national interest can be seen to coincide with a collective, international interest ... What this seems to suggest is that [harmonization] can work most effectively in areas where actors operate in a self-interested manner and these are not only areas where values are congruent but where the operational goals of governments coincide.[48]

Therefore, to summarize, this study employs the following questions as its analytical framework in the case studies that follow:

1. What is the extent of liberalization, deregulation and privatization in each area investigated, and what have been the pressures and public policy priorities for such liberalization?
2. What are the main problems of governance, or 'risks' that have arisen from this liberalization, in terms of a frustration of other aspects of public policy?
3. Who are the main protagonists of risk, and what is the extent of their transnationalization?
4. Through what means of international cooperation are the risks being addressed?
5. What attempts are being made at the level of municipal law to mitigate risk (domestication)?
6. In what ways are the municipal laws of the United States and the European Union becoming harmonized in these areas?

SUMMARY

This book explores mechanisms of governing international society not from the top down as has been the norm since the mid-1800s, but from the bottom up through the assimilation of states' municipal legal structures. This is due to the fact that an important aspect of governing international society is controlling civil society actors. In the areas investigated in this book, states are not the principal agents of destabilization; it is the activities of private individuals – be they criminals, international bankers, or Internet users – that threaten certain values and policies of governments. And as this book will show, as civil society actors have become transnationalized to a greater extent,

---

[48] Harrison and Mungall, ibid., pp. 58 and 65.

civil society regulations have become transnationalized as well. The mechanism of domestication and harmonization examined here differs fundamentally from institutionalized governance at the level of public policy coordination because the contingency/threat that underlies this form of governance operates at a different level.

A central issue that arises from the case studies here is nothing less than the fact that domestication and harmonization are empowering the state – which argues against the strong thesis of globalization – in the sense that it provides assurances that similar legislation in other states, in this case, in the United States and the European Union, will be enforced separately by each. Domestication and harmonization are methods of responding to some transnational challenges while working within the states system. By states system is generally meant 'several states that are so connected as to seem to constitute one body but whose members retain sovereignty'.[49] Here, it means a system of more or less self-contained legal communities, whose politically independent (sovereign) authorities articulate laws (including rules, norms and administrative procedures). However, the globalized economy increasingly presents states with challenges and opportunities that are the same (depending on their level of integration into its various systems), and the evidence presented here shows that the legal frameworks of the United States and the European Union in certain issue areas are becoming increasingly similar as well. Otherwise distinct units at the political level of authority, the laws of states are converging on an administrative level.

The idea of assimilated legal/administrative spaces that transcend sovereign borders raises interesting questions about international order. International cooperation through policy coordination takes as given the assumption that states are differentiated political entities based on the existence of a common rationality which belongs to the state (reason of state, *raison d'état, stattsreason, ragione di stato*).[50] The emergence of a different kind of international governance outlined in this book is due to the fact that disorder in the issue areas investigated is now threatened by transnationally mobile civil society actors whose reach has been extended by the relaxation of public policy and the development of technology. Is it at all surprising that the 'empire of

---

[49] Martin Wight, quoting Pufendorf, in *System of States*, London: Leicester University Press, 1977, at p. 21.

[50] The ideas in this section derive largely from conversations with Stefan Rossbach, for which I am grateful.

civil society' is being accompanied by an 'empire of law'?[51] Contemplations of mechanisms of governance that transcend sovereign state borders originated, in the main, from cosmopolitan projects for the creation of a supranational political authority. Possibly, if the integrative forces of the liberalized and deregulated international system continue to assimilate states at the level of municipal law, world governance will not come from the 'top' at all, and a form of international governance will emerge that will not look at all like it had been anticipated since the 1300s. This is a development of the argument on which this book will end in proposing an agenda for future research.

[51] The first reference is, of course, to Justin Rosenberg's *Empire of Civil Society*, op. cit.; the second is to James Harrington's 'empire of law'. See H. F. Russell-Smith, *Harrington and His Oceana: A Study of a 17th Century Utopia and Its Influence in America*, Cambridge: Cambridge University Press, 1914.

CHAPTER 3

HARMONIZING THE REGULATION AND SUPERVISION OF INTERNATIONAL BANKS

Finance has become 'globalized', to the extent that states that are integrated into the international financial system are susceptible to shocks emanating from outside at great speed. The risks that inhere in international finance are numerous, and much has been written about the challenges to regulatory authorities presented by international currency trading and international banking. This chapter begins by surveying such risks to provide substance to the discussion that follows. It is argued that the risks presented by international banking have been confronted through concurrent processes of domestication and harmonization. Attention is focused on the series of Concordats of the Basle Committee on Banking Regulation and Supervisory Practices.[1] Particular attention is given to the manner in which the Committee's Minimum Standards of 1992[2] have provided a basis for the harmonization of national legislation, the United States' Foreign-Bank Supervision Enhancement Act of 1991[3] and the European Union's

---

[1] Known as the 'Basle Committee', this is an informal consultative group under the auspices of the Bank for International Settlements at Basle, Switzerland, comprising representatives of the central banks of Belgium, Canada, France, Germany, Great Britain, Italy, Japan, The Netherlands, Switzerland, the United States, Luxemburg, and Sweden.

[2] Bank for International Settlements, Committee on Banking Regulation and Supervisory Practices, *Minimum Standards for the Supervision of Banking Groups and their Cross-Border Establishments*, 1992. Hereafter 'Minimum Standards'.

[3] United States Foreign Bank Supervision Enhancement Act of 1991, FBSEA, Pub. L. No. 101–242, sections 201–215, 105 Stat. 2236–305, Washington, DC: Government Printing Office, 1991.

Directive on the Supervision of Credit Institutions on a Consolidated Basis.[4]

THE PROBLEM: FINANCE AND RISK

Much has been written about the risks to state sovereignty in the globalized financial system. Some writers have written of a 'stateless' transnational financial system, 'delinked' in some fundamental way from the control and perhaps even the oversight of states. Phil Cerny has referred to 'the crystallisation and consolidation of a genuinely transnational and increasingly autonomous financial market'.[5] In the words of Eric Helleiner, 'All states have been losing power to the international markets in the financial arena making their management of such markets more difficult in recent years.'[6] Others perhaps somewhat overstate the point, such as Gregory Millman, who in journalistic style commented that 'the new markets in risk baffle old-school bankers, humiliate presidents, and elevate twenty-something traders to a rankless power from which they determine the fate of nations. They are a sign of capital's triumph over all social constraints.'[7] Finally, one must not overlook Charles Kindleberger's succinct statement (though in a different context) that 'the nation-state is just about through as an economic unit'.[8]

Such arguments relate to the foreign currency market, where approximately US$1.2 trillion is traded every day.[9] The position of central banks *vis-à-vis* the market has been expressed succinctly by Andrew Walter:

---

[4] Council Directive 92/30 of 6 April 1992 on the Supervision of Credit Institutions on a Consolidated Basis, *Official Journal of the European Communities*, L110, 52, Brussels, 1992.

[5] Phil Cerny, 'The political economy of international finance', in Cerny (ed.), *Finance and World Politics*, Aldershot: Edward Elgar, 1993, p. 13.

[6] Eric Helleiner, 'States and the future of global finance', *Review of International Studies*, vol. 18, no. 1, 1992, p. 49.

[7] Gregory J. Millman, *Around the World on a Trillion Dollars a Day: How Rebel Currency Traders Destroy Banks and Defy Governments*, London: Bantam Press, 1995, p. xvii.

[8] Charles Kindleberger, *American Business Abroad*, New Haven: Yale University Press, 1969, p. 207.

[9] Millman, op. cit.

> At the end of 1989 ... international interbank deposits (net of redepositing) were $3.5 trillion. Since the total foreign exchange reserves of central banks were almost $800 billion by mid-1990, it was clear by then that the international interbank market easily dominated the official sector. Central bank reserves are less than the equivalent of *two days'* turnover in the world's foreign exchange markets, which indicates that one central bank or even a number of central banks intervening together in exchange markets cannot hope to oppose a concerted onslaught on a particular currency or currencies by the exchange markets.[10]

Walter continued, 'the global financial revolution has been characterised by a dramatic shift in the balance of power away from national and international public authorities towards the private market'. This challenge is rather new, as it pertains only under a system of deregulated finance, which began following the breakdown of the Bretton Woods system in 1971.

The other side of the argument is that while central bankers may regard some currency trading as being akin to a virus which occasionally attacks its host, one should bear in mind that with the exception of very few viruses which mutate quickly, they do not destroy the organisms which give it life. While there is no doubt that currency markets discipline governments – and little doubt that this was the intention of neo-liberal orthodoxy – it is straining the argument to suggest that currency traders are likely to be inclined, not to mention sufficiently organized, to attack the entire foundations of the financial system from which they profit. Systemic risk does not necessarily follow from floating exchange rates without state-imposed capital controls.[11]

Another risk inherent in the present globalized system which has prompted much commentary relates to the risks posed by new financial instruments, derivatives.[12] It has been said that derivatives are 'any

---

[10] Andrew Walter, *World Power and World Money: The Role of Hegemony and International Monetary Order*, London: Harvester Wheatsheaf, 1993, p. 199.

[11] Indeed, as Hirst and Thompson noted, the financial system before the First World War was in many ways more deregulated and remained more or less stable. See Paul Hirst and Grahame Thompson, *Globalisation in Question*, Cambridge: Polity Press, 1996.

[12] Many writers have stressed that the volume of trading in derivatives presents a systemic risk. See, for instance, Stephen Zamora, 'Regulating the global banking network – what role (if any) for the IMF?', *Fordham Law Review*, vol. 62, 1994, at p. 1953; and Peter E. Millspaugh, 'Global securities trading: the question of a watchdog', *George Washington Journal of International Law and Economics*, vol. 26, 1992, at p. 355.

financial product that is difficult to understand', including exchange-traded instruments, such as options and futures with standardized contracts for size, maturity and delivery, and over-the-counter (OTC) instruments, which are customized to the specific needs of parties, including forwards, swaps, swaptions, caps, floors and collars, leveraged swaps and structured notes.[13] Of these, it has been said that there is 'no generally accepted meaning to the term derivative', and that the computer-designed hybrids can 'scare anyone silly'.[14]

Derivatives have given rise to a number of risks. Some are not new to international finance, such as credit risks, which obtain when a counterparty is unable to meet the terms of the contract through insolvency and default; event risk, which occurs when a contract is frustrated due to a political upheaval or natural catastrophe; or legal risks, which occur when changes in the law affect transactions, such as occurred when the High Court declared the interest rate swaps undertaken by Hammersmith and Fulham Borough Council to be *ultra vires*, as local authorities did not have the power to enter into such contracts. The result of this was that banks lost a total of £550 million from contracts with local authorities.[15] Neither are operational risks new; Barings Bank was not the first in history to operate with lax management oversight and poor auditing systems.[16] However, a new risk in international finance to which these financial instruments give rise is intellectual risk, in the sense that many bankers – the managing directors of Barings Bank being a case in point – do not understand fully the new instruments. As *The Economist* commented: 'To control money, you must know what "money" is – and, thanks partly to innovation and the growth of international finance, that is no longer clear.'[17]

---

[13] A full discussion of these is outside the scope of this study. For a comprehensive examination of each, see Saul S. Cohen, 'Financial services regulation: a mid-decade review: colloquium: the challenges of derivatives', *Fordham Law Review*, vol. 63, 1995, at p. 1993.

[14] Ibid., p. 1993 and p. 2000.

[15] Ibid., p. 2012.

[16] In this case, the trader Nick Leeson was able to disguise losses of US$1 billion incurred on foreign-exchange markets by establishing a secret account and reporting profits to the head office. For an interesting account of the mismanagement of banks throughout history, see Russell Taylor, *Going for Broke: How Banking Mismanagement in the Eighties Lost £ Thousands of Billions*, London: Simon & Schuster, 1993.

[17] 'Fear of finance', *The Economist*, op. cit., p. 29, note 9. This cites the growth in the global stock of derivatives from US$1.1 trillion in 1986 to US$6.9 trillion in 1991. See also 'Banks and derivatives markets: a challenge for financial policy', *IMF Survey*, 21 February 1994, pp. 49–51.

However, there is another side to this argument as well. While new financial instruments in the world of derivatives are risky, they generally do not pose a systemic risk to the financial system. In fact, many have argued that these instruments were designed to minimize risks to international commercial operations; the risks are accepted by those who speculate in exchange markets. For instance, Andrew Walter commented that 'new instruments such as financial futures and options unbundle and redistribute risk to those more willing to bear it, thereby lending greater stability to the system'.[18] The Economists Roundtable agreed that 'the use of over-the-counter derivatives does not justify the current fear that they might cause a systemic meltdown'.[19] The current fear of derivatives, and of the securitization of banking in general, could be based on the fear of a repetition of the bank failures of the 1930s when banks engaged in securities operations. However, recent studies, such as that of the US Comptroller of the Currency, have concluded that 'studies have consistently demonstrated that the securities activities of banks had little, if anything, to do with the collapse of the banking system in 1933'.[20]

Another risk in international finance concerns the 'denationalization' of money. Money passes freely from one territory to another, but does so potentially through payments systems regulated by divergent national laws.[21] In the execution of an electronic fund transfer (EFT), for example, 'payment' is deemed by British banks to be the point at which the funds are transferred by the recipient bank into the account of the payee. The practice of Continental banks, on the other hand, is that the funds cannot be recalled after reaching the recipient bank.[22] As Tommaso Padoa-Schioppa and Fabrizio Saccomanni summarized:

> Settlements reflect the heterogeneity of domestic payment systems in terms of regulation, payment techniques, working hours, and finality ... there is no lender of last resort, nor is there a supervisory authority;

---

[18] See Walter, op. cit., p. 210. This echoes the statement of Alan Greenspan, Chairman of the Federal Reserve Board: 'the economic function of [derivatives] is to allow risks that formerly had been combined to be unbundled and transferred to those most willing to assume and manage each risk component'. Cited in Cohen, op. cit., p. 2004, at note 61.

[19] Cited in Cohen, op. cit., p. 2009, at note 78.

[20] Cited in Richard Dale, *International Banking Deregulation: The Great Banking Experiment*, Oxford: Blackwell, 1992, p. 27.

[21] See Millman, op. cit., p. 250.

[22] Ibid., p. 37.

> currencies are traded largely outside of their country of issue, and multiple clearing and settlement arrangements coexist.[23]

In addition, the courts have failed to agree on the law applicable to Eurocurrency transactions.[24] In *Libyan Arab Foreign Bank v. Bankers Trust Co.*[25] the United States attempted in 1986 to freeze the assets of Libya in response to its support of terrorist activities. Among these assets were US dollars held in an account of the London branch of Bankers Trust, which was a foreign branch of an American bank not separately incorporated in the United Kingdom. In complying with the Executive Order of President Reagan Bankers Trust refused an instruction to transfer $130 million from London to Libyan Arab Foreign Bank (LAFB). However, Justice Evans in the High Court in London found in favour of the plaintiff, LAFB, on the grounds that these deposits were subject to British law, even though they were denominated in US dollars. Thus, in this case, it was held that deposits are subject to the law of the place that is host to the branch of the foreign bank where the deposit is made. And this despite the fact that such a large Eurocurrency transaction is normally conducted through CHIPS or FedWire which would involve an instruction from the London branch to New York to perform the transaction, thus bringing the centre of gravity closer to New York as the applicable law. However, in a similar case involving US sanctions, Judge Knapp in *Wells Fargo Asia Ltd. v. Citibank* found that New York law would be the applicable law to a Eurocurrency transaction because the performance of the transfer would have to occur in a clearing house in New York. He stated:

> Since Eurodollar transactions denominated in US dollars customarily are cleared in New York, the rationale for application of New York law becomes even stronger. If the goal is to promote certainty in international financial markets, it makes sense to apply New York law

---

[23] Tommaso Padoa-Schioppa and Fabrizio Saccomanni, 'Managing a market-led global financial system', in Peter B. Kenen (ed.), *Managing the World Economy: Fifty Years After Bretton Woods*, Washington, DC: Institute for International Economics, 1994, p. 254.

[24] 'Eurocurrency' is the generic name of an account held in a different denomination than that issued by the government of the place where the deposit is held. Thus, the term Eurocurrency would apply to US dollars held outside the United States, to sterling held outside of the United Kingdom, and so on. The rise of the Euromarkets is explained in greater detail below.

[25] The details of this case are discussed at length by Peter S. Smedresman and Andreas F. Lowenfeld, 'Eurodollars, multinational banks, and national laws', *New York University Law Review*, vol. 64, 1989, at pp. 751–61.

> uniformly, rather than conditioning the deposit obligations on the vagaries of local law, and requiring each player in the Eurodollar market to investigate the law of numerous foreign countries to ascertain which would limit repayment of deposits to the foreign branch's own assets.[26]

In reviewing this and other cases, Harry Windecker concluded that the Euromarkets seem to have evolved 'a new species of transnational currency ... not only unregulated by an international authority, but also beyond the regulatory reach of any single country'.[27] Thus, since the courts have failed to agree on a single governing law for Euromarket transactions, there are indeed important risks associated with such international banking transactions. However, this does not denote a systemic risk. While the fact that the legal framework to govern particular transactions may change is dangerous, it is dangerous mainly to the participants involved in the litigation – as is true of any litigation – and it frustrates the attempt by governments to use their currency as weapons of economic statecraft. However, it is unlikely that the structure of the Euromarkets will come crashing down as a result.

Thus, in summary, while there are both new risks in international finance, and old ones that present themselves in new ways, they do not by themselves pose a systemic risk to the international financial system; while they could be regarded as presenting a condition for systemic risk, they are not sufficient to cause systemic risk. Rather, it is imprudent lending – the traditional activity of banks – which poses the greatest risk to the international banking system. As *The Economist* stated, 'As the recent spate of write-offs by banks around the world has shown, it is lending that is most fraught with risk.'[28] It went on to show how Citicorp wrote off US$736 million of North American property loans in 1991, and US$1.4 billion in 1992, whereas this class of lending comprised only 5 per cent of its loan portfolio.

There have always been risks in lending, the main categories of which are credit risk and liquidity risk. Credit risk pertains in a situation where a counterparty is not able to reimburse the bank when its obligation to do so falls due. Liquidity risk relates to the inability of banks to raise sufficient funds (liquid or capital) to meet current

---

[26] Quoted in ibid., p. 772.

[27] George H. Windecker, 'The Eurodollar deposit market: strategies for regulation', *The American University Journal of International Law and Policy*, vol. 9, Fall 1993, p. 278.

[28] 'New tricks to learn: survey of international banking', *The Economist*, 10 April 1993, p. 14.

needs.[29] And banks are uniquely vulnerable to contagious collapse. The threat of rapid international contagion has grown along with the growth of lending and the volume and speed of payments systems. A systemic risk to the international financial system can arise from the illiquidity or insolvency of a large bank which could lead to a series of bank failures due the downstream effects of these banks being unable to meet their obligations to others, and to a crisis of confidence among depositors which would precipitate a 'run' on the banks.

One such threat of systemic risk occurred in the Latin American Debt Crisis[30] which began in autumn 1982 when Mexico announced that it could not repay its debts. This was followed by similar threats of default by thirty other Latin American countries in 1983. Among them, Brazil announced that it would not pay the interest of US$9 billion for 1987; Honduras fell behind by US$15 million on its US$3 billion debt; Costa Rica fell behind US$12 million in interest payments; and Peru, Bolivia and Cuba simply stopped paying interest on their debts.[31] Many major banks with a high exposure of risk to sovereign debt were stricken by panic.

The Debt Crisis threatened to undermine the confidence in the international banking system by undermining the stability of the world's largest banks, which could have precipitated severe repercussions. Indeed, Citibank, the largest US bank at the time, was the largest player in Lesser Developed Country (LDC) debt.[32] It is worth recalling in this context Lord Keynes' maxim: 'If one owes a million to a bank, it is one's problem; but if one owes ten million, it is the bank's problem.'

The Debt Crisis is also an illustration of safety and solvency risks. At the root of the Debt Crisis was the fact that there was too much credit being made available in relation to the bank's reserves. Indeed, Midland Bank had lent a total of US$4.7 billion to Latin American

---

[29] See Dilip K. Das, 'Contemporary trends in the international capital markets', in D. K. Das (ed.), *International Finance: Contemporary Issues*, London: Routledge, 1993, p. 23.

[30] For a good overview of the debt crisis within the context of the evolving monetary/finance system of the 1970s and 1980s, see E. A. Brett, *International Money and Capitalist Crisis*, London: Heinemann, 1983, esp. pp. 175–222; Stephen Gill and David Law, *The Global Political Economy: Perspectives, Problems, and Policies*, Hertfordshire: Harvester Wheatsheaf, 1988, pp. 182–88.

[31] See 'Is anybody paying?', *The Economist*, 14 March 1987, p. 82.

[32] See Matthew Shepherd, 'US domestic interest and the Latin American debt crisis', in Richard Stubbs and Geoffrey Underhill (eds), *Political Economy and the Changing Global Order*, London: Macmillan, 1994, pp. 302–12.

states, which was greater than its total capital of US$4 billion.[33] Moreover, the loans were made without adequate risk assessment. When the loans were advanced, there was a general belief in the credit worthiness of sovereign borrowers. Walter Wriston, the former chief executive of Citicorp, famously wrote in a newspaper article in 1982, 'A country does not go bankrupt.'[34] The banks also believed that they had limited their exposure through syndicated loans which was thought to minimize the exposure of each individual bank.[35] Syndication made all of the banks involved feel secure in the belief that someone was checking adequately the risks, while in reality none was.

Credit and solvency risks are inherent in banking, but can have far-reaching repercussions in the intricate nexus of payments and settlements in the present electronic system. One example of this is the collapse of the Drexel Bank in February 1990, due to the fact that it was rolling over US$30 million in short-term borrowing without adequate capital reserves. As Alexandre Lamfalussy, the general manager of the Bank for International Settlements, explained, 'the failure of Drexel Burnham Lambert might have blocked the [international] payments mechanism, with widespread repercussions'.[36] In 1974, Bankhaus Herstatt was shut in the middle of a US$620 million foreign exchange transaction before the New York settlement system opened for business, which threatened to ignite a series of payments failures. And, in 1985, the Federal Reserve had to lend a record US$22.6 billion to the Bank of New York to avert a serious crisis when it faced a settlement problem due to a computer failure.[37] Gerald Corrigan, the Chairman of the international advisory council of Goldman Sachs, has stated that these payments systems 'constitute an extraordinarily complex chain of financial flows and resulting credit interdependence that I dare say nobody fully understands'.[38]

Thus, the danger to the system as a whole has increased along with the increase in the volume of capital in circulation in the private market, the interdependence of financial institutions, and the speed at

---

[33] See Mario Marcel and Gabriel Palma, *The Debt Crisis: The Third World and British Banks*, London: Fabian Research Series No. 350, 1987, p. 13.

[34] Cited in 'New tricks to learn', *The Economist*, op. cit., p. 1.

[35] Banks have since developed sophisticated models to measure risk, such as the Bankers Trust RAROC (Risk-Adjusted Return on Capital) system.

[36] Quoted in Millman, op. cit., p. 238. See also Dale, op. cit., p. 162.

[37] Dale, op. cit., p. 15.

[38] 'New tricks to learn', *The Economist*, op. cit., p. 17.

which vast sums of money are transmitted. John Pattison, the senior vice-president of the Canadian Imperial Bank of Commerce, summed up: 'Financial technology, electronic markets, payments and settlements systems ... increase the danger of financial instability being transmitted from institution to institution and from country to country'.[39] The sheer volume of international lending and the speed of interbank transactions have grown to such an extent that credit, solvency and safety risks increasingly can pose systemic risks. As Padoa-Schioppa and Saccomanni observed: 'Systemic risk in fact is bound to grow to the extent that the total amount of gross transactions to be settled increases in relation ... to central bank money balances ... A systemic risk has outgrown individual risk.'[40]

Thus, it may be conceptually convenient for purposes of exposition to separate credit, solvency and safety risks. However, in reality one bank's liquidity problem becomes another bank's credit risk when the interbank market is as interdependent as it has become. It is also true that each kind of risk can be contained, as indeed the Citibank exposure and Drexel failure were. But this does not alter the fact that large bank failures have been contained at considerable costs to the lenders of last resort, their governments, and to taxpayers.

This discussion of risks lays the foundations for the following argument. For it is precisely due to these credit, solvency and safety risks that banking regulators responded with international guidelines for the regulation of international banking. The first Basle Concordat[41] was enunciated in 1975 in the wake of the failure of Bankhaus Herstatt; the Revised Concordat[42] was formulated in 1983 in response to the

---

[39] Quoted in Bruce Zagaris and Scott B. MacDonald, 'Money laundering, financial fraud, and technology: the perils of an instantaneous economy', *George Washington Journal of International Law and Economics*, vol. 26, 1992, p. 76.

[40] Padoa-Schioppa and Saccomanni, op. cit., note 35, p. 254.

[41] Bank for International Settlements: Basle Committee on Banking Regulation and Supervisory Practices, Basle Concordat on Principles for the Supervision of Banks' Foreign Establishments. This original Concordat was not released to the public until 1981. See International Monetary Fund, *International Capital Markets: Recent Developments and Short-Term Prospects*, Occasional Paper no. 7, 1981, pp. 29–32. Hereafter 'Basle Concordat'.

[42] Committee on Banking Regulations and Supervisory Practices, *Revised Basle Concordat on Principles for the Supervision of Banks' Foreign Establishments, International Legal Materials*, vol. 22, 1983, at p. 900; and Committee on Banking Regulations and Supervisory Practices, Principles for the Supervision of Banks' Foreign Establishments, reprinted in *International Monetary Fund Survey*, vol. 12, 1983, p. 201. Hereafter 'Revised Concordat'.

failure of Banco Ambrosiano in 1982; the Basle Capital Adequacy Accord[43] of 1988 arose due to concern about the under-capitalization of US banks involved in the Debt Crisis; and Minimum Standards for the Supervision of International Banking Groups and their Cross Border Establishments (Minimum Standards)[44] were released in 1992 in the wake of the scandal at the Bank of Credit and Commerce International in 1991.

NOTHING NEW UNDER THE SUN? SOVEREIGNTY AND THE MARKET

Before proceeding to discuss these in detail, however, it is necessary to interject with a response to the 'lost sovereignty' thesis, and the suggestion that states are at the mercy of an 'autonomous' financial system. For if one accepts out of hand that states have lost the power to avert serious banking crises or to impose proactive prudential supervisory mechanisms, one accepts that the ability of states to exert effective authority over their territory has been denigrated in the face of transnational civil society actors and electronic impulses. But states do not have to accommodate themselves to the power of civil society actors in the international financial system (in this case, international bankers), nor is there any good reason why they must remain continually behind the times by reacting to crises.

The strong 'lost sovereignty' thesis can easily construct a 'straw man' of sovereignty. That is, without an historical appreciation of the interplay between statesmen and financiers, it is relatively easy to overstate the extent to which states ever have enjoyed absolute sovereignty over finance, and thus also to overestimate the extent to which the relationship between states and financiers is truly 'new' in the era of so-called globalization. There always has been an inherent tension *within* the interests of states; on one hand has been the need for liquidity to underwrite economic growth, while on the other hand has been the need to minimize risks and to maintain confidence in the system. The fundamental difficulties experienced in regulating a liberal international finance system are not, in essence, new. This tension is

---

[43] Committee on Banking Regulation and Supervisory Practices, *International Convergence of Capital Measurement and Capital Standards*, in *International Legal Materials*, vol. 30, 1991, pp. 980–1008. Hereafter 'Capital Adequacy Accord'.
[44] Minimum Standards, op. cit.

manifest from the earliest attempts to construct a market system, to the policies that states undertook to permit the 'globalization' of finance in the 1970s, to the newest measures taken in the 1980s and 1990s.

Therefore, the following will show that there always has been such an interdependence between statesmen and financiers, although in various historical periods the relative power of the parties has varied, and that states have always held conflicting interests between liquidity and stability. The important point is worth restating, that the turbulence that has prompted much of the claims about lost sovereignty is precisely what has prompted states to reassert a greater degree of control.

The following outlines a brief history of international finance from the consolidation of the states system to the present. By no means does it aspire to a comprehensive review, which is not possible within the confines of these pages. Thus, it is important to state here that the central organizing concept around which the following survey was written is that of state interests in regulating finance. The main point is that the motivations for the domestication of control over banking through the passage of national law is due precisely to the fact that the risks in the present international banking system are greater due to the increased volume and speed of transactions; the corresponding harmonization of national legislation is due to the fact that contagion and systemic risks which do not respect state borders are such that no state's law alone can address effectively the problems of regulation. The argument is that globalization is driving the process of transnational harmonization.

One opponent of the globalization school, Stephen Krasner, recently lamented: 'Change, globalisation, transnationalism, the erosion of the state ... New, new, change, change ... Globalisation is not new.'[45] In a critical reply to Krasner, Susan Strange agreed that:

> There is a tension between the principle of national self-determination and the principle of openness in the world economy ... That coexistence of a political system founded on the principle – or myth – of national autonomy and an economy founded on the principle of free movement of capital, technology and goods and services.[46]

---

[45] Stephen D. Krasner, 'International political economy: abiding discord', *Review of International Political Economy*, vol. 1, no. 1, Spring 1994, p. 13.

[46] Susan Strange, 'Wake up, Krasner! The world *has* changed', *Review of International Political Economy*, vol. 1, no. 2, 1994, p. 212.

It is interesting that both sides of the debate should accept the fact that sovereignty never has been absolute.

While it has been said that 'a currency and an army had historically been twin pillars of national sovereignty',[47] surely Napoleon's maxim that 'soldiers march on their stomachs' indicates the extent to which statesmen depended upon sources of finance to be able to exercise such a basic element of sovereign power as warfare. As E. J. Hobsbawm commented, the states of Europe in the mid-1800s could 'take no action, pursue no policy, and undertake no war if the House of Rothschild set its face against it'.[48] Though this is somewhat overstating the point, one important instance of this power of finance over the power of a state to undertake an autonomous policy occurred in March 1831 when the House of Rothschild pressured the Austrian government not to commence hostilities by advancing the government a long-term loan that would be recallable if war were to break out in the following three months.[49]

Indeed, most states of Europe attempted to maintain good relations with financiers, wary of not only the fact that the latter could refuse to advance loans if the sovereign risk were to become too great, but also that bankers could transfer their assets to another state which offered a more accommodating business climate. Bankers had developed very early an unwritten maxim, 'put not your trust in princes'. Sovereign default is as old as sovereign lending itself: King Edward III defaulted on a loan granted by Ferussi and Bardi to finance England's share of the Hundred Years War, which led to the bankruptcy of the lender.[50]

It is also the case that states never have been able to regulate entirely international financiers. The banking house of the Rothschilds was oftentimes masterful at evading government restrictions. The five brothers managed not only to flout the Continental Blockade by conducting transactions with Britain, but, aware of the fact that their post was being intercepted by the French Imperial State Police, they undertook deliberate campaigns of misinformation. The banking house minimized the risks associated with the transfer of physical money across state boundaries – both through theft and expropriation – by becoming the first truly multinational corporation with a central

---

47 Millman, op. cit., note 19, p. 101.

48 E. J. Hobsbawm, *Industry and Empire*, London: Penguin, 1969, p. 41.

49 See Karl Erich Born, *International Banking in the 19th and 20th Centuries*, Warwickshire: Berg Publishers Ltd., 1977, p. 41.

50 See Charles Kindleberger, *A Financial History of Western Europe*, London: Allen and Unwin, 1984.

accountancy procedure whereby money could be transferred simply through book-keeping entries. While outwardly the banks were legally independent companies which had to conform to the statutory requirements of the states in which they operated, the branches were regarded for accountancy purposes as a single enterprise.[51]

In recounting the 'great era' of the Rothschilds from 1853–1856 Karl Erich Born explained:

> All European powers owed them money in this period. This is not to say that the equilibrium between the powers and peace in Europe was dependent on the Rothschilds and the scale of their influence. What matters is that the two factors were mutually interdependent: on one hand, the balance between the European states was a precondition for the international scope of the Rothschilds' business; on the other, their financial power was in itself a weighty factor within the European system during these decades. Their financial power was just as vital to the state bureaucracies and the standing armies.[52]

The phrase 'mutually interdependent' belies, at a very fundamental level, the basis of the relationship between statesmen and financiers. Any international economic system – the present era of 'globalization' included – is determined by the level of interdependence between states, merchants and particularly financiers. For what is the international political economy if not an outgrowth of the internal systems of economy of the largest and most influential states, in the sense that international policies have reflected their domestic priorities? This is no less true whether we are considering the mercantile system which accompanied the process of building the modern nation–state in the sixteenth century, the period of liberalization in Europe in the mid-1800s, the construction of the post-war Bretton Woods system, or the modern era of globalization.

Indeed, this interdependence underlay the beginnings of capitalism which coincided with the process of state-building.[53] Both mandated the development of a national economy which involved principally the monopolization of force, legitimation, bureaucratization and monetization. This process was not instantaneous, and the monarchs could not

---

[51] See Count Corti, *The Rise of the House of Rothschild* (translated from the German by Brian and Beatrix Lunn), London: Victor Gollancz Ltd., 1928.

[52] Born, op. cit., p.38.

[53] See Immanuel Wallerstein, *The Modern World-System: Capitalist Agriculture and the Origins of the European World-Economy in the Sixteenth Century*, New York and London: 1974.

accomplish it on their own. It depended on the cooperation of, broadly speaking, a group of three key actors: kings, nobles, and commercial bourgeoisie – the infamous triumvirate which Herman Schwartz referred to as 'lawyers, guns and money'.[54] Nobles depended on the kings to defend their 'turf' from external invasions; the kings, in turn, were dependent on these groups to collect taxes and to maintain localized civil order. Whilst the state apparatus was still small, the kings depended on nobles and merchants to carry out their policies. Merchants and landowners turned this to their advantage to gain policies that were in their interests, which manifested in measures to protect nascent industry, and to privilege certain merchants.

The power of the state in the era of mercantilism therefore depended on a series of compromises. However, it is important to note that despite the largely interdependent relationship between the members of the key troika, their relationship was also a tense one. Most notably, to consolidate the national economy the kings desired monetization, and this was resisted by the nobles who feared that this would enable the kings to by-pass them in the collection of taxes and thus marginalize their influence. Once done, however, the kings enjoyed rights of seigniorage, for instance in determining the value of their money, as illustrated most markedly by the Great Debasement of Henry VIII in the mid-1540s. However, it should be noted that while this policy was profitable in the short term, even at this early stage of a monetized economy the ensuing inflation and loss of confidence in the credit system showed that governments could not disregard market forces.[55] The need to maintain a stable currency and confidence increased markedly as the volume of trade and investment grew at a phenomenal rate under the liberal international economy of the mid- to late 1800s.[56]

The liberal international political economy from the mid-1800s to the outbreak of the First World War also came about due to the interdependence between commercial interests and governments of the major European states.[57] The Industrial Revolution had caused a shift in

---

[54] Herman Schwartz, *States Versus Markets: History, Geography, and the Development of the International Political Economy*, New York: St Martin's Press, 1994.

[55] See Millman, op. cit.

[56] In fact, it has been argued that the international economy grew faster in this period than it is during the present era of 'globalization'. See Hirst and Thompson, op. cit.

[57] For greater detail, see A. G. Kenwood and A. L. Lougheed, *The Growth of the International Economy, 1820–1980: An Introductory Text*, London: George Allen & Unwin, 1983; and William Ashworth, *A Short History of the International Economy Since 1850*, 3rd edn, London: Longman, 1981.

the commercial and political power-base from farmers to industrialists. The steam engine was unveiled in Britain in the same year as the publication of Adam Smith's *Wealth of Nations*.[58] The newly created commercial bourgeoisie criticized the old system, which Smith had referred to as the 'mercantile system of economy': one that was based on power and privilege for political reasons rather than for reasons of economic efficiency. This new community that was excluded from the field of privilege maintained by government control demanded a relaxation of commercial regulation and free trade.[59] With Smith's justification of liberalization for the common good, the new industrialists attacked the protected landed interests, which culminated in such measures as the repeal of the Corn Laws in 1846, and Gladstone's Budget of 1860 which abolished most tariffs and laid the foundations for the Cobden-Chevalier Treaty with France which eventually led to generally free trade in Europe by the 1870s.

In this period of rapid commercial expansion brought about by technological advancement and liberalization,[60] governments faced the problem of ensuring sufficient liquidity in the credit system to underwrite the growth of trade while ensuring confidence in the system. Internationally, there was a need for stability in exchange rates, which was provided by the gold standard administered by Britain. Major European currencies became fixed to sterling, and the system proved to be relatively stable. International liquidity was provided by the British government, which maintained a conscious policy of running a balance-of-payments deficit in order to provide the international financial system with a counter-cyclical flow of liquidity.[61]

Domestically, it was necessary to reconcile the need for the circulation of an easily transportable currency, namely bank notes, with the need to maintain confidence in the value of those notes. Banking therefore became more heavily regulated. In the United Kingdom, the

---

[58] Adam Smith, *An Inquiry into the Nature and Causes of the Wealth of Nations*, New York: Modern Library, 1937.

[59] See Charles Kindleberger, 'The rise of free trade in Europe', in Jeffrey Frieden and David Lake (eds), *International Political Economy: Perspectives on Power and Wealth*, London: Routledge, 1995.

[60] The value of world trade grew from £280 million in 1800 to £800 million in 1850, and foreign direct investment grew from £420 million in 1850 to £9,500 million in 1914.

[61] See, for instance, Robert Gilpin, *War and Change in World Politics*, Cambridge: Cambridge University Press, 1981.

Bank Act of 1833 enabled the rise of joint-stock banks, which could offer fixed rates of interest on deposits, and thus encouraged investment. However, banks were required to hold gold reserves to cover the notes in circulation. For, in the economic crisis of 1816–17 following the Napoleonic wars, over 90 private issuing banks went bankrupt as holders of bank notes created a 'run' on the banks by attempting to convert their notes to gold. In the words of Born,

> [This] revealed a dilemma in which many private issuing banks had been placed. They were unable to satisfy business needs if they pursued a cautious policy in issuing notes; on the other hand, they jeopardised their capacity to convert the notes into ready money if they issued large quantities of them.[62]

Thus, Peel's Bank Charter Act of 1844 applied David Ricardo's theory of money whereby two-thirds of the notes in circulation were to be covered by gold.[63] However, it is interesting to note that the government found it necessary in economic crises, such as in 1847, 1857 and 1866, to not apply this regulation and allow the Bank of England to act as a lender of last resort or face the consequences of strangulating the economy of liquidity at a time when it was most needed.[64] Thus, as early as the first attempts to organize a liberal economy there surfaced a tension between the government's interest in providing sufficient liquidity necessary for growth, and its interest in regulating the financial system to promote confidence. This dilemma persists in the globalized international financial system. The pressures for getting that balance right are now greater than ever, for the consequences of not doing so are far greater.

The consequences of getting this balance wrong were seen in numerous booms and busts under the gold standard, but none more catastrophic than that of the Great Depression of 1929–39.[65] At that time, the United States had replaced Britain as the world's largest creditor nation, but funds were flowing mainly into the United States due to its demand for the repayment of wartime debts and to its high interest rates without a mechanism for redistributing the money back

---

[62] Born, op. cit., p. 7.

[63] In the United States, the National Currency Act of 1863 mandated that national banks were required to maintain liquid reserves of 25 per cent of deposits and notes in circulation.

[64] Kindleberger, *A Financial History of Western Europe*, op. cit., pp. 91–2.

[65] On which, see Charles Kindleberger, *The World in Depression, 1929–1939*, London: Allen Lane & Penguin Press, 1973.

into the international economy. These policies made it difficult for debtors to earn dollars to repay their debts or to buy from the United States. Thus, US policies deprived the international monetary system of a mechanism for a counter-cyclical flow of liquidity.[66]

US policies also deprived its domestic economy of much needed credit. At the time, there was overproduction in basic commodities, especially in agriculture, but speculation had maintained prices artificially high. The Federal Reserve decided that it would not respond to the inflow of gold by creating more money, as would pertain under the principles of the gold standard. Rather, the United States reduced the money supply in order to discourage people from buying stocks in an attempt to stem speculative transactions. At the beginning of 1928, prices began to fall, the speculative bubble burst and the stock market crashed in October 1929. At the same time, Germany was experiencing hyperinflation which led to a series of bank failures, precipitated notably by the Nordwolle crisis in June 1931. This caused a flight of money from Germany, and sparked a series of bank failures which quickly spread to Britain, France and the United States. In 1929–33, 9,000 – one-fifth – of US banks failed.[67]

This crisis led to the greater involvement of the state in the finance system. Regulation of the domestic banking system in the United States, for instance, occurred on 6 March 1933 when President Roosevelt temporarily closed all banks by invoking the Enemy Trading Act. Following an investigation, the Glass-Steagall Banking Act was passed in June 1934 which separated banking and securities activities. And, recognizing that the severity of the crisis was due in large part to the lack of an effective lender of last resort, the Act strengthened the powers of the Federal Reserve in two important ways. It was granted the power to adjust the level of liquid reserves deposited with it by national banks to ensure sufficient reserves for it to step in as lender of last resort, and it also established the Federal Deposit Insurance Company to protect depositors.[68]

The other important lesson of the Great Depression was that there

---

[66] Ibid.

[67] Dale, op. cit., pp. 1–6. As opposed to only 641 bank closures from 1934 to 1973. See Timothy A. Canova, 'The transformation of US banking and finance: from regulated competition to free-market receivership', *Brooklyn Law Review*, vol. 60, 1995, p. 1300.

[68] The evolution of domestic regulatory regimes is outside the scope of this study. But see David Gowland, *The Regulation of Financial Markets in the 1990s*, Aldershot: Edward Elgar, 1990. See also Born, op. cit., pp. 276–79; Dale, op. cit., pp. 21–6.

was a greater need for concerted regulation by governments of the international financial system. Not only would speculative movements of capital need to be controlled, but states would have to agree to refrain from resorting to the competitive devaluation of their currencies as part of their armoury in international commercial warfare. President Roosevelt's 'bombshell' announcement, to use the phrase of his Secretary of State Cordell Hull,[69] of a 10 per cent devaluation of the US dollar on the eve of the London Economic Summit of 1931 was one instance where, in the words of Charles Kindleberger, when each nation retaliated, and turned inwards to protect itself, the welfare of the system and of each state went 'down the drain'.[70]

Following the Second World War, international cooperation was expressed in the Bretton Woods system of the International Monetary Fund (IMF) and International Bank for Reconstruction and Development (IBRD – World Bank) established in 1944, and the General Agreement on Tariffs and Trade (GATT) of 1947. This system aimed to promote stable economic growth through trade liberalization while avoiding the harsh dislocations that can accompany unbridled liberalism. The domestic goals of full employment and social stability were married to the growth of industry by subordinating the international financial system to a supportive role to underwrite international trade.[71]

The principles of the IMF system reintroduced a gold standard, with the US dollar as the reserve currency fixed to gold at a rate of US$35 per ounce. All other currencies were fixed to the dollar. The Articles of Agreement provided that currencies would be convertible for international trade transactions. The post-war planners wished above all to avoid large international flows of capital for the purpose of buying stocks or currencies for speculative purposes. The Bretton Woods Agreement created a heavily regulated international financial system which, in the words of the US Treasury Secretary Harry Dexter White, would 'drive the usurious moneylenders from the temple of

---

[69] Cordell Hull, *The Memoirs of Cordell Hull*, vol. I, London: Hodder & Stoughton, 1948.

[70] Charles Kindleberger, *The World in Depression*, op. cit., p. 242, note 82.

[71] See Richard N. Gardner, *Sterling-Dollar Diplomacy in Current Perspective: The Origins and Prospects of Our International Economic Order*, New York: Columbia University Press, 1980; and John Gerrard Ruggie, 'international regimes, transactions and change: embedded liberalism in the postwar economic order', in Stephen Krasner (ed.), *International Regimes*, Ithaca, New York: Cornell University Press, 1983.

international finance'.[72] The system of fixed exchange rates also depended on preventing capital flows following higher rates of interest. In the words of John Maynard Keynes, 'the whole management of the domestic economy depends on being free to have the appropriate rate of interest without reference to the rate prevailing elsewhere in the world. Capital control is a corollary to this.'[73] Thus, there were no obligations to make currencies convertible for capital transactions; indeed, states imposed IMF-sanctioned controls on the movement of capital.

During the entire operation of the Bretton Woods system, however, there remained the age-old tension between ensuring sufficient liquidity in the international financial system while maintaining stability and confidence. The United States acted to correct the 'dollar shortage' which followed the war through the Marshall Plan of 1948 and thereafter provided the system with a counter-cyclical flow of liquidity, much the same way as Britain had done under its gold standard, by running a balance-of-payments deficit. These deficits initially were regarded as desirable due to the need for dollars, and controllable due to the health of the US economy.

However, by the 1960s the United States began to print dollars to finance military spending and particularly the Vietnam War. In 1960, official dollar holdings exceeded gold reserves for the first time, and by 1971 official dollar holdings exceeded US gold stocks by over 300 per cent.[74] So long as there was confidence in the health of the US economy, this 'dollar overhang' was considered manageable. However, growing US trade deficits began to reflect a loss of US competitive advantage as other economies had now fully recovered from the war. The US balance-of-payments deficit had grown from US$1.9 billion in 1965 to US$10.6 billion in 1971.[75] This led to the dilemma whereby the volume of dollars would have to be stemmed to ensure confidence in the system, but on the other hand, this could have precipitated a lack of credit in the system. Notably, while this was termed the 'Triffin

---

72 Quoted in Gardner, ibid., p. 73.

73 J. M. Keynes, *The Collected Writings of J.M. Keynes: Vol. 25 – Activities 1940–44: Shaping the Postwar World, The Clearing Union*, London: Cambridge University Press, 1980, pp. 148–9, quoted in Eric Helleiner, 'Explaining the globalisation of financial markets: bringing states back in', *Review of International Political Economy*, vol. 2, no. 2, Spring 1995, p. 318.

74 Joan Spero, *The Politics of International Economic Relations*, 3rd edn, New York: St. Martin's Press, 1985, p. 68.

75 Ibid., p. 69.

Dilemma', announced by economist Robert Triffin, this essential problem had always existed in a growing liberal economy.

Several multilateral remedies were attempted, such as the creation of a secondary reserve currency, composed of a pool of currencies in the IMF, called Special Drawing Rights (SDR). These were intended as a temporary measure to take pressure off the United States to permit it to control its deficits. However, the pool of SDRs proved to be too small to meet requirements, and in any case, the US deficits continued to amass. By August 1971, as the official value of the dollar and its actual value had diverged to such an extent that gold was flowing out of the United States, President Nixon reneged on the Articles of Agreement of the IMF and suspended the convertibility of dollars to gold. This culminated in the legalization of a new system of exchange rate flexibility in the Jamaica Agreement of 1976, which was followed by the dismantling of capital controls, beginning with the United States in 1974, the United Kingdom in 1979, and most other countries of the OECD in the 1980s. As Helleiner stated, '[d]uring the 1980s, governments across the advanced industrialised world abolished external capital controls which had been in place for a half century giving market actors a degree of freedom unparalleled since the 1920s'.[76]

At the same time that the United States undermined the government-controlled monetary system (G-IMS, relating to exchange rates), it also paved the way for the development of the M-IMS (market-led international monetary system).[77] As the US balance of payments worsened, it instituted a series of capital controls which led to the holding of dollars in banks outside of the United States. In 1964, the United States passed the Interest Equalization Tax to discourage foreign borrowers from raising money in the US market; the Foreign Credit Restraint Program of 1965 limited American bank loans to foreign borrowers; and the Foreign Investment Program of 1968 restricted US corporations from using domestic dollars to fund foreign

---

[76] Helleiner, 'Explaining the globalisation of financial markets', op. cit., p. 328. See also Herman Schwartz, op. cit., p. 238.

[77] The events which led the financial system from this heavily regulated one to the 'explosion' of finance have been recounted by a number of scholars. See in particular Susan Strange, *Casino Capitalism*, London: Blackwell, 1986; Eric Helleiner, 'Explaining the globalisation of financial markets', op. cit., pp. 315–41; Phil Cerny, *Finance and World Politics*, op. cit.; and Geoffrey Underhill, 'Markets beyond politics? The state and the internationalisation of financial markets', *European Journal of Political Research*, vol. 19, no. 2–3, 1991.

investments.[78] These measures encouraged the establishment of an off-shore dollar market, which became known as the Euromarket.[79]

Other deposits, mainly the surpluses of oil-producing states (OPEC) and short-term deposits of multinational corporations, fuelled the development of the Euromarket. The American Federal Reserve Act of 1937 did not permit banks to pay interest on sight-deposits, and interest rates on time-deposits could not exceed the rate set by the Federal Reserve. It was thus more profitable to deposit dollars in accounts outside of the United States. At the time, US banks were required to hold 3 per cent reserves which meant that they had to charge higher interest rates to cover the cost of reserves.[80] However, banks outside of the United States (including branches of US banks) that did not have to comply with such reserve requirements could charge lower rates for dollar-denominated loans. The Euromarket grew at over 25 per cent per annum through the 1970s. Between 1971 and 1984, the Eurocurrency market grew from US$85 billion to US$2,200 billion. By 1988, the Euromarkets comprised US$4 trillion, which exceeded the domestic deposit market of the United States by US$1 trillion.[81]

There are two important consequences of the rise of the Euromarkets. The first is the shift in the financial system from one depending on a state to manage the flow of international liquidity to a system whereby liquidity is provided by private banks. Whereas previous international financial systems were threatened with a lack of credit, there is now, if anything, excess international liquidity, and this is provided by private bank lending. In 1980, the US interbank loan market stood at US$74 billion, and this more than doubled by 1995 to US$170 billion. The international interbank lending market had grown to US$5.8 trillion by June 1995.[82]

---

[78] For further details on this, see Francis A. Lees, *International Banking and Finance*, Basingstoke: Macmillan, 1974, pp. 100–06.

[79] The name derives from the telex sign-off of a Soviet dollar-denominated bank account in London, Eurobank. This Soviet dollar holding was necessary for international commercial transactions by the USSR, since oil and other commodities are denominated in US dollars. The fear that the United States would seize these funds if they were kept on United States soil prompted the USSR to keep dollars outside of the US.

[80] Born, op. cit., p. 203; Lees, op. cit., pp. 297–312.

[81] Windecker, op. cit.; Smedresman and Lowenfeld, op. cit., p. 744.

[82] 'International banking: coping with the ups and downs', *The Economist*, Survey, 27 April 1996, p. 15.

The consequence of this increase in liquidity, along with a revolution in technology, is an increase in competition among banks and between banks and non-bank financial organizations. Indeed, such competition was one of the reasons for the imprudent loans to developing countries which underlaid the Debt Crisis.[83] The consequences of this, in the words of Hirst and Thompson, are that 'contagion risk, market risk, and systemic risk have all increased, presenting new and important regulatory problems for governments'.[84] And, as Richard Dale commented:

> It is becoming more difficult to ensure banking stability, partly because the internationalisation of the financial services industry has removed the protective bulkheads separating one banking jurisdiction from the other. The implication is that there is increasing potential for cross-border contagion within the global banking system.[85]

This relates to the second important consequence of the Euromarkets, which is regulatory arbitrage, or competition in regulatory laxity. That is, as one state deregulates, financial industries in another state feel they are at a competitive disadvantage, and lobby for deregulation.[86] US dollars comprise over 75 per cent of the Euromarket, and these are not subject to US reserve requirements, legal limits on the rate of interest paid on deposits, or depositors' insurance.[87] Sovereignty over such matters stops at the nation's borders. International banks, unless otherwise prevented, can exploit differences in national priorities and regulation – as indeed they always have done. Depositors seek out the highest rates of interest, and borrowers seek the lowest – meaning that there can be a strong pressure for a 'race to the bottom' among national legislation. Thus, it has been said that the 'expansion of global finance promotes deregulation'.[88] Will Hutton likened this competition in regulatory laxity to a '1990s version of Gresham's Law', whereby good regulation is driven out by poor regulation. He argued,

---

[83] 'One prominent central banker' is quoted as saying: 'There is ... undoubted over-capacity in the financial sector which is leading to unrealistic undercutting of fees and margins in much the same way as we saw very low spreads being offered to Third World borrowers in the 1970s.' Cited in Dale, op. cit., p. 174, in note 27.

[84] Ibid.

[85] Ibid., p. 192.

[86] See Timothy A. Canova, 'The transformation of US banking and finance: from regulated competition to free-market receivership', *Brooklyn Law Review*, vol. 60, 1995, esp. pp. 1307–09.

[87] Smedresman and Lowenfeld, op. cit., p. 734, note 37.

[88] 'Fear of finance', *The Economist*, op. cit., p. 12, note 26.

'Deregulated banking drives out regulated banking and all of us pay the price.'[89]

It is true, for instance, that pressure from US banks for deregulation led in December 1981 to International Banking Facilities (IBFs) so that banks on US soil could compete with offshore banking. However, it is important to recognize that the 'race to the bottom' in regulation has taken place mainly outside the OECD countries. As Don Marshall explained, 'Competition between states to attract and retain finance-capital has intensified, with peripheral countries seeking to make their sites more attractive to investment.'[90] Indeed, as Mary Footer noted, international transactions as much as 90 per cent of all transactions in some banking centres.[91] There are many offshore financial centres (OFCs) such as the Bahamas, Bermuda, Antigua, Cayman Islands and Barbados which maintain lax regulatory regimes. However, the OECD countries control more than 80 per cent of the lending market, and their banks' share of the world total of assets and liabilities has continued to grow while that of offshore centres has grown less quickly, and those of developing countries have remained almost static.[92]

The states of the OECD also welcome the increase in private liquidity to underwrite the growth of international trade and foreign direct investment and to service their deficits. Just as the increase in international trade that accompanied the liberal international trade system of the mid-1800s required an increase in liquidity in the credit system, the present era of growing trade and foreign investment mandates access to finance. And competition in the financial market is seen as desirable to rationalize the efficiency of financial institutions as well as to create a dynamic, competitive credit sector. To take the United States as an example, the number of foreign banking establishments there doubled from 345 offices in 1980 to 738 in

---

[89] 'Tight regulation of the economy has kept the high-rolling Tokyo market from breaking the bank, but as the falls continue the odds are shortening on a financial catastrophe', *The Guardian*, 10 September 1990, p. 10.

[90] Don D. Marshall, 'Understanding late-twentieth-century capitalism: reassessing the globalisation theme', *Government and Opposition*, vol. 31, no. 2, 1996, pp. 193–215; see also Marshall, 'Tax havens in the Commonwealth Caribbean: a merchant capital-global finance connection', *Global Society: Journal of Interdisciplinary International Relations*, vol. 10, no. 3, 1996, pp. 255–80.

[91] Mary E. Footer, 'GATT and the multilateral regulation of banking services', *International Lawyer*, vol. 27, 1993, p. 343.

[92] *Industry and Trade Summary: Commercial Banking*, USITC Publication 2638 (SV-4) June 1993, p. 26.

1991, and foreign establishments increased their assets in the United States by 320 per cent from US$198 billion to US$832 billion, which is approximately 25 per cent of the US lending market.[93] It has been estimated that US corporations have borrowed a total of US$222.4 billion from foreign banks, which is approximately half the amount that US banks have listed in commercial and industrial loans. Foreign capital is therefore an important source of liquidity.[94]

While it may not have been the intention of the US government in the 1960s and 1970s to drive dollars into offshore bank accounts, it did believe that the Euromarket would provide a quasi-Keynesian 'clearing house' function to redistribute money from surplus nations to deficit nations. According to Eric Helleiner, by the mid-1960s, 'US officials were in fact actively encouraging US banks and corporations to move their operations to the offshore London market'[95] so that American banks would not lose business while at the same time the government could pursue its policies of adjusting its economy. The British government was keen to promote London as a financial centre, and bankers in the City were 'eager to capture international business without being constrained by sterling controls'.[96] Helleiner concluded that the 'globalization' of finance was supported by states through 'granting freedom to market actors through liberalisation initiatives ... [and] choosing not to implement more effective controls on financial movements'[97] because it suited their interests.

However, the major states also retain an interest in the stability of the financial system due to the costs involved for them as lenders of last resort in the event of a crisis. As Dale explained, 'Major financial centre countries have developed a strong aversion to bank failures. This attitude is rooted in the fear of contagious deposit runs and destabilisation of the domestic financial system.'[98] Thus, states' interests are not only to ensure sufficient credit to underwrite a growing liberal international economy, but to ensure that this private credit system operates prudently at the same time. And no state can do so by acting alone. As Richard Dale commented, 'in a regime of self-

---

93 Ibid.

94 See L. Todd Gibson, 'The Foreign Bank Supervision Enhancement Act of 1991: short run consequences en route to the long term goal', *Case Western Reserve Journal of International Law*, vol. 27, 1995, pp. 124–5.

95 Helleiner, 'Explaining the globalisation of financial markets', op. cit., p. 321.

96 Ibid., p. 320.

97 Ibid., p. 316.

98 Dale, op. cit., pp. 14–15.

contained national banking systems, borders act as natural firebreaks in the sense that contagious financial disturbances are unlikely to spread beyond national frontiers. However, the internationalisation of banking has removed this safeguard.'[99] The result of this, as expressed by *The Economist*, is that 'national bank regulators are bound to have a tough time tackling an increasingly international problem: systemic risk ignores borders'.[100]

THE IMPETUS TO DOMESTICATION AND HARMONIZATION

The previous section has shown several things that may be summarized as follows. The first is that it has always been the case that 'the task of regulators is to strike a balance between costs and benefits – i.e., between instability and efficiency',[101] or as stated here, between sufficient liquidity to underwrite a growing liberal economy and the stability and confidence on which the economy also depends.

Related to this, it has also been shown that bankers and statesmen always have had an interdependent relationship, although the balance of power among the parties has varied from time to time. Also raised in this connection (flagged here, but not pursued until later in this book) was the point that international systems of governance always have reflected the domestic priorities of the largest states in the system. For instance, liberalization in the mid-1800s was promoted due to domestic pressures in Britain brought by the Industrial Revolution, and the form in which international finance evolved grew out of Britain's policies of maintaining a gold standard. Similarly, the pressures in the United States during the Great Depression and the transfer of hegemony from Britain prompted the form of the mechanisms of the Bretton Woods system.

It was also pointed out that the risk of systemic crisis and contagion risks have increased. Thus, the task of regulating the globalized international financial system has been shifted squarely to the regulation of private finance. It is crucial to restate this at this juncture in the terms of the thesis being developed. It is precisely the increased contagion and systemic risks presented by the speed and volume of

---

99 Ibid., p. 16.
100 'Coping with the ups and downs', *The Economist*, op. cit., p. 9.
101 'Fear of finance', *The Economist*, op. cit., p. 24.

transfers in international banking that, first, have intensified states' long-held interests in promoting stability, and second, led to the realization that no state can do it alone. As expressed by Zamora, 'while banking is an international industry, banking regulation is almost entirely national'.[102]

Indeed, there was little reason to harmonize regulations for banking supervision prior to Bretton Woods because social safety nets were not yet in place and the lessons brought only with the Depression were not yet learned. Similarly, there was little reason for the harmonization of banking supervision during the time that Bretton Woods functioned. The post-war arrangements established at Bretton Woods were a G-IMS: the international financial system was based on monetary and exchange rate policies. The Articles of Agreement of the IMF did not address the oversight and operation of private banks, nor did it address the issue of international banking supervision.[103] There was little need for this in a system which operated on the basis of capital controls.

Such controls, once removed, raised the question of how states would respond to this gap in institutionalized regulation. When the problem became one of disciplining civil society actors because international banks had taken over the function of providing liquidity in the increasingly liberal international economy, it was at a time that it had to be confronted on an international scale because regulators realized that risks did not apply brakes at sovereign boundaries. In attempting to meet the challenge in international fora, the problem has arisen that international banking takes place under different regulatory regimes, and the questions that needed to be resolved concerned such things as which state should act as a lender of last resort where subsidiaries of foreign banks are involved, and what should be a prudent level of capital reserves for banks.

Therefore, the liberalism unleashed after the collapse of Bretton Woods' capital controls shifted the focus of regulation efforts from 'high politics' and treaties in multilateral institutions such as the IMF to a concentration on disciplining civil society actors (international banks) through domestication (the passage of national laws) and more functional coordination among bank regulators leading to harmonization of national laws. The following section outlines the initiatives that have been taken at the international level among bank regulators through the Basle Committee, which operates under the auspices of the

---

[102] Zamora, op. cit., p. 1959.

[103] Ibid., p. 1953.

Bank for International Settlements; these, it has been said, 'represent the most significant efforts to date'.[104] The section after that examines how the United States and the European Union have domesticated control over international banks through their domestic legislation at the same time that they have harmonized their laws by acting within the confines of broad principles elaborated in the Basle Committee.

INTERNATIONAL BANKING REGULATION

The first Basle Concordat of December 1975[105] was promulgated in the wake of the collapse of the Bankhaus Herstatt in 1974. The bank had engaged in fraudulent book-keeping practices, and its failure occurred while it was engaged in a foreign exchange transaction of US$620 million. This not only threatened to ignite a series of payments failures, but raised difficult issues in the manner in which foreign creditors were to be compensated. In the end, foreign creditors' claims were settled unsatisfactorily which demonstrated that greater international regulation of banks was required.[106]

Thus, the Basle Committee was formed to provide a forum for consultation and cooperation among the central bankers of the G-10 states, to provide for an exchange of information about bank supervision, and to lead to a greater harmonization of their banking laws. The first task was to agree that 'no foreign banking establishment should escape supervision'. To do this, the Committee had to clarify the respective roles of the regulators in the home state, that is the situs of the bank's head office, and those of the host state, where the bank's foreign establishment is located. The 1975 Concordat declared that 'the supervision of foreign banks should be the joint responsibility of the home and host authorities'.[107] Thus, a 'central tenet of the Concordat was the joint responsibility of home and host banking regulators in regulating international banks'.[108]

---

[104] Thomas F. McInerney III, 'Towards the next phase in international banking regulation', *DePaul Business Law Journal*, vol. 7, 1994, p. 155.

[105] Basle Concordat, op. cit.

[106] For details of the Herstatt failure, see Duncan E. Alford, 'Basle Committee Minimum Standards: international regulatory response to the failure of BCCI', *George Washington Journal of International Law and Economics*, vol. 26, 1992, p. 246.

[107] Basle Concordat, op. cit., pp. 29–30.

[108] Alford, op. cit., p. 249.

The Concordat dealt mainly with liquidity[109] and solvency.[110] It was decided that a bank's liquidity should follow local practices, irrespective of whether the entity was established as a branch or subsidiary. Thus liquidity should be under the purview of host authorities. The solvency of the foreign branch was allocated between home and host authorities depending on the type of establishment. A foreign branch's solvency was deemed to be directly related to the solvency of the parent establishment. Foreign branches were considered to be a part of the parent bank and thus 'indistinguishable from the parent bank as a whole'. Thus, a branch's solvency would be a matter for the supervision of the home authorities. However, foreign subsidiaries, deemed to be separate corporations, were to be governed by host authorities.

Though a welcome first step, the original Concordat contained many ambiguities. First, the designation of the host supervisor as the authority responsible for the solvency of a foreign banking establishment was not consistent with the practice among most industrialized country bank regulators which measured solvency on the basis of 'consolidated supervision'. The principle of consolidated supervision follows the logic that the home authority is in the best position to see the entire picture of a bank's operations worldwide and depends on information from the various host state regulators to construct this picture. The conflict between the Concordat and normal practice among regulators caused confusion. More importantly, while the Concordat dealt with supervision in smoother times, it left unclear which regulator should take action to contain a major bank failure. Most 'important and dangerous', according to Duncan Alford, was the 'mistaken belief that lender of last resort responsibility accompanied supervisory responsibility. The Committee never intended the Concordat to deal with lender of last resort responsibility.'[111] These shortcomings became apparent when regulators attempted to deal with the collapse of the Banco Ambrosiano in 1982, which led to a Revised Concordat in 1983.[112]

Banco Ambrosiano was an Italian bank whose Luxemburg subsidiary had made imprudent loans of US$1.4 billion to Latin American companies which left it US$450 million short in its liabilities to its

---

[109] Liquidity is defined as a bank's ability to convert assets into cash without diminishing the assets' value.

[110] Solvency is the ability of a bank to generate sufficient cash to pay its liabilities.

[111] Alford, op. cit., p. 249.

[112] Revised Concordat, op. cit, p. 901.

creditors. The bank consequently collapsed in 1982. The ambiguities in the original Concordat led to a dispute between Luxemburg and Italy over who should have exercised supervision of the bank, and who should be the lender of last resort.[113]

The Revised Concordat did not replace the original Concordat. It reiterated the general principles that 'no foreign banking establishment should escape supervision' and that 'the supervision should be adequate'.[114] However, it did state explicitly that it did not address lender of last resort responsibility.[115] Solvency of a branch remained the responsibility of the home authority, but both home and host authorities would be responsible for the solvency of a subsidiary. Both host and home supervisors would have responsibility for ensuring liquidity.[116] The manner in which the Revised Concordat allocated responsibilities was through the adoption of the principle of consolidated supervision.

Under consolidated supervision, the home authority would be responsible for monitoring the overall exposure of the bank, taking into account its operations throughout the world. It was believed that 'banking supervisory authorities cannot be fully satisfied about the soundness of individual banks unless they can examine the totality of each bank's business worldwide through the technique of consolidation'. The Revised Concordat continued,

> The principle of consolidated supervision is that parent banks and parent supervisory authorities monitor the risk exposure … of the banks or banking groups for which they are responsible, as well as the adequacy of their capital, on the basis of the totality of their business wherever conducted.[117]

However, host authorities were deemed to have primary responsibility for supervising branches and subsidiaries.

Crucially, the Revised Concordat did not designate primary responsibility for supervising holding companies. It stated, '[w]here

---

[113] For details, see Alford, op. cit., pp. 251–2; and Daniel M. Laiffer, 'Putting the super back in the supervision of international banking, post-BCCI', *Fordham Law Review*, vol. 60, 1992, p. 470, in note 18.
[114] Revised Concordat, op. cit., p. 903.
[115] It has been suggested that this was deliberate to encourage discipline among banks. Moreover, central banks had accepted that they would act either solely or in concert to prevent a major international liquidity crisis, as indeed they have done. See Helleiner, 'Explaining the globalisation of financial markets', op. cit., pp. 332–3.
[116] McInerney, op. cit., p. 160; Alford, op. cit., p. 255.
[117] Ibid., p. 161.

holding companies are at the head of groups that include separately incorporated banks operating in different countries', there is no requirement for consolidated home supervision of the institution.[118] This was an important loop-hole exploited later by the Bank of Credit and Commerce International (BCCI), as outlined below.

The second important principle adopted by the Revised Concordat was that of 'dual key' supervision. Under this approach, parent and host authorities could assess the quality of each other's supervision. If a host country considered the supervision of the home regulators to be inadequate, it was empowered to prohibit or discourage the operation of banks in its jurisdiction. Conversely, if a home authority considered the supervision of the host regulators to be inadequate, it should 'either extend its supervision, to the degree that is practicable, or it should be prepared to discourage the parent bank from continuing to operate the establishment in question'.[119] This principle was adopted to discourage the sort of dispute that arose between the regulators of Italy and Luxemburg. If a similar situation were to arise, both regulators would share responsibility for failing to 'catch' the laxity of the other.[120] Moreover, there was an intention to stop competition in regulatory laxity. As explained by Alford:

> The 'dual key' system, as envisioned by the drafters of the Revised Concordat, should have encouraged nations to make their bank supervision practices equivalent to those present in the most stringently regulated financial centres. This kind of convergence will occur, however, only if bank regulators are prepared to lock out weakly regulated banks from expanding into inadequately regulated jurisdictions.[121]

Another important product of the Basle Committee was the Capital Adequacy Accord. This was formulated primarily due to pressure from the United States, which was concerned about the undercapitalization of US banks involved in the Debt Crisis, as well as the fact that Japanese banks were undercapitalized relative to US banks, and hence in a better competitive position.[122] As Walter commented, 'In order to

---

[118] Revised Concordat, op. cit., p. 904.

[119] Ibid.

[120] See Alford, op. cit., p. 252; McInerney, op. cit., p. 160.

[121] Alford, op. cit., p.253. A similar point is made by Laifer, op. cit., p. 470.

[122] The Accord in fact grew out of a bilateral Accord between the US and the UK. On the genesis of the Accord, see J.J. Norton, 'The work of the Basle Supervisors Committee on bank capital adequacy and the July 1988 report on "International Convergence of Capital Measurements and Capital Standards" ', *International Lawyer*, vol. 23, 1989, pp. 245–63.

strengthen the capital base of US banks without further endangering their competitiveness, US authorities pursued an international accord which would create a "level playing field".'[123] As expressed by Zamora, the goals of the Capital Adequacy Accord were:[124]

1. To require banks to maintain higher levels of capital reserves through the maintenance of capital-to-asset ratios that are 'risk based' (i.e., that reflect the real credit risks as well as the risks of banks' increasingly important off-balance-sheet positions); and
2. To establish a level playing field so that a bank based in one country will not receive a competitive advantage by enjoying a lower capital adequacy standard than a bank located in another country.

The Basle Committee viewed capital reserves as a means to minimize the credit risk of banks and thereby to ensure their safety and soundness.[125] To that end, it promulgated a framework for measuring capital adequacy and formulated minimum standards to which banks should adhere. It distinguished between two 'tiers' of capital: 'core capital', which is basic equity, and 'supplementary capital', which is less easily evaluated capital. It has been said that the Basle Committee's 1988 Capital Accord was a 'most impressive achievement',[126] and that it was even 'probably the most significant international agreement to date in the field of bank supervision'.[127] Indeed, Dale reported that the capitalization of banks had been declining steadily. For instance, in 1840, the average equity-capital-to-total-assets ratio for US banks was about 50 per cent, and this fell to only 5 per cent among the 25 largest US banks in 1989.[128] Banks now are required to hold capital equal to at least 8 per cent of their risk-weighted assets and have 'tier one' capital equal to at least 4 per cent of their risk-weighted assets.[129] Moreover, there is some flexibility built into the ratio formula to permit authorities to assess market and interest rate risks and to adjust the level of reserves accordingly. Thus 'riskier banks will be subject to higher capital requirements'.[130]

---

123 Walter, op. cit., p. 228. See also 'Coping with the ups and downs', *The Economist*, op. cit., p. 40.

124 Zamora, op. cit., p. 1958.

125 See Gibson, op. cit., p. 136.

126 Padoa-Schioppa and Saccomanni, op. cit., p. 258.

127 Hirst and Thompson, op. cit., p. 132.

128 See Dale, op. cit., p. 170.

129 McInerney, op. cit., p. 161.

130 Ibid., p. 161.

Finally, the Basle Committee's Minimum Standards for the Supervision of International Banking Groups and their Cross-Border Establishments[131] was formulated in response to the closure of BCCI in 1991 in a coordinated action among the regulators of eight states. Apparently, BCCI had been engaged in all manner of fraud and illegal activities.[132] Among these were fraudulent book-keeping entries such as fictitious loans (to the tune of US$1.3 billion), unrecorded deposits (of approximately US$600 million), and shuttling of funds between subsidiaries in an attempt to conceal huge losses. BCCI also had pled guilty to money laundering activities in Tampa, Florida, for which the Federal Reserve Board issued a cease and desist order to prohibit the bank from operating in the United States. Finally, the bank allegedly had acquired illegally and controlled secretly four banks in the United States.[133] The precise details of these activities are less important to the present discussion than are the loopholes that permitted them and the consequent Minimum Standards that were adopted in response.

BCCI was able to evade supervision due to its complex corporate matrix. BCCI was a holding company headquartered in Luxemburg. Its principal operations were in Luxemburg (BCCI S.A.) and the Cayman Islands (BCCI Overseas Ltd), which permitted it to use separate auditors in two states which had relatively strong bank secrecy requirements. Moreover, under Luxemburg law, a holding company was not considered to be a bank, and in any case, the Revised Basle Concordat had left ambiguous the responsibility for supervising a holding company. Thus, BCCI did not have a 'home base', and therefore was not subject to any consolidated supervision. In fact, it has been suggested that the corporate organization of BCCI appears to have been designed precisely to evade supervision.[134]

The severity of the loopholes which allowed a US$20 billion bank effectively to evade supervision, to jeopardize US$8.7 billion of international trade transactions, and to accumulate liabilities of US$10.64 billion while retaining assets of only US$1.1 billion cannot be overstated.[135] To address these loopholes, the Basle Committee's Minimum Standards formulated strict regulations. There are four:[136]

---

[131] Minimum Standards, op. cit.

[132] See Peter Truell and Gary Gurwin, *BCCI: The Inside Story of the World's Most Corrupt Financial Empire*, London: Bloomsbury Publishing, 1992.

[133] Alford, op. cit., pp. 259–62; Laifer, op. cit., pp. 478–9.

[134] Laiffer, op. cit., p. 466.

[135] For these figures, see Laiffer, op. cit., p. 467; and Alford, op. cit., p. 265.

[136] See McInerney, op. cit., p. 163; Alford, op. cit., p. 267.

1. All international banks and banking groups should be supervised by a 'home country' regulator.
2. The creation of a cross-border banking establishment should receive the prior consent of both the host-country supervisory authority and the bank's, and, if different, the banking group's home-country supervisory authority.
3. Supervisory authorities should possess the right to gather information from the cross-border banking establishments of the banks or banking groups for which they are the home-country supervisor.
4. If a host-country authority determines that any one of the foregoing minimum standards is not met to its satisfaction, that authority could impose restrictive measures necessary to satisfy its prudential concerns consistent with these minimum standards, including the prohibition of the creation of banking establishments.

In effect, the principles of consolidated supervision by home country regulators and the dual-key approach of home and host country regulators assessing each other's practices are reinforced. But, as McInerney stated, 'What BCCI makes clear is that home country supervision only makes sense where that jurisdiction has i) comparable supervisory standards, [and] ii) a capacity to implement and enforce such standards.'[137] The regulators of the Cayman Islands, for instance, have a staff of only eighteen to supervise all the banking establishments in its jurisdiction. Some have fewer, and many OFCs are less inclined to be vigilant in supervising banks, lest they drive investment from their states.[138] Thus, the Minimum Standards state that 'all international banks should be supervised by a home-country authority that capably performs consolidated supervision',[139] which is without doubt more strongly worded than the original Concordat which states only that all international banks should be supervised 'adequately'. However, it is left purposely flexible to permit home and host country regulators to formulate an approach to consolidated supervision which best fits each individual case.

There are important new requirements in the Minimum Standards, such as that an international bank must obtain permission from both its home and host country regulators prior to opening a cross-border

---

[137] McInerney, op. cit., p. 152.

[138] Indeed, the Basle Committee is comprised of the bank regulators of only the G-10 states, which control 80 per cent of the world's banking assets.

[139] Minimum Standards, op. cit., p. 270.

establishment. Particularly important is that host country regulators must first determine that the bank operates prudentially, that is, that it has sufficient capital and risk-management procedures. The host regulator must also determine whether the home country has given its permission to the establishment of the cross-border operation, and whether the home country has the capacity to exercise consolidated supervision *prior* to permitting the bank to establish in its jurisdiction. Finally, the host regulator should *prevent* the establishment of the bank in its jurisdiction if it is not so satisfied.[140]

This last element is designed to be *proactive* in nature. International banking regulation always has followed serious banking crises, and this perhaps only serves to fuel the arguments of many writers of 'lost sovereignty' that states must remain behind the times, largely relegated to a reactionary position, and largely unable to regulate effectively the 'autonomous' financial system which 'hovers above' and from time to time drops risks into their sovereign jurisdiction.

This proactive 'lock out' provision has raised a host of issues, among which are fears of a polarization of the international financial system into zones of banking activity that are regulated according to Minimum Standards and those that are not. Another issue is the manner in which the interest of states in prudence expressed in the Minimum Standards conflicts (or not) with their other interests in liberalizing financial services through the services negotiations of the World Trade Organization and the General Agreement on Trade in Services (GATS). Such issues will be developed in Chapter 6 in the context of the geographic spread of harmonized municipal laws. What is important at this juncture is to relate the manner in which the United States and the European Union have attempted to 'domesticate' control over international banks through the passage of national legislation, and to illustrate the manner in which such legislation, drafted under guidance from the general statements of principle enunciated in the Basle Committee, has become assimilated across the Atlantic.

---

[140] The Basle Committee has since issued guidelines that build upon the Minimum Standards. The *Core Principles for Effective Banking Supervision*, released for comment on 9 April 1997, details twenty-five basic principles which the Comittee deems necessary for a prudential supervisory system to be met. These include 'a suitable legal framework' and 'adequate resources' for banking supervisors, as well as a list of policies and procedures that must be set in place by banks and home country supervisors relating primarily to risk management.

NATIONAL LEGISLATION

From 1978 under the US International Banking Act (IBA),[141] branches of foreign financial institutions operating in the United States were given equal treatment as national establishments.[142] That is, foreign establishments could gain approval from either federal or state regulators to operate in the United States.[143] However, the IBA was amended in 1992 by the Foreign Bank Supervision Enhancement Act (FBSEA)[144] which requires the Federal Reserve Board to regulate all foreign banks even if they operate under a state charter. The result of this according to Duncan Alford is that 'the regulatory burden on foreign banks operating in the United States will probably increase'.[145] In particular, the FBSEA establishes uniform standards for the entry of foreign banks into the United States, including home country supervision and managerial and operational standards.

Crucially, the FBSEA grants regulators the power to refuse entry of a bank or to expel a bank from the United States if it is not satisfied that it is subject to consolidated supervision by a home country which

---

141 International Banking Act of 1978, 12 U.S.C. 3101–3108.

142 The principle of 'national treatment' is that no foreign establishment will be given less favourable treatment than a national institution. According to the Act, foreign banks in the United States are 'entitled to the same powers and subjected to the same restrictions as similarly situated US-based banks'. The IBA was passed because foreign banks were enjoying a competitive advantage by being permitted to branch across state lines even if they were chartered as a state bank, whereas similar American banks were prevented from doing so under the MacFadden Act. As Daniel Laifer stated, 'unlike domestic banks, foreign banks could cross state lines, engage in non-banking activities, hold equity in US securities firms, benefit from lower capitalisation requirements, ignore federal reserve requirements and interest rate ceilings, and decline FDIC insurance and related assessments'. See Laifer, op. cit., note 118, p. 466, note 56; Alford, op. cit., p. 244; Gibson, op. cit., pp. 119–23.

143 A foreign establishment could choose among several different types of entities, such as an agency, a representative office, a branch or a subsidiary. Different regulatory regimes would apply. For instance, under the MacFadden Act, national banks which belong to the Federal Reserve System are prohibited from branching across state lines. The intricacies of the system of state banks and national banks (and the various supervisory institutions, such as the Federal Reserve Board, the Office of the Comptroller of the Currency, and the Federal Deposit Insurance Corporation) are not directly pertinent to the overall argument elaborated here. But see Dale, op. cit.; Laifer, op. cit., pp. 471–8; and Carl Felsenfeld, 'Electronic banking and its effects on interstate branching restrictions – an analytic approach', *Fordham Law Review*, vol. 54, May 1986, pp. 1019–61.

144 Foreign Bank Supervision Enhancement Act, op. cit.

145 Alford, op. cit., p. 245.

is capable of such supervision, or if it is not satisfied that the home country supervisors will share information with the Federal Reserve Board about the bank, or, of utmost importance, if the home country supervisor does not apply 'the *same* financial, managerial, and operational standards that govern US banks'.[146] As stated by Virgil Mattingly Jr., General Council for the Board of Governors of the Federal Reserve System, '[The FBSEA] ensures that foreign bank operations in this country are regulated, supervised and examined in the same manner as US banks.'[147] In other words, if the bank is not regulated to the same extent as a bank subject to the supervision of the Federal Reserve Board, that bank is considered not to be supervised adequately. It has been said that, 'in effect ... the FBSEA seals the nation's borders, preventing entry of institutions which cannot demonstrate that they undergo consolidated supervision in their respective home country'.[148]

The FBSEA was promulgated in the wake of the collapse of BCCI and in conformity with the Basle Committee's Minimum Standards.[149] The intention was to 'keep poorly managed, poorly capitalised or inadequately supervised banking institutions from operating in the United States'.[150] The FBSEA is therefore an attempt to domesticate control over destabilizing risks in the international financial system. There are similar provisions in the legislation of the European Union.

As part of Project 1992,[151] the European Commission implemented

---

[146] Laifer, op. cit., p. 494. Emphasis added.

[147] Quoted in Gibson, op. cit., p. 126.

[148] Ibid., p. 128.

[149] Zamora, op. cit., p. 1960.

[150] Alford, op. cit., p. 279. The Federal Reserve Board takes into account five aspects of the supervision provided by home supervisors: '1) ensuring that individual banks which they oversee have adequate procedures for monitoring and controlling domestic and international activities; 2) collecting regular reports (e.g. audits) on the condition of the parent bank, and the subsidiaries and offices outside the home country; 3) collecting information regarding the relationship between the parent bank and its foreign and domestic affiliates; 4) collecting financial reports that are consolidated on a worldwide basis; and 5) evaluating prudential standards (e.g. capital adequacy) on a worldwide basis.' See Gibson, op. cit., p. 131.

[151] For a comprehensive discussion of the economic, legal and political milieu in which the following Directives were drafted, see Joseph Jude Norton, 'The European Community banking law paradigm: a paradox in bank regulation and supervision – reflections on the EC Second Banking Directive', in Norton, Chia-Jui Cxheng and Fletcher (eds), *International Banking Regulation and Supervision: Change and Transformation in the 1990s*, Dordrecht: Martinus Nijhoff, 1994, pp. 49–80.

a Second Banking Directive[152] and a Directive on the Supervision of Credit Institutions on a Consolidated Basis.[153] The Second Directive has three main objectives: 1) the harmonization of capital requirements and monitoring of liquidity; 2) mutual recognition by domestic supervisory authorities of the duty to promote harmonization; and 3) allowing home country control through coordination of domestic efforts.[154] The centre-piece of the Second Directive is the creation of a 'single passport' or 'single banking licence' whereby a bank from one Member State of the European Union need not be separately authorized by the host country to carry on banking activities in its territory; indeed, it need not even be subject to supervision by the host country. The 'single passport' operates on the basis of an eventual harmonization, and mutual recognition of Member States' supervisory practices. Adequate home country supervision obviates the need for host country supervision.[155]

To protect an internal banking market, the Directive on the Supervision of Credit Institutions on a Consolidated Basis follows the Basle Committee's Minimum Standards on consolidated supervision. It establishes the 'principle that supervision of a credit institution operating in several Member States is provided by the competent authorities of the Member States in which the head office of the credit institution is situated'. The essential features of this Directive are strikingly similar to those of the FBSEA. As outlined by Laifer, these are:[156]

1. Authorizing and supervising on the basis of home-country control;
2. Necessary harmonization of capital requirements law, standards of experience for management, and monitoring of liquidity and solvency;

---

[152] Second Council Directive on the Coordination of the Laws, Regulations and Administrative Provisions Relating to the Taking-up and Pursuit of the Business of Credit Institutions and Amending Directive 77/780/EEC, 89/646/EEC, *Official Journal*, no. 1, 386, 1989. The Commission has also promulgated a Solvency Ratio Directive and Own Funds Directive and a Draft Capital Adequacy Directive, among others, to regulate the single financial services market envisioned in the Project 1992.
[153] Council Directive 92/30 of 6 April 1992 on the Supervision of Credit Institutions on a Consolidated Basis, *Official Journal of the European Communities*, 1992, (L110), 52.
[154] McInerney, op. cit., pp. 150–1, note 119. For detailed explanation of this Directive, see Caroline Bradley, '1992: The case of financial services', *Journal of International Law and Business*, vol. 12, 1991, esp. pp. 141–50.
[155] Dale, op. cit., pp. 156–61; Alford, op. cit., pp. 274–9.
[156] Laifer, op. cit., pp. 490–1.

3. Mutual recognition by the national supervisory authorities that each will follow this harmonization;
4. The theory of home-country control through coordination of national supervisory activities.

And, like the FBSEA, 'this system requires a member state to deny authorisation or to rescind current authorisation for banks "clearly" attempting to evade regulation in one country because of expectations of lesser regulation in another market'.[157] Like the FBSEA, the European Union is reserving the right to 'lock out' banks that are not adequately supervised.

CONCLUSION

This chapter has questioned the view that the 'globalized' financial system which arose following the demise of Bretton Woods has created an international financial system that operates 'up there', in an ethereal plane which somehow hovers above national supervision and oversight, and challenges sovereign control. It argued that the main social and economic risks to states from the internationalization of private finance are in international banking, owing particularly to the fact that some banking regimes are more lax than others and that the liberal international financial system integrates economies into contagion and systemic risk emanating from anywhere in the system.

The newest measures embodied in the Minimum Standards are designed to enable states proactively to protect their economic and societal security by locking out banks that present such risks. It was shown that, faced with a security threat emanating from the liberal international financial system, the United States and the European Union are attempting to 'domesticate' responsibility for controlling the risks in international banking by disciplining through municipal law the private actors involved. Both the US FBSEA and the EU's Consolidated Supervision Directive empower state authorities to decline to grant a

---

[157] McInerney, op. cit., p. 176. Foreign banks would fall within the jurisdiction of the Second Banking Directive if they establish subsidiaries. Branches, on the other hand, remain the subject of individual Member State regulation. See Sarah A. Wagman, 'Laws separating commercial banking and securities activities as an impediment to free trade in financial services: a comparative study of competitiveness in the international market for financial services', *Michigan Journal of International Law*, vol. 15, 1994, pp. 1010–11.

licence to, or 'lock out', a foreign banking establishment to operate in their territory due to a lack of information sharing by the home supervisors, which ostensibly was designed to lock out banks headquartered in states which maintain strict bank secrecy laws or lax regulation.

In a critical review of 'globalization', Paul Hirst and Grahame Thompson raised a pertinent question relating to the work of the Basle Committee. They asked, 'in an era of increased ideological emphasis on market-led solutions ... why create new coordinative bodies to regulate and manage markets and transactions when such regulation and management are supposed to be increasingly frowned upon by policy-makers?' They concluded that 'national governments have not proved powerless in the face of an overwhelming "globalisation" of international finance. Indeed, they have joined together to organise an effective supervision of the new situation.'[158]

As to the reasons for this, Hirst and Thompson offered the demand on the part of governments and banks for stability due to a fear of an 'organisational loss of control'.[159] Similarly, Padoa-Schioppa and Saccomanni observed that, 'with the intensification of international integration, the perception of a need for firmer rules and institutions has become more acute'.[160] There indeed has been a dove-tailing of a range of pressures and interests to create this demand: the role of private banks in providing international liquidity since the breakdown of Bretton Woods; the increased potential for systemic risk in the intricate cobweb of international payments; states' desire to protect social safety nets for depositors; and states interests in maintaining a deregulated (read privatized) liberal international financial system. This would seem to confirm the neo-liberal thesis on how the demand for regularity and predictability can lead to the creation of international regimes to dispel anarchy from aspects of international relations.[161]

However, this does *not* explain the reason for one response to be chosen over another. While the demand for stability may be a necessary condition for action, it is insufficient to explain why states pursued informal discussions in the Basle Committee to enunciate general principles that would be given effect in harmonized systems of

---

[158] Ibid., pp. 134–5.

[159] Hirst and Thompson, op. cit., p. 132.

[160] Padoa-Schioppa and Saccomanni, op. cit., p. 265.

[161] See Robert Keohane, 'The demand for international regimes', in R. Keohane (ed.), *International Institutions and State Power*, London: Westview Press, 1989, pp. 101–31.

municipal law. There is a certain rationality of governance here. The tension within states' interests between providing liquidity to underwrite economic growth and ensuring confidence is not new, and this tension always has been governed through national law, such as Peel's Bank Act. The same rationality of governance is being applied to these same interests, only the laws now have a transnational orientation. But the fact that governments sharing similar interests and subject to similar pressures have promoted the assimilation of their laws is important: integrated liberalism is integrating national systems of law.

The question whether an integrated liberal system privileging the involvement of private actors transnationally is leading to transnationally assimilated legal structures in other areas is intriguing. More intriguing is whether sufficient evidence of generalizability would support the contention that in the transatlantic community is emerging an 'empire of law', meaning an assimilated system of law administered by local authorities. Thus, let us now turn in the next chapter to a second case study, one dealing with criminal law: the legislation in the United States and European Union to control money laundering.

CHAPTER 4

HARMONIZING THE CONTROL OF MONEY LAUNDERING[1]

The previous chapter outlined some threats to the international financial system presented by transnational banks. Those threats may arise innocently, as through the interruption of electronic payments systems which could spark contagion risks, negligently through imprudent decisions taken by bankers, or criminally from fraud and the evasion of regulation, as in the case of BCCI. There are other, perhaps more subtle and understated, but nevertheless dangerous consequences of the globalization of the financial system, namely the avenues which it provides for transnational criminals to launder the proceeds of their illicit activities.

This chapter outlines recent international initiatives in the United Nations and the Basle Committee which have provided a framework under which regional and national initiatives have been taken. Like the supervision of international banks, the approach taken to discipline transnational criminals has been through the passage of municipal legislation within the general statements of principle agreed in international fora. The legislation in the United States and the United Kingdom (within the confines of European Union Directives) is surveyed. This case study supports the argument being developed here that states which are presented with threats by civil society actors, empowered by technology and deregulation (globalization), are attempting to domesticate control over transnational criminals, which has as its corollary the harmonization of their laws.

This chapter begins by outlining in general terms the nature of money laundering, which is defined here as any attempt to conceal the beneficial ownership of funds. Several mechanisms of money

---

[1] This chapter builds on earlier work. See Jarrod Wiener, 'Money laundering: transnational criminals, globalisation, and the forces of "redomestication"', *Journal of Money Laundering Control*, vol. 1, no. 1, May 1997, pp. 54–66.

laundering are discussed. While some readers may be disappointed that a step-by-step guide is not provided, the purpose of this is to illustrate the logic behind the anti-money-laundering legislation in the United States and the European Union. It is shown that once money becomes translated into electronic impulses that contain information about the money, it is exceptionally difficult to trace as it navigates its way through electronic systems in and out of several states' jurisdictions. Efforts therefore have been aimed at stopping money laundering at the 'placement' stage, as it is when the money is first introduced to the banking system that suspicious activities are perhaps most obvious.

It is shown that there are public policy incentives for wishing to control money laundering, and that the nature of money laundering itself has determined functionally the manner in which states have attempted to control it, i.e., by domestication. To stop money laundering at the placement stage requires national laws to criminalize money laundering. But to find the money launderers requires information from banks, and the legislation in both the United States and the United Kingdom is emphatic in its provisions that hold banks responsible for 'assisting' money laundering, which is a criminal offence, unless they report anything suspicious. Thus, there is here not only an attempt to domesticate through municipal laws the transnational threats, but an attempt to privatize the function of policing the financial system for dirty and hot money.[2]

This chapter also points to several difficulties that have been experienced by the United States and the United Kingdom as they implemented the legislation, particularly as this relates to changes in the traditional banker–customer relationship. In law, the relationship between a bank and its customer is a contractual one, and the bank's primary responsibility has been to keep the affairs of the customer confidential unless the bank is required by court order to provide specific information. The requirement of banks to report suspicious activities has altered this, and therefore it is shown that it is not only the anti-money-laundering legislation proper that is becoming harmonized, but many related ancillary points of law, such as the nature of the banker–customer relationship.

---

[2] 'Dirty' money generally refers to money derived from illegal activities, while 'hot' money is money that is stolen.

THE PROBLEM: WHAT IS MONEY LAUNDERING?

It has been estimated that the turnover from organized crime in the United States amounted to between US$170 and US$250 billion in 1989, and that the world-wide figure approached US$1 trillion.[3] Of course, this pales in comparison to the estimated US$1 trillion that is transferred on global money markets daily, and seems even more insignificant in light of the vast amounts transferred through the electronic interbank payments systems. However, by comparison, the aggregate profits of the top fifty Fortune 500 companies totalled US$33.9 billion in 1993.[4] Large-scale money laundering does threaten the integrity of global financial institutions and in particular the confidence that the international financial system must maintain. Moreover, money laundering may frustrate governments' attempts to implement fiscal policy, since large-scale movements of funds may be counter-intuitive to the anticipated behaviour of rational investors. That is, governments predict the movement of capital on the basis of such things as changes in the interest rate, whereas money may move in and out of a state for no other reason than because it is in flight. Of course, all this is quite apart from the fact that money laundering enables criminals to reap the profits from other illegal activities, including economic crime, such as firm fraud and commodity futures trading abuses, and of course trafficking in drugs and arms.

Although money laundering is by no means a new activity, the issue recently has become 'securitized'.[5] No doubt, this is due in some measure to a desire on the part of governments to tackle their social problems, such as drugs, by attacking the profits of crime, as well as to their desire to minimize tax evasion. Recent attention is perhaps also due to the fact that money laundering has become much easier since the removal of government capital controls. As Bruce Zagaris and Scott B. MacDonald commented,

---

[3] For the US estimates, see B. A. K. Rider, 'The financial world at risk: the dangers of organized crime, money laundering and corruption', *Managerial Auditing Journal*, vol. 8, no. 7, 1993, pp. 3–14. For the global figure, see Matthew B. Comstock, 'GATT and GATS: a public morals attack on money laundering', *Journal of International Law and Business*, vol. 15, Fall 1994, pp. 139–77.

[4] Rider, ibid.

[5] The reader is referred to the opening comments on this subject in the Introduction, particularly the statements by US President Bill Clinton and former UN Secretary-General Boutros Boutros-Ghali.

> Open economies, growing interdependence and the sheer instantaneity of financial transactions can be, and is being, abused by those who intentionally seek to conceal the source of their earnings ... As new technology allows information to move faster around the globe in new forms, so money can also move faster and in more mysterious ways'.[6]

Criminals take advantage of the speed and complexity of electronic fund transfers (EFTs) to conceal the source of the funds. It has been said that large volumes of money are transferred in international electronic networks 'with little more documentation than an ordinary sales slip'[7] which greatly frustrates the construction of a paper trail. The simplest EFT takes place between two clearing banks. However, many EFTs involve numerous intermediary banks and many payment orders. Intermediaries sometimes use different protocols to complete the transfer, which can leave bits of information out along the way, and sometimes the intermediaries will not even know the name of the originator or the payee, only the name of the two banks on either side of the chain. This can make the construction of a paper trail especially difficult for law enforcement officials, and hence also makes EFTs a preferred medium for money laundering.[8] As Edward Kelly, Governor of the Federal Reserve Board, testified before a House Banking and Financial Services Committee on Organized Crime and Banking, 'It is indeed a problem in the electronic age to be able to effectively monitor the enormous numbers of very, very rapid transactions that take place.'[9]

INTERNATIONAL EFFORTS

International initiatives to control money laundering began in 1985 with the United Nations International Conference on Drug Abuse and

---

[6] Bruce Zagaris and Scott MacDonald, 'Money laundering, financial fraud, and technology: the perils of an instantaneous economy', *George Washington Journal of International Law and Economics*, vol. 26, 1992, p. 63. See also Thomas F. McInerney III, 'Towards the next phase in international banking regulation', *DePaul Business Law Journal*, vol. 7, Fall 1994, pp. 143–71.

[7] George H. Windecker, 'The Eurodollar deposit market: strategies for regulation', *The American University Journal of International Law and Policy*, vol. 9, Fall 1993, p. 366.

[8] Sarah Jane Hughes, 'Policing money laundering through funds transfers: a critique of the regulation under the Bank Secrecy Act', *Indiana Law Journal*, vol. 67, Winter 1992, p. 283.

[9] Testimony of Edward Kelly before the House Banking and Financial Services Committee (Rep. Jim Leach, Chair), *Federal News Wire*, 28 February 1996.

Illicit Trafficking, which led to the adoption in 1988 of the United Nations (Vienna) Convention Against Illicit Traffic in Narcotic Drugs and Psychotropic Substances.[10] This was adopted by 106 nations and ratified by 75 and the European Union. Under the Convention, states agreed, among other things, to criminalize the laundering through international means of the proceeds from the sale of illicit drugs; to empower their courts to seize financial records to assist a money laundering investigation; and to cooperate in mutual legal assistance and the extradition of persons accused of money laundering.

In December of 1988, the Basle Committee on Banking Regulations and Supervisory Practices issued a general statement of principles known as the 'Know Your Customer' rule. This expressed a consensus among banking regulators that efforts to stop money laundering must begin at the national level in the form of legislation aimed at the banking community. This is due to the fact that once dirty and hot money has entered the banking system, it is very difficult to distinguish a transfer of funds derived from illicit activities from *bona fide* transactions.

Sophisticated attempts to conceal the source of money can involve hundreds, perhaps thousands, of bank accounts in numerous jurisdictions in an attempt to create as complex a web of transactions as possible – a process known as layering. This makes it difficult to trace transactions by presenting law enforcement authorities with administrative barriers against obtaining financial details, and by making it difficult to obtain other evidence and to freeze assets. It is by no means impossible to do so; cases of large-scale money laundering are uncovered regularly. For instance, in October 1995, a large ring was uncovered in which the origin of nearly US$93 million was disguised through a complex web of bank accounts in the United States, Hong Kong, Australia, Switzerland, Singapore, and Taiwan.[11] One month later, 12 individuals in Turkey, Germany, US, and the Netherlands were apprehended for allegedly laundering approximately US$9 million.[12]

Money laundering activity can also be discovered at the integration

---

[10] United Nations Convention Against Illicit Traffic in Narcotic Drugs and Psychotropic Substances, UN Doc. E/CONF. 82/15 (1988), in *International Legal Materials*, vol. 28, 1989, p. 493.

[11] 'Drug barons laundered millions through HK banks', *Reuters Report*, 30 October 1995.

[12] 'International drug-smuggling ring smashed', *Deutsche Presse-Agentur*, 10 November 1995.

stage, which is the final stage of the process where the money is finally rendered clean. For instance, the Cali drug cartel has established 'paper companies' which 'sold' (on paper) such commodities as leather goods and jewellery. These establishments shipped token amounts of goods for over-inflated sums of money so that their audits would record large profits. However, officials cannot observe every business to see if they are actually shipping goods, and that bills of lading correspond to the value of each shipment. Moreover, since this form of integration can entail tax liabilities, it is not used often. More often, criminals use a pool of consolidated 'dirty' money as collateral on a loan on which they default.

It is useful to illustrate the complexity of money laundering operations with this account from Daniel Laiffer writing on the activities of the Bank of Credit and Commerce International:

> Drug money was first deposited in a non-BCCI bank in any city in the US. The money was then wired to an account at BCCI in Tampa that was set up for the laundering operation. From Tampa the money was transferred by wire through a non-BCCI New York bank to BCCI headquarters in Luxembourg. From there the money was wired to BCCI in London, where it was placed in a certificate of deposit. This certificate of deposit was used as a basis to generate a loan in the Bahamas to a phony corporation set up by the drug dealers. From the Bahamas the money was wired back to the undercover account in Tampa, where is was transferred by wire to the BCCI branch in Uruguay. From Uruguay, the money was transferred as cash into Colombia.[13]

However, even a very complex scheme such as this one must start with funds deposited in some bank account in some state's territory. As Barry Rider commented, 'money in flight will be most noticeable when it "splashes" first into the pool'.[14] Thus, money laundering operations are more noticeable, and thus easier to stop, when the money is first introduced into the system – the 'placement' stage – since deposits without an apparently *bona fide* commercial reason more easily arouse suspicion at the point of face-to-face contact with the bank.

It is this philosophy which has guided the approach of the US and the UK authorities, two states with stringent anti-money-laundering legislation. Both states place the onus of vigilance on banks, in

---

[13] Daniel M. Laiffer, 'Putting the super back in the supervision of international banking, post-BCCI', *Fordham Law Review*, vol. 60, 1992, p. 1042.

[14] Barry A.K. Rider, 'Taking money launderers to the cleaners'. Unpublished, 1 April 1995, p. 13.

conformity with general principles that were enunciated by bank regulators in the Basle Committee. Those principles enunciated a consensus that banks should undertake to obtain proper identification for customers, and maintain record keeping and internal systems for reporting suspicious transactions. In July 1989, the G7 established a 26-nation Financial Action Task Force on Money Laundering (FATF) to recommend standards for legislative and regulatory measures to control money laundering. In February 1990, the FATF issued a report which endorsed the Basle Committee's 'Know Your Customer' rules, and recommended various measures to implement them, such as the abolition of secret bank accounts, and greater coordination among law enforcement officials. International efforts continue. The Basle Committee and the International Organisation of Securities Commissions coordinated a joint report on 15 November 1995 outlining 'Know Your Customer' guidelines which reinforce the original Basle Committee's recommendations.[15]

In addition, the Federal Bureau of Investigation has called for the integration of intelligence data bases and coordination of asset seizures among nations to fight cross-border money laundering.[16] There have also been international conferences of law enforcement officials involving the FBI, New Scotland Yard, the Serious Fraud Office and Interpol in an attempt to devise mechanisms to streamline legal and diplomatic channels in transnational criminal investigations.[17] However, there still remain administrative barriers to obtaining financial details, obtaining other evidence, such as bank records, and freezing assets is difficult since there are national sovereignty barriers in the form of different national regulatory regimes for obtaining information, different bank secrecy laws, and different criminal procedures for freezing and confiscating assets. Law enforcement officials are presented with administrative barriers precisely because the compartmentalized Westphalian system has generated differentiated legal jurisdictions, while the forces of globalization unleashed by the state through deregulation and liberalization have enabled civil society actors (in this case criminals) to skip over their moats of sovereignty.

---

15 'Government; central banks, markets, foreign exchange; economic news', *AFP-Extel News*, 13 November 1995.

16 'Global cooperation crucial in fight against fraud', *The Reuter European Business Report*, 8 November 1995.

17 'Fraudbusters press for more powers', *The Times*, 6 November 1995.

NATIONAL LEGISLATION

The United States was perhaps the first state to enact strict anti-money-laundering legislation. Its efforts began with the Money Laundering Act of 1986. Subsequent legislation includes the Anti-Drug Abuse Act of 1990, the Annunzio-Wiley Anti-Money Laundering Act of 1992, and the Money Laundering Suppression Act of 1994.[18] Through these, the United States has taken very seriously the principle that banks should endeavour to know their customer, and that they should police the financial system 'on the ground' for suspicious financial activity.

Banks in the US are obliged to obtain proper identification of customers and to report all large transactions. Under the Currency and Foreign Transaction Reporting Act (CFTA) provisions of the Bank Secrecy Act of 1970 (BSA), all financial institutions are required to file a Currency Transaction Report (CTR) for any transactions of any financial instruments totalling more than US$10,000, including a payment, receipt, transfer inside the United States or to foreign bank accounts. It is an offence wilfully to violate any record-keeping requirements under the CFTA, to fail wilfully or negligently to file a CRT, or wilfully to make false statements in a report filed under the CFTA.

However, this automaticity in the US law does not mean that US financial institutions are relieved of the burden of deciding whether or not a particular transaction is suspicious. Banks not only have to make reports for transactions over US$10,000, but they must guard against attempts by customers to evade the mandatory reporting requirements. The common technique for evasion is 'structuring' which refers to the breaking up of large transactions into more numerous, smaller value ones in an attempt to fall under the US$10,000 mandatory reporting threshold. It is an offence not only for anyone to structure, but to assist – a provision aimed at the bank itself – in structuring transactions in a way that will evade the reporting requirement.

Legislation in the United Kingdom also places the onus of vigilance on banks consistent with the philosophy of attempting to stem money

---

[18] On the US legislation, see G. Philip Rutledge, 'Bank secrecy laws: an American perspective', unpublished; Jonathan J. Rusch, 'Hue and cry in the counting-house: some observations on the Bank Secrecy Act', *Catholic University Law Review*, vol. 37, Winter 1988, pp. 465–88; and Frank C. Razzano, 'American money laundering statutes: the case for a worldwide system of banking compliance programs', *Detroit College of Law Journal of International Law and Practice*, vol. 3, 1994, pp. 277–307.

laundering at the placement stage.[19] For instance, the laundering of money derived from drug-related crimes was criminalized by the Drug Trafficking Offences Act 1986. The Drug Trafficking Act 1994 re-enacted and consolidated the laws relating to the laundering of money derived from trafficking drugs. Section 50 of the 1994 Act made it an offence for anyone to assist another to retain, control, conceal, or disguise money if that person knew or suspected that it derived from drug trafficking. Section 52 made it an offence to fail to disclose such knowledge or suspicion to the appropriate authorities. Section 53 made it an offence to 'tip off' a person about an actual or impending investigation.

The Northern Ireland (Emergency Provisions) Act of 1991 criminalized the laundering of money connected with terrorist activities. This made it an offence for anyone to assist another to retain (Section 53), conceal, convert, transfer or to move from the jurisdiction of the courts (Section 54) the proceeds of terrorist activities if that person had knowledge of, or suspected the source of the funds as having derived from terrorist activities.

The Criminal Justice Act 1993 (CJA) implemented the European Community's Council Directive on Prevention of the Use of the Financial System for the Purposes of Money Laundering,[20] which itself was drafted in conformity with Article 3(1)b of the 1988 United Nations (Vienna) Convention.[21] The CJA made the laundering of proceeds of all serious offences a crime. Section 93A outlines several

---

[19] For a thorough and concise exposition of the following Acts, see Leonard Jason-Lloyd, 'Money laundering – the complete guide', *ms.* See also Ross Cranston, 'Bankers' duty of confidentiality: English law', paper presented to the Cambridge International Symposium on Economic Crime, 11 September 1995. The Sections cited relate to banks, financial advisors, or others who assist the criminals for the purposes of this exposition. The Sections pertaining to the criminals themselves have been omitted.

[20] European Directive on the Prevention of the Use of the Financial System for the Purposes of Money Laundering. Council Directive 91/308, *Official Journal of the European Communities*, (L166) 1991, p. 77. For a discussion of this, as well as the laws implemented by other European states, see Scott E. Mortman, 'Putting starch in European efforts to combat money laundering', *Fordham Law Review*, vol. 60, 1992, at p. 429.

[21] On the Criminal Justice Act 1993, see Robert Finney, 'UK money laundering law after the reports of 1993', *Butterworths Journal of International Banking and Finance Law*, December 1993, pp. 530–7; Monica Bond, 'Money laundering', *Accountants Digest*, no. 324, September 1994; Michael Clarke, 'How will the money laundering regulations work?', *Journal of Financial Regulation and Compliance*, vol. 31, no. 1, 1995, pp. 36–42; and Gerard McCormack, 'Money laundering and banking secrecy', *The Company Lawyer*, vol. 16, no. 1, 1995, pp. 6–10.

related offences of direct relevance to banks and other financial services institutions: first, to facilitate the retention or control of monies derived from criminal activities; second, to conceal such proceeds by its removal or transfer from the jurisdiction of the courts; and third, to fail to disclose knowledge or suspicion of money laundering. Finally, Section 93D made it an offence to 'tip off' a person about an actual or impending investigation.

It may be that individual bankers are in the best position to monitor and to report suspicious financial transactions. However, the attempt to stop money laundering at the placement stage has exerted considerable pressure on banks, and indeed on the tradition of the laws in these countries. Several issues arise in this connection.

The first issue is the extent to which the requirement of a banker to report to the authorities not only knowledge, but 'suspicion' of illicit activities on the part of his or her customer conflicts with the duty of confidentiality of a banker which arises out of the contractual relationship with a customer. It is an established principle in English common law that the relationship between a bank and its customer is a contractual one, and that a bank has a legal duty arising out of this contract to protect the confidentiality of a customer's financial details.[22] In the words of Bankes LJ in *Tournier v. National Provincial and Union Bank of England,* this duty extends 'at least to all the transactions that go through the account ... [even] beyond the period when the account is closed ... [and] extends to information obtained from other sources than the customer's actual account'.[23]

However, while this duty of non-disclosure is a legal one arising out of contract, this duty is deemed to be 'not absolute, but qualified'. In *Tournier,* Bankes LJ outlined four qualifications: 'a) where disclosure is under compulsion by law; b) where there is a duty to the public to disclose; c) where the interests of the bank require disclosure; d) where the disclosure is made with the express or implied consent of the customer'.[24] One could argue that the disclosure under the legislation

---

[22] In fact, T.G. Reeday opens *The Law Relating to Banking* (4th edn, Butterworths, London, 1980) not with a general chapter on the nature of banking *per se,* but on the general nature of the law of contract. The nature of this relationship was confirmed in *Foley v. Hill* ([1848] 2 H.L. Cas.28), and *Joachimson v. Swiss Bank Corporation* ([1921] 3 K.B. 110). See Lord Chorley and P.E Smart, *Leading Cases in the Law of Banking,* 4th ed, London: Sweet & Maxwell, 1977, esp. pp. 1–6.

[23] [1924] 1 K.B 461, in Chorley and Smart, ibid., pp. 6–10, at p.7.

[24] Ibid. As to the second qualification, see *Weld-Blundell v. Stephens;* on the third, see *Sunderland v. Barclays Bank Ltd,* in ibid., pp. 8–14.

concerning money laundering falls within the remit of the first *Tournier* qualification. After all, Sections 50 and 52 of the Drug Trafficking Act 1994 and Sections 12 and 53 of the Prevention of Terrorism Act provide immunity for bankers from the consequences of a breach of contract or confidence. And the first *Tournier* qualification is the only one that Report of the Review Committee on Banking Services (Jack Report) recommended should not be altered.[25]

This is not as straightforward as it appears. There is a clear distinction between the traditional concept of disclosure by 'compulsion by law' and the sort of reporting that is required under the new legislation. The distinction turns on the meaning of the concept of 'compulsion'. Traditionally, this meant complying with a demand by sequestrators for disclosure promptly and accurately. Megrah and Ryder explained that 'compulsion by law' under the first *Tournier* qualification 'must be confined to the regular exercise of the proper officer or actual legal power to compel him to disclose'.[26] For instance, Diplock, LJ, in *Parry-Jones v. Law Society* stated that 'the duty of confidence is subject to the overriding duty of the banker at common law to disclose and answer questions as to his customer's affairs when he is asked to give evidence on them in the witness box in a court of law'.[27] Similarly, Donaldson J in *Eckman v. Midland Bank Ltd.* held that the bank should disclose no more than what it is compelled to by law or court order, which means the bank should not volunteer information.[28] It is this meaning of compulsion that was meant to apply to disclosures under, for instance, the Bankers' Books Evidence Act 1879 and the Companies Act 1948, which related to disclosure following an order from the court to obtain evidence for the purpose of court proceedings.[29] This led Megrah and Ryder to conclude that 'it would be obviously improper for a banker to give information or other facilities with regard to his customer's account to any party in a litigation except under *compulsion of the court*', whether in the witness box, or under a court order.[30]

---

[25] See Cresswell, Blair, Hill and Wood, *Encyclopaedia of Banking Law*, London: Butterworths, 1995, pp. C-57-C-60.

[26] Maurice Megrah and F.R. Ryder, *Paget's Law of Banking*, 8th edn, London: Butterworths, 1972, p. 167.

[27] [1968] 1 All E.R. 177, at p. 180. Cited in Chorley and Smart, op. cit.

[28] [1974] Q.B. 76. Cited in Chorley and Smart, op. cit., p. 13.

[29] See also *Williams and Others v. Summerfield* [1972] 2 Q.B 513, in Chorley and Smart, op. cit., pp. 11–12.

[30] Megrah and Ryder, op. cit., emphases added.

In effect, the Criminal Justice Act 1993 and the 1993 Money Laundering Regulations entail a wholesale shift in the spirit of the law in the United Kingdom. The new legislation relating to money laundering operates according to a suspicion-based reporting system. Banks are forced to report any unusual activity in an account if there does not appear to be a good commercial reason for it.[31] This places the onus on the banks to make inquiries to satisfy themselves of the legitimacy of a transaction, on pain of being found to be 'assisting' a money launderer. It is important to note that the criminal offence of assisting relates only to the proceeds from drugs or terrorist activities. However, it is an offence to fail to report any unusual activity, and this relates both to the directors of a financial institution as a whole and to individual employees of the institution for failing to report internally. The solution to this is to maintain internal procedures for reporting and maintaining records, which will be returned to below.

There has also been some controversy as to whether the BSA contravenes a bank's duty of confidentiality to its customers. In the United States, an individual's right to privacy is enshrined in the Constitution, and American common law generally follows the decision in *Tournier*. The constitutionality of the BSA was challenged on the grounds that the maintenance of records as required under the BSA constituted an unreasonable seizure, but was upheld by the US Supreme Court in *California Bankers Association v. Schultz* and *US v. Miller*.[32] A significant difference between US law and UK law is that while 'tipping off' is an offence in the United Kingdom, the Right to Financial Privacy Act (RFPA) requires that a US bank notify a customer of a government request for financial information. However, amendments to the RFPA through the Financial Institutions Reform, Recovery and Enforcement Act of 1989 have tempered this to permit a delay in such notification (where notification would result in the endangerment of life, or interfere with an investigation by enabling a person to flee from persecution, destroy evidence or intimidate a witness) without fear of civil liability under the RPFA.[33] All of these qualifications have led G. Philip Rutledge to state that 'despite the

---

[31] See S. Taylor, 'Knowing too much and saying too little, the risks to banks', paper presented to the Cambridge International Symposium on Economic Crime, 11 September 1995.

[32] Cited in Rutledge, op. cit.

[33] Rusch, op. cit., p. 482.

mis-named BSA, there is no bank secrecy in America in the traditional sense'.[34]

Thus, in both the United States and the United Kingdom it is not the civil liability for breach of confidence that banks fear most, but the criminal charge of assisting in money laundering. In both countries, the burden of policing the system for 'suspicious' transactions is forced on the individual banks.

The question thus is, what is 'suspicious'? This raises the difficult issue of what is due diligence. The defence for a banker or financial advisor in the UK and the US for failing to report money laundering could be that he or she did not know or suspect that the monies in question derived from criminal activities. But this raises the question of what is 'knowledge'? The onus is on the prosecution to show that the banker knew, or deliberately turned a blind eye to the source of the funds, or neglected to act with reasonable probity. But what is 'reasonable'? And what cost should the bank bear in its effort to act with probity?

In the context of 'structuring' in the United States, the BSA states that 'multiple currency transactions shall be treated as a single transaction if the financial institution has knowledge that they are by or on behalf of any person' and result in a transaction 'totalling more than $10,000 during any one business day'.[35] Therefore, it is a defence if the institution can claim that it did not know that a person was structuring transactions. Yet, the US Treasury will impute knowledge to the institution if the transactions are kept in an automated or manual system to trace cash-in and cash-out transactions.

One might argue that it is reasonable to assume that a bank should be able to notice a transaction of US$10,000 in a single business day. However, as Jonathan Rusch argued, the concept of 'knowledge' includes the concept of 'wilful blindness', which means that 'if a person has his suspicions aroused but then deliberately omits to make further inquiries because he wishes to remain in ignorance, he is deemed to have knowledge'.[36] Not only that, the US Court of Appeals for the First Circuit in *United States v. Bank of New England* held that a court could ascribe 'collective knowledge' theory to the institution as the 'total knowledge of the banks' employees acting within the scope of their employment'.[37] Furthermore, in *Bank of New England*, the court

---

34 Ibid.
35 See Rusch, op. cit., note 65.
36 Ibid.
37 Ibid., p. 482 note 70.

upheld an inference of specific intent to evade the CTR by the failure of an employee of a bank to make further investigations or to report a transaction about which he or she was suspicious.

Therefore, the vigilance of the bank to report extends much further than the obvious case of the same person making a number of transactions in succession in the same day. Does it extend to the case of a person carrying out transactions with regularity over a period of time which individually fall below the reporting requirements? Does it extend to a case where two people enter a bank together and make two transactions separately which individually fall below the $10,000 reporting limit but which together breach the $10,000 reporting threshold? The law is unclear, but the incentive built into the law is for banks to err on the side of caution. For instance, Section 1103(C) of the BSA exempts an institution from liability to the customer under federal, state, and local law if it chooses voluntarily to disclose such activity 'even if the bank does not know which law may have been violated'.[38]

The incentive is therefore for banks, released from their contractual duty of confidentiality when complying with the BSA, to report anything and everything for fear of being liable for a failure to file a CTR with imputed collective knowledge. The US approach to reporting is perhaps more burdensome than the UK's because of the requirement to report automatically under the CTR – even of large, well established and respected companies – as well as anything that arouses suspicion. The number of CTR filings have increased from 707,000 in 1984 to 5 million in 1987 to 11 million in 1995. And it has been estimated that US banks spend US$100 million annually in the fight against money launderers.[39]

The strain on bureaucratic channels is self-evident. In reaction to this, the US Treasury's Financial Crimes Enforcement Network has attempted to determine which companies can be exempt from US$10,000 reporting rules to lower current annual average reports.[40] Along with this, the American Bankers Association has been preparing 'Know Your Customer' procedures for banks, along with 'Money Laundering Manuals' to help banks recognize customers of bad character.[41]

---

[38] Ibid., p. 483.

[39] Razzano, op. cit.

[40] '2,000 firms may be exempted from filing currency reports', *The American Banker*, 9 November 1995, p. 14.

[41] 'Money laundering manual will surface in December', *The Regulatory Compliance Watch*, (American Banker-Bond Buyer), 13 November 1995, vol. 5, no. 43, p. 12.

While this certainly alleviates the overload on information channels from the banks to the Treasury, it does very little to ease the burden on US banks. How is a bank to distinguish between a *bona fide* commercial enterprise and a 'paper company' that has been established for the sole purpose of money laundering? There can be significant financial costs involved in 'knowing your customer'. As Martin S. Kenney pointed out, the 'old school' method of due diligence, in other words nineteenth-century practice, relied on personal references. Business transactions today are more impersonal, in the sense that 'corporate webs, transactional complexes and multi-jurisdictional activities present the need for a creative and lateral methodology for due diligence'.[42] A harmonized verification system does not exist to assess the credentials of customers. Rather, there are numerous disparate commercial on-line database searches, such as the Dunn and Bradstreet Basic Business Searches, Dunn and Bradstreet Legal Searches, Dow Jones Full Text Searches, Disclosure Database Searches, and criminal record checks. All of these are expensive, and place an undue cost on individual banks. Business has also been impersonalized with the advent of electronic technologies. For instance, forged or stolen cards can be used to purchase fictitious or overvalued goods from a 'paper company', which transfers legitimate money from the credit company to the criminals.[43]

The concept of 'suspicion' in the United Kingdom is defined in a similar manner to that in the United States, which includes the concept of wilful blindness. Reporting in the United Kingdom has also increased dramatically. The British Bankers Association stated that the number of reports to the National Criminal Intelligence Service exceeds 20,000 annually.[44] This is significantly less than in the United States. The UK approach is also somewhat less cumbersome to financial institutions, in that there is no requirement for automatic reporting of large transactions and banks are not subject to routine audits. However, banks are required to follow the British Bankers Association Guidance Notes for Banks and Building Societies which were drafted to give some guidance in constructing internal reporting structures and in deciding what to report to the authorities.[45] Banks and other financial institutions are required to maintain identification

---

[42] Martin S. Kenney, 'How and how well do you know your customer?', ms.

[43] See Zagaris and MacDonald, op. cit., p. 62.

[44] As reported in Finney, op. cit., p. 532.

[45] The Regulations are reproduced in Monica Bond, op. cit., pp. 9–32.

and verification procedures (Regulations 7–11), record-keeping (Regulations 12 and 13), internal reporting procedures and to train employees in the procedures and in the laws relating to money laundering (Regulations 5 and 14) and to take other procedures 'as may be reasonably necessary for the purposes of ... preventing money laundering'. Banks must now be wary of such things as persons acting through intermediaries, and to ensure that they know the true identity of a new customer. In the case of a one-off transaction if money laundering is suspected banks must report if a single transaction exceeds Ecu 15,000, or if it appears that a transaction for over Ecu 15,000 is being structured. Institutions which do not implement internal procedures in this way can face a criminal charge under Regulation 5(3), regardless of whether money laundering has occurred or not.

Such a system places unprecedented burdens on financial institutions. The financial costs involved have been estimated for each large building society at £60,000 initially, with £23,000 recurring annually.[46] The firm Nabarro Nathanson which specializes in assisting financial institutions to comply with these regulations estimated that the market for legal services in the UK is worth £200 million.[47] Moreover, as Finney pointed out,[48] although the disclosure under the CJA in good faith absolves the financial institution of liability to the customer for a breach of confidence, this does not preclude actions for defamation or negligence. Even more important for present purposes is that the new measures to control money laundering sit uncomfortably with the traditions in banking in these states.

CONCLUSION

One could argue that, as far as transnational crime is concerned, the deregulated international financial system represents an 'ethereal plane' that hovers above national supervision and oversight. As Barry Rider observed, 'There really is no international capability at present to deal

---

[46] Finney, op. cit., p. 535. Duncan E. Alford has even suggested that the costs outweigh the benefits. See Duncan E. Alford, 'Anti-money laundering regulations: A burden on financial institutions', *North Carolina Journal of International Law and Commercial Regulation*, vol. 19, 1994, p. 437.

[47] 'Funny money: catching the money launderers', *Law Casebook 1996*, p. 28.

[48] Finney, op. cit., p. 533.

with serious organised crime at its own level of operations.'[49] It remains the case that it is more difficult for law enforcement agencies to coordinate their efforts and to share information than it is for the criminals, who exploit the fact that states guard their sovereignty and maintain differentiated legal systems to shield their operations. Criminals' money flows alongside legitimate money in the international clearing systems. The deregulation of finance and advances in technology – globalization – have blown the sails of such international civil society actors (criminals) while the representatives of the authority of the state (law enforcement officials) are still forced to traverse the murky moats of due process. It is doubtful that moats of sovereignty were ever truly effective at disciplining all individuals all of the time, but the machines that have accompanied the advances of liberalism have put states on the defensive to a greater extent.

It should be pointed out that international efforts have enunciated general statements and principles of best practice, which are voluntary. Thus, these international agreements do not supersede such things as bank secrecy rules, nor do they permit the sanctioning of transgressors who do not implement fully their international undertakings. However, the fact that the governments of the United States and those of the European Union share similar interests in controlling money laundering has prompted them to tackle the problem. The manner in which they have done so – through domestication – is mandated by the fact that it is more effective to implement measures at the placement stage. This is quite apart from the fact that governments are released from the burden of doing so by privatizing the task of policing the financial system.

This chapter has shown that the United States and the United Kingdom (as an example of a state acting in conformity with European directives) are attempting to domesticate control over an undesirable dimension of globalization by passing national legislation. The harmonization of that legislation is a function of informal discussions in functionally specific international fora, i.e., meetings of bank regulators and law enforcement officials. The fact that these states share similar interests and are subject to similar pressures has promoted the assimilation of their laws. Therefore, it can be said – at one level of abstraction from globalization which emphasizes deregulation and technology – that integrated liberalism is integrating national systems of law. In this case, not only are the laws relating to the control of

---

[49] Rider, 'The financial world at risk', op. cit., p. 11.

money laundering similar, such as criminalizing money laundering, but other aspects of national governance are also becoming harmonized, such as mandatory reporting and the maintenance of internal records by banks, the definition of knowledge and due diligence, and the immunities under civil law. And the meaning of legal compulsion under the new money laundering legislation is different in spirit to the traditional common law qualifications to confidentiality in the banker–customer relationship. Transnational pressures are creating the need for similar responses, such as criminalizing the act of money laundering, and this, in turn, requires that the various related aspects of legislation be adopted as well.

CHAPTER 5

HARMONIZING COPYRIGHTS ON THE INTERNET

Communications technologies, and particularly the Internet, epitomize the compression of territory through an increase in speed.[1] While the telephone and television have become commonplace in many societies, and have impacted on the development of global society, digital technology and computer-mediated communication have blurred the traditional distinction between text, audio and film media. Digitization enables all three signals to be carried together, thereby fusing heretofore distinct media – publishing, common carriage (telephone) and broadcasting.[2]

With the rapid development of such technology, and its migration from the government and scientific communities to the commercial realm, the US government has actively promoted the development of an 'information superhighway', citing the benefits of such technology to education, business, the economy, and society at large. As early as 1991, the US High Performance Computing Act[3] promised that the National Information Infrastructure (NII) will 'revolutionize the way we work, learn, shop, and live, and will provide Americans the information they need, when they need it, and where they need it – whether in the form

---

[1] The 'information revolution' has been the subject of much commentary. For a very good synthesis from an International Relations perspective, see Keith Webb, 'The Internet as an object of interest for international relations', in Stephen Chan and Jarrod Wiener (eds), *Twentieth Century International History: A Reader*, London: I.B. Tauris, 1998.

[2] See, for instance, 'The route to faster networks', *The Economist*, 19 January 1991, pp. 99–100; 'The computer industry runs out of room', *The Economist*, 29 June 1991, p. 71; 'Telecoms alliances: called together', *The Economist*, 19 October 1991, p. 130; 'Harsh new world', Survey of the Computer Industry, *The Economist*, 27 February 1993, pp. 15–19; 'A mighty morphing', *Time International*, 16 January 1995, p. 40.

[3] US Congress, High Performance Computing Act of 1991 (P.L.102–194), Washington, DC: Government Printing Office, 1991.

of text, images, sound, or video'.[4] To accomplish this, the National Economic Council and the Office of Science and Technology inaugurated such agencies as the Information Infrastructure Task Force (IITF), chaired by the Secretary of Commerce, and an inter-agency High Performance Computing, Communications, and Information Technology Committee.[5] From 1991 to 1993, the United States amended its telecommunications legislation, which dated from the 1930s, to permit common (telephone) carriers to provide video services over telephone cables,[6] most notably in a ruling in July of 1992 of the Federal Communications Commission (FCC).[7] Alliances among communications industries followed quickly with the intent of creating 'Full Service Network' interactive entertainment systems, such as that unveiled by Time-Warner in cooperation with Silicon Graphics, AT&T, and Scientific Atlanta among others.[8]

The European Commission also has promoted an agenda to create an integrated network for most of the reasons cited by the US, with the addition of regional 'social cohesion' and the further development and consolidation of the regional market.[9] The European Commission inaugurated several projects, such as 'Esprit' for the development of information technology, 'Race' for communications technology to create a fibre-optic integrated broadband network for Europe, and in particular 'Impact' programmes (Information Market Policy Action) to coordinate the development of an integrated 'European Information

---

[4] Federal Coordinating Council for Science, Engineering, and Technology, High Performance Computing and Communications, 'Toward a National Information Infrastructure', Washington, DC: Office of Science and Technology Policy, 1993.

[5] Office of Management and Budget, 'Information resources management plan of the Federal Government', Washington, DC: Government Printing Office, 1992, p. 2.

[6] US Congress, HR 1504: 'Communications competitiveness and Infrastructure Modernization Act of 1993'; US Congress, S.1086: 'Telecommunications Infrastructure Act of 1993'. See Peter F. Cowhey, 'The international telecommunications regime: the political roots of regimes for high technology', *International Organization*, vol. 44, Spring 1990, pp. 169–99.

[7] 'Now you're talking', *The Economist*, 25 July 1992, p. 73.

[8] 'Ready for prime time?', *Time International*, 26 December 1994–2 January 1995, pp. 86–7.

[9] See, for instance, 'Proposal for a Council decision on inter-administration telematic networks for statistics relating to the trading of goods between Member States', COM(93) 73 final, Brussels: Office for Official Publications of the European Communities, 1993; 'Proposal for a Council decision on a specific programme of research, technological development and demonstration in the areas of advanced communications technologies and services (1994–1998)', COM(94) 68 final, Office for Brussels: Official Publications of the European Communities, 1994.

Society'. Developments in Europe have been slower than in the United States, however, due in part to the slower process of deregulation of national monopolies and higher charges for the use of telephone services than in the US,[10] although many European communications companies have invested in fibre-optic networks in anticipation of legislation similar to that of the US.[11]

However, legislation in both the United States and the EU – not to mention in states that are not as committed to developing information societies – has been slower to react in the context of governing what is transmitted on these networks. It has been asserted that the Internet is 'the closest thing to true anarchy that ever existed',[12] and in a special issue on the Internet, *Time Magazine* stated that the Internet 'crosses national boundaries and answers to no sovereign. It is literally lawless.'[13] The flow of information over the Internet is exceedingly difficult to control. While it may be overstating the case to suggest that the Internet answers to no sovereign (for it certainly does in many instances), the technology has raised serious questions about territorial conceptions of law, particularly relating to jurisdiction.[14]

There has been a myriad of court cases regarding the Internet, and a host of issues debated in the context of the Internet, ranging across questions of privacy, censorship, free speech, the protection of information, access to information, the security of electronic commerce, computer security, and crime, to name but a few.[15] Almost each of these issues has concerned whether there ought to be government intervention in the application of existing laws or the elaboration of new ones to the digital environment. And each debate, with few

---

[10] Whereas the United States had deregulated its common carriers in 1984 by breaking up AT&T, European carriers remain, for the most part, national monopolies. The European Commission attempted to deregulate information services delivered by telephone in 1990, but this was challenged by Belgium, Italy, Spain and Greece. See 'Telecoms regulation: the last stand', *The Economist*, 22 February 1992, pp. 85–6.

[11] Eighty-three cable companies had already laid 29,000 kilometres of fibre optics by July 1995 in Britain alone: 'Wiring the world', *Time International*, 17 July 1995, p. 61.

[12] Clifford Stoll, quoted in 'The strange new world of the Internet: battles on the frontiers of cyberspace', *Time Magazine*, 25 July 1994, p.53.

[13] Special Issue, 'Welcome to cyberspace', *Time International*, Spring 1995, p. 7.

[14] See Michael J. Wagner and Matthew G. Allison, 'Internet law', *The National Law Journal*, 7 July 1997, p. B05. Available: www.ljx.com/internet/0707juris.html.

[15] There is no lack of references here. See David J. Loundy, 'E-Law 2.0: computer information systems law and the system operator liability revisited', *Murdoch University Electronic Journal of Law*, vol. 1, no. 3. Available: www.murdoch.edu.au/elaw/issues/v1n3/loundy.txt

exceptions, has encountered the dilemma of jurisdiction and the efficacy of national action without parallel international action.

Some issues can be resolved by one state acting singly. For instance, a state that is sensitive to the problem of 'hacking'[16] and that wishes to enforce its laws relating to the protection of personal information could mandate that computers containing personal information meet certain security and encryption criteria. In this case, the legislation would relate to technical standards of security, and these standards would be enforceable due to the fact that the law governs persons who maintain the computer systems, and these persons are located on the territory of the state over which the state has jurisdiction.

However, other issues are not so easily resolvable within a national context. For instance, a state that is sensitive to the proliferation of pornography available on computer networks conceivably could legislate that pornographic material on all Internet sites within the state be removed and enforce the law. However, even assuming that everyone within the state complies with the law, this would not necessarily reduce the supply of pornographic material than can be viewed on the Internet from sites located outside of that state.

This chapter deals with one issue that has been the subject of intense debate and numerous court cases, that of enforcing copyrights for material on the Internet. This case study was chosen because it meets the criteria of globalization – in the sense of deregulated, permeable borders, a loss of protective-jurisdictional sovereignty, susceptibility to actions occurring outside of the state with domestic implications – that were seen to be present in the other cases examined. Technology permits infringements of copyrights on a scale greater than ever before, from many quarters of international society, thus challenging territorial legislation. The fact that State A has adequate copyright laws for the digital environment does not prevent a person located in State B from accessing material stored on a computer within State A and making copies; converting into digital form printed text that is protected by copyright in State A and transmitting it over the Internet to people in third states; maintaining the infringing material on an Internet site for others to access; or from removing the identity of the author or right holder and incorporating significant portions of a digitized text, recording, or computer program into another work.

This chapter begins by outlining the essential rationale for the

---

16 'Hacking' is a term that refers to the unauthorized access of a computer, usually from a remote system.

modern system of intellectual property protection, and moves on to explain in more detail the ways in which digitized communication challenges the current practice of balancing the rights of producers of intellectual property with society's access to information. This chapter finds that the European Commission and the US government were under similar pressures to adapt their intellectual property legislation, and that the legislation considered – much of it had yet to come into force at the time of this writing – was very similar. Due to the trans-border flows of information on the Internet, both the United States and the EU realized the sub-optimal nature of purely national or regional solutions. Informal consultations took place in the G7 and OECD that aided the 'steering' of parallel national action. For instance, the concluding statement of the G7 ministerial Conference on the Information Society in Brussels on 25–26 February 1995 stated:

> Providing high levels of legal and technical protection of creative content will be one of the essential conditions to ensure the necessary climate for the investment needed for the development of the Information Society. Thus, there is a need for internationally recognized protection for the creators and providers of materials that will be disseminated over the Global Information infrastructure.[17]

Similarly, the OECD stated that the protection of intellectual property rights 'may prove difficult if copyright procedures are only left to national determination' and that 'greater harmonisation of IPR regimes in different countries would facilitate this process'.[18]

THE ESSENCE OF INTELLECTUAL PROPERTY RIGHTS

Intellectual property protection, which includes copyrights, patents and trademarks, is a means to accord legal protection to an inventor from others copying his or her work and detracting from his or her

---

[17] Chair's Conclusions of the G7 Ministerial Conference on the Information Society, Brussels, 25–26 February 1995. Document dated 7 November 1994 obtained from Larry Irving, Assistant Secretary of Commerce for Communications and Information.

[18] Organization for Economic Cooperation and Development, Committee for Information, Computer and Communications Policy, 'Global information infrastructure – global information society (GII-GIS): policy requirements', OECD/GD(97)139, Paris, 22 August 1997, p. 55. Available: www.oecd.org/dsti/iccp/gii-gis.htm.

rewards.[19] It accords an inventor a monopoly right to exploit his or her invention in the case of a patent, or expression of an idea in the case of a copyright, for a definite period of time.

The rationale for granting intellectual property rights has a long history, and dates perhaps to the first patents that were granted in Venice in 1474. The logic of protecting inventions gained currency in the mercantile era, mainly through systems of patronage, for instance through the UK Statute of Monopolies in 1623. The primary purpose of the early monopolies was to encourage the development of national industry by rewarding an industrialist for his invention, or for bringing to the state an industry or an industrial application that was developed in another state by granting him an exclusive licence to produce a particular good. The first copyright law, England's Statute of Anne of 1710, had as its stated purpose 'the Encouragement of learned Men to write useful Books', with the implication being that learned people would not express their ideas in writing or bring other acts of creativity into the public domain if their private work could not be protected from copying. To encourage the flourishing of ideas and literary works, the expression of ideas is protected by copyright.[20]

When the patronage system was challenged,[21] the modern system of intellectual property attempted to reach a compromise, or balance, between the need to reward a person for developing and putting into use an invention, generally through permitting that person to reap monopoly prices, and society's interest not only in enjoying that product or the fruits of more technologically advanced industrial processes, but in having knowledge disclosed publicly. This rationale has its roots in the various philosophies that arose to influence the modern system of intellectual property rights.[22] One is the 'natural

---

[19] As a general source on intellectual property law, readers are referred to W. R. Cornish, *Intellectual Property: Patents, Copyrights, Trade Marks and Allied Rights*, London: Sweet & Maxwell, 1989.

[20] In practice, however, the Act was devised in reaction to pressure from publishing houses to protect the interests and profits of publishers, not those of the creators of the work, the authors. As Cornish put it, copyright protection stemmed 'from commercial exploitation rather than literary creation pure and simple', Cornish, op.cit., p. 246.

[21] The case of Darcy v. Allin (1602) is generally cited as having laid the foundations for that challenge. See David I. Bainbridge, *Cases and Materials in Intellectual Property Law*, London: Pitman Publishing, 1995, pp. 131–3.

[22] The early philosophies – and arguments – about the merits of intellectual property protection can be found in H. I. Dutton, *The Patent System and Inventive Activity During the Industrial Revolution*, Manchester: Manchester University Press, 1984; and

law' thesis, which regarded the concept of property, which included ideas, as sacrosanct. The use of the ideas of another without compensation was regarded as theft, and it was believed that it was the duty of the state to enforce rights to such intellectual property. Another is the 'reward by monopoly' thesis that argued that inventors should be rewarded for the usefulness of their inventions. Following Jeremy Bentham, it was believed that there are two different kinds of labour, one that is knowledge-intensive in the creation of a good, and another that, by copying the inventions of the first, can produce the same goods at lower labour cost. It was argued that products of the former should be protected from the free-riding of the latter. The third rationale was the 'monopoly-profit incentive', which held that there is a direct link between intellectual property protection and innovation, and that the general good of society is enhanced through development, progress and private profit. Finally, the 'exchange for secrets' thesis was based on a concept of social contract between the inventors and society; the former offered knowledge of new techniques, and the other, temporary protection. The modern system of intellectual property protection that grew out of these ideas rewards inventors for innovations or the expression of new ideas by granting them a limited monopoly in exchange for putting into use and bringing into the public domain new ideas.

PROBLEMS OF COPYRIGHT ON THE INTERNET

A host of 'literary and artistic' creations are considered copyrightable, ranging across text, music, films, databases, sculptures and paintings.[23] The basic axiom of copyright is the protection of the expression of an idea, not the protection of the idea itself. So long as a work is 'original', it is protected. Unlike the meaning used in patent law, 'originality' for

---

contd.
Edith Tilton Penrose, *The Economics of the International Patent System*, Baltimore: Johns Hopkins Press, 1951, esp. pp. 19–41. It remains the case that not all commentators are convinced that intellectual property protection through law is the most effective means to reward innovation. See, for instance F. M. Sherer, *Industrial Market Structure and Economic Performance*, 2nd edn, Chicago: Rand McNally, 1980, esp. pp. 442–8.

[23] The full scope of copyrightable 'literary and artistic works' is set out in Article 2(1) of the Berne Convention for the Protection of Literary and Artistic Works, 9 September 1886. Revised by the Paris Convention, 24 July 1971. Hereafter 'Berne Convention'. Available: www.wipo.org.

copyright does not require a novel or inventive step. Rather, originality, for instance under the UK Copyright Designs and Patents Act, 1988, means that the work must not have been copied, and that it exhibits an investment in time or intellect which displays 'skill, judgement and labour'. Thus, in the United Kingdom such things as translations and compilations which satisfy this criteria are protected by copyright.[24] In some legal systems, a work need not necessarily be 'published' to enjoy copyright protection, although there is generally a criteria of 'fixation'; in other words, the work must exist in a permanent form.[25] 'Publication' used to arise in the United States under the 1976 Copyright Act only when a transferee is authorized to sell, lease, or otherwise distribute copies of a work.[26] However, under the Berne Convention for the Protection of Literary and Artistic Works,[27] to which the United States became a member in 1989, copyright arises with the creation of the work. Unpublished works are therefore protected. The fact that works are unregistered in the United States does not invalidate copyright, but plaintiffs cannot seek statutory damages in the event of an infringement if the material is not deposited with the Copyright Office.

The Internet and electronic communications raised serious questions as to whether electronic texts were copyrightable, given that there was no established standard of sufficiency for 'fixation' prior to transmission. For instance, the situation could arise that a performer would not have copyright of his or her performance unless the performance were recorded by the performer to give it a 'fixed' quality. Thus, is an electronic mail message, perhaps a poem, considered to be fixed 'text' or a performance if the sender does not save the message as a document in his own computer or print the message in hard copy prior to transmission? Is an email message a 'live' transmission? Does the fact that the message is fixed in binary code on a computer qualify for fixation even if the message is fleeting through the network? Is fixation affected if the standard procedure of a bulletin board operator is to erase all messages after four weeks, three days, or two hours?

These questions gave rise to serious doubts about whether information on the Internet was copyrightable. The thin case material

---

[24] The Berne Convention, 1971, left 'as a matter for legislation of the countries in the Union' to decide whether certain works are copyrightable, such as databases.

[25] Cornish, op. cit., pp. 268–85.

[26] Jenevra Georgini, 'Through seamless webs and forking paths: safeguarding authors' rights in hypertext', *Brooklyn Law Review*, vol. 60, Fall 1994, p. 1199.

[27] Berne Convention, op. cit.

did not clarify the issues. For instance, in the case of *United States v. LaMacchia*, an MIT student distributed approximately US$1 million worth of pirated software over the Internet. The US government charged the defendant with conspiracy to commit wire fraud, not with the infringement of copyright. As Ilene Knable Gotts and Alan D. Rutenberg pointed out, this left 'unclear whether the copyright laws consider such transmissions as "copying" or "distributing".'[28] Thus, while one could have expected copyright law to apply to copying on the Internet protected works, it did not follow that the uploading of work to an electronic distribution system was, in fact, copying (would the persons receiving the software be copying?).

The NII Working Group on Intellectual Property Rights suggested that such a transmission can be considered both a communication and a performance, depending on the 'primary purpose of the recipient'.[29] The question of how one is to decide the primary purpose of a party downloading the material leads to the murky area of imputing intention. The issue becomes cloudier still with regard to hypertext, which can incorporate text, sound and motion video clips. Hypertext blurs the distinction between the traditional concept/construct or idea/expression dichotomy, and hypertext links challenge notions of authorship.[30] It has even been said that 'Intellectual Property law cannot be patched, retrofitted or expanded to contain digitized expression any more than real estate law might be revised to cover the allocation of broadcast spectrum.'[31] Notwithstanding the ambiguity in the law, and the fact that this thesis was advanced more or less

---

[28] Ilene Knable Gotts and Alan D. Rutenberg, 'Navigating the global information superhighway: a bumpy road lies ahead', *Harvard Journal of Law and Technology*, vol. 8, Spring 1995, p. 296.

[29] The Working Group on Intellectual Property Rights, National Information Infrastructure Task Force, *Intellectual Property and the National Information Infrastructure: A Preliminary Draft of the Report of the Working Group on Intellectual Property Rights* (1994).

[30] Indeed, there is also an issue of the blurring of copyright and patent. For all of these issues, see: Debora Halbert, 'Computer technology and legal discourse: the potential for modern communication technology to challenge legal discourses of authorship and property', *Murdoch University Electronic Journal of Law*, vol. 1, no. 2. Available www.murdoch.edu/elaw/issues/v1n2/halbert.txt; and J. H. Reichman, 'Charting the collapse of the patent-copyright dichotomy: premises for a restructured international intellectual property system', *Cardozo Arts and Entertainment Law Journal*, vol. 13, no. 2, 1995. Available: http://yu1.yu.edu/cs1/journals/aelj/articles/13-2/reichman.html.

[31] J. P. Barlow, 'The economy of ideas: a framework for rethinking patents and copyrights in the digital age', *Wired*, vol. 2, no. 3, 1994, p. 85.

convincingly by some, the approach favoured by governments has been for adaptation, rather than for a wholesale change of existing laws.

This issue was settled in the United States and the United Kingdom: electronic texts are copyrightable as they are fixed, even if they exist in electronic form only without existing in a 'hard-copy', or paper form. Files on CD-ROMS, floppy disks and computer memory have been deemed to be of suitable fixation as they contain works which exist in a pattern of zeroes and ones.[32] However, there was by no means international agreement on this issue. While US and UK law expressly requires 'fixation' as an element of copyright, many continental European systems view fixation as 'satisfying evidentiary requirements or do not demand it at all'.[33]

The next problem with copyright on the Internet, and perhaps a more serious one, is that of identifying and tracing infringement. That an electronic text is recognized in law to be protected by copyright may not dissuade a person intent on copying it, particularly if that person is outside of the jurisdiction of the state that has made the law. Moreover, for a copyright holder to claim compensation for copying presently, the plaintiff must prove that, 'directly or indirectly, the defendant's alleged infringement is taken from the work ... in which he claims copyright',[34] and this is generally more difficult than defending a patent or trademark, for instance, which grant more strict monopolies.

Copying is neither novel nor particular to the Internet – it became a widespread problem with the proliferation of the photocopy machine, and with the printing press before that. However, the new technologies raise two important problems. The first is the ease with which copies can be made. While the Gutenberg press certainly eased the copying of texts on a large scale, typesetting a printing press to make copies involved considerable time and expense. The photocopier amplified the problem of cheap copies, but by no means to the same extent as digital technology. Digitization increases the volume of copies that can be made of a work, the speed with which the copies can

---

[32] Gotts and Rutenberg, op. cit., p. 298. See also Senator Patrick J. Leahy, 'New laws for new technologies: current issues facing the subcommittee on technology and the law', *Harvard Journal of Law and Technology*, vol. 5, no. 1, Spring 1992, pp. 1–23.

[33] Melville B. Nummer and Paul Geller (eds), *International Copyright Law and Practice*, cited in Robert A. Rosenbloum, 'The rental rights directive: a step in the right and wrong directions', *Loyola of Los Angeles Entertainment Law Journal*, vol. 15, Summer 1995, pp. 547–74, at p. 551.

[34] Cornish, op. cit., p. 287.

be distributed and the geographical area and the directions in which the copies can traverse simultaneously. There are approximately 30 million to 40 million personal computers connected to the Internet world-wide, and it has been estimated that this number is growing at a rate of 10 per cent a month.[35] A work – even a work that has appeared in print and is copyrighted – can be scanned and uploaded to a bulletin board system, and copied by thousands, if not millions, of users. Moreover, digitization greatly eases the extent to which pieces of text can be incorporated into other documents, for instance in common wordprocessing software, without attribution to the creator of the text.

The second problem is that of identifying and catching infringers. Anonymous remailers[36] can make it almost impossible to identify the person who placed the copyright-infringing material on a bulletin board in the first place, and they enable Internet users to distribute texts incognito. Moreover, the Internet crosses borders more stealthily than a person carrying copyrighted material through a customs port or distributing through the postal service.

This has led to the question of who should be liable for the infringement of copyright on the Internet. Early cases in the United States tended to gravitate towards placing strict liability on the system operators.[37] The case of *Playboy v. Frena* involved a user of a commercial bulletin board service who scanned pictures from *Playboy* magazine into digitized form and uploaded these to a bulletin board, where they could be copied by other users. *Playboy* sued the system operator. The system operator argued that it did not know that the user did not own the copyright for the material. The court found in favour of *Playboy*, on the established principle that knowledge

---

[35] Reliable figures are difficult to obtain given the exponential growth of Internet usage. In 1994, it was estimated that 25 million people in 137 countries were connected and that the number of articles available was rising at a rate of 35,000 per month. See European Commission, Directorate General XIII, Information Market Observatory, 'The Internet and the European information industry', IMO Working Paper 94/3, September 1994. One estimate of current figures can be obtained from ITM Solutions' Internet Usage Statistics, available at: www.lsilink.com/usage_regions.html.

[36] An 'anonymous remailer' is an electronic mail system that permits a user to log in, normally free of charge, to send by proxy an email message. The technical data of the email message that normally contains the identification of the sender is removed and substituted with the word 'anonymous'. Such remailers are administered either by people concerned with safeguarding anonymity and free speech, or anarchists.

[37] This refers to such services as America Online or Compuserve, which are also called 'content providers'.

(scienter) is not an essential element of copyright infringement (innocent infringement), and decided that the system operator should have strict liability for copyright infringement. It stated, 'innocent infringement is still infringement nonetheless'.[38]

The deregulated telecommunications industry and system operators consequently became concerned about being contributorily liable for copyright infringement on their networks, particularly when the court cases began to proliferate where system operators were being sued for contributory infringement. These cases included *Sega Enterprises Ltd. v. MAPHIA* for facilitating the unauthorized uploading of Sega video games; *Frank Music Corp v. Compuserve*, for the unauthorized uploading and downloading of sound recordings; and *Religious Technology Center v. NETCOM* where the Church of Scientology sued for the unauthorized uploading of copyrighted materials.[39] As these cases were emerging – and perhaps to give some direction to the courts – the Clinton administration, through the NII Working Group on Intellectual Property Rights, produced a White Paper in which it recommended that systems operators should be strictly liable as direct infringers, as held in *Playboy*. It stated:

> On-line service providers have a business relationship with their subscribers. They – and perhaps only they – are in a position to know the identity and the activities of their subscribers and stop unlawful activities. And, although indemnification from their subscribers may not reimburse them to the full extent of their liability and other measures may add to their cost of doing business, they are still in a better position to prevent or stop infringement than the copyright owner. Between these two relatively innocent parties, the best policy is to hold the service provider liable.[40]

That the US government should have preferred to place strict liability on system operators is understandable, for at least four important reasons. First, this would *identify, de facto*, the infringer out of a range of potentially 30 million users. Second, this would *localize* the infringer on

---

[38] *Playboy Enterprises, Inc. v. Frena*, 839 F.Supp, 1552 (M.D. Fla. 1993). Details of the case may be found in Dan L. Burk, 'Patents in cyberspace: territoriality and infringement on global computer networks', *Tulane Law Review*, vol. 68, no. 1, November 1993.

[39] See William Galkin, 'Jumping the gun on sysop liability', *The Computer Law Report*, no. 13, 6 November 1995. Distributed by Galkin@aol.com.

[40] Information Infrastructure Task Force, 'Intellectual property and the National Information Infrastructure: the Report of the Working Group in Intellectual Property Rights', Washington, DC: Department of Commerce, 1995, p. 123.

the territory of a state and enable injured parties to have recourse to the law. It is notable that this strategy is akin to localizing the act of money laundering at the placement stage and holding banks liable for it. Like the bank officials who are liable for aiding and abetting money laundering if they do not take every reasonable step to find money laundering activity taking place in their bank, the system operator would be liable if it did not take every reasonable step to ensure the protection of copyrights on its system. Thus, third, this would *privatize* the policing of the system, much as the anti-money-laundering legislation privatized the task of policing the international financial system of dirty and hot money. The bank is required to 'Know Your Customer', and the system operator would be required to know crucial information about its users.

Finally, and related to this, placing liability on the system operator would have lent itself most easily to the adaptation of extant laws to the new digital environment. The additional legislation could be relatively *minimalist*, and this would be accompanied by a series of private contracts between the system operator and users wherein the system operator would attempt to deflect the burden and hold users responsible. As I. Trotter Hardy stated: 'Strict liability will force the system administrator of each BBS service to determine the most advantageous mix of preventative measures for that BBS, including the need to ensure user solvency, to perform message screening, to limit uploading.'[41] This already occurs in many instances. Lexis Council Connect, for instance, requires subscribers to sign an initial contract which permits the copying of their messages, which resolves some issues ahead of time. Contracts could require customers to state that they will place nothing obscene, libellous, or previously copyrighted onto the Internet, much like book contracts which give publishers recourse to authors of books. One could argue that such a system of contracts could be unwieldy to administer, given the potential number of users. But this is not necessarily so, if, for instance, they were to take the form of 'contracts of adhesion' that are placed on software packages: by using the system, the user consents to be bound by the terms of the contract. In other words, there could be shrinkwrap licences for cyberspace. A legal compulsion to 'Know Your Internet User' would allow the copyright holder to sue the service provider,

---

[41] I. Trotter Hardy, 'The proper legal regime for cyberspace', *University of Pittsburgh Law Review*, vol. 55, September 1994, p. 1043.

and a private contract would then permit the service provider to recover damages from the user.

All of these reasons for placing liability on the system operator are quite rational, at least from the point of view of the government. However, another court decision accepted that the very great volume of up-loads to the large commercial systems – such as America Online, Prodigy, and Compuserve – and the inability to screen reliably the content of each and every up-load (either for defamatory content or copyrighted material) makes it unreasonable to place strict liability on system operators, as held in *Chubby, Inc. v. Compuserve, Inc.*[42] An analogy could be made that bulletin board systems are more like bookshops or libraries which are not required to review every book that they carry and which are not contributorily liable unless they carry such material knowingly.[43]

While the US government and the European Commission were attempting to create 'virtual libraries' and a whole host of other services through computer networks, the uncertainty about the protection of information on the networks – in their own states, let alone internationally – could cause people to refrain from placing their works at the disposal of network users, and thus frustrate public policy. The United States, for instance, identified the need for the 'development of high-speed, highly accurate systems for converting printed text, page images, graphics, and photographic images into electronic form'[44] to make the digital or 'virtual library' a reality. The networking of computers holding such information, as in today's Internet, and the advances in fibre-optic cables make it technologically possible for scholars, researchers, students and the general public to access vast electronic databases with a great wealth of information. However, a 'virtual library' puts the material within easy grasp of the pirate with relatively inexpensive computer equipment. More worryingly, the commonplace technology of a computer, digital scanner, and modem can empower an anarchist with the inclination to send books to whoever wants them, with the potential of making him the greatest copyright infringer in history. An individual can download a manuscript, a database, or a computer program that is stored in a

---

42 776 F. Supp.135 (S.D.N.Y 1991).

43 See Hardy, op. cit.

44 H.R. 1757, op. cit. Section 310 (b)(1) and (2): Applications for Libraries. See also Executive Office of the President, 'Technology for America's growth: a new direction to build economic strength', Washington, DC: US Government Printing Office, 1993.

computer, and make an endless number of copies, sell these copies, or incorporate parts of a work into his or her own work without crediting the author. Any of this would violate the rights of the author of the work. For these reasons, it has been said that 'the most significant area of intellectual property law impacting the NII concerns copyright protection'.[45]

Thus, the age-old dilemma of encouraging work to be put in the public domain in return for protection resurfaced, but it was amplified greatly by the fact that copying benefits from advances in technology and that the technology crosses borders. As expressed by the 1995 European Commission IMPACT Programme: 'The fear of uncontrollable copying is probably the single biggest factor in discouraging information providers from making their services available over networks such as the Internet.'[46]

While copying has always been a problem – and is the very reason why copyright law came into existence – it is unlikely that one person can access, say, a thousand popular titles by post or by collection through travel and reproduce and distribute these without a great investment in time and capital. The new information technologies have empowered individuals at the same time that they have interconnected states, leading to an erosion of the power of the state to apply its national law to individuals reaching transnationally into its territory from their armchairs. The Internet compresses space and thereby challenges the enforcement of national laws. That infringement can take place on an international scale, among states with differing standards of protection, as quickly and easily as it could occur within one state's borders requires that attention turn in the following section to an examination of the international regime for the enforcement of copyrights.

THE INTERNATIONAL MILIEU

One could argue that established practice regarding the international recognition of copyrights applies whether it relates to respecting the rights which subsist in a printed work accessible by postal order or in an electronic work accessible through the Internet. However, this was

---

45 See Gotts and Rutenberg, op. cit.

46 European Commission IMPACT Work programme, 1995, 'Key legal and regulatory issues'.

not the case prior to the definition, in 1996, that electronic texts are copyrightable in the major international treaty, the Berne Convention administered by the World Intellectual Property Rights Organization (WIPO).[47] As this section will explain, although the Berne Convention now recognizes digital works to be subject to intellectual property rights protection, it does not mandate uniform systems of protection since the Convention operates on the principle of national treatment.

The WIPO Copyright Treaty was adopted at a Diplomatic Conference on Certain Copyright and Neighbouring Rights Questions in Geneva from 2 to 20 December 1996 (hereafter WIPO treaty).[48] Acknowledging, in its Preamble, 'the profound impact of the development and convergence of information and communication technologies on the creation and use of literary and artistic works', the treaty recognizes copyrights for computer programs and databases, 'whatever may be the mode or form of their expression' thereby including electronic transmission.[49] Explicit reference to the Internet and particularly the World Wide Web is made in Article 8 of the treaty which deals with the communication rights. This provides that

> authors of literary and artistic works shall enjoy the exclusive right of authorizing any communication to the public of their works, by wire or wireless means, including the making available to the public of their works in such a way that members of the public may access these works from a place and at a time individually chosen by them.[50]

Finally, and perhaps foreshadowing the greater use in future of technological means for protecting the copying of digital works, Article 11 provides for legal remedies in the event of the circumvention of such technical measures.[51]

This WIPO treaty is significant in that it outlines copyrightable subject matter in the digital environment, and it provides that signatories shall 'undertake to adopt, in accordance with their legal

---

[47] The other major international treaty, the Universal Copyright Convention (UCC) of 1952 administered by UNESCO, had a smaller membership, and was created largely on the insistence of the United States which did not join the Berne Convention until 1989.

[48] World Intellectual Property Organization, *WIPO Copyright Treaty*, CRNC/DC/94, Geneva, 23 December 1996.

[49] Article 4 'Computer Programs', and Article 5, 'Compilations of Data (Databases)'. *WIPO Copyright Treaty*, ibid.

[50] Article 8, 'Right of Communication to the public', *WIPO Copyright Treaty*, ibid.

[51] Article 11, 'Obligations concerning technological measures', *WIPO Copyright Treaty*, ibid.

systems, the measures necessary to ensure the application of this Treaty'.[52] However, the treaty does not increase the extent to which copyrights in general are protected since this treaty incorporates and builds upon the Berne Convention, and the Berne Convention operates on the basis of 'national treatment'. The principle of national treatment means that works of foreign authors in a member state of the Berne Union are accorded protection to the same extent as nationals under the law of that particular state. For instance, the Berne Convention is not *law* in the United States; the Convention merely gives nationals of other member countries the right to be recognized as having the same rights under US laws as US nationals, and to sue in US courts under US law. National treatment does not result in a harmonized system of law; it only guarantees a foreigner equality before the law in a national context and leaves to each state the method of incorporating principles into law.

There are two main problems in constructing an international regime of copyright protection on the principle of national treatment, and these relate to differences in the specific provisions of national law (which reflect differing national attitudes), and to mechanisms of enforcement. While the WIPO Treaty, and Berne Convention generally, outline in broad terms what is to be protected and the term of the protection, they permit exceptions in national law and also leave to the national context the definition of numerous detailed aspects of law that follow from the broad principles. The WIPO Treaty provides an exception to rights granted to authors in cases of reproduction that 'do not conflict with a normal exploitation of the work'.[53] What is 'normal' is open for interpretation and argument in a national court. For example, individual states will define in their laws the meaning of 'transient reproduction', and on-line service providers became concerned after the conclusion of the treaty that 'cache' systems of a computer which store temporarily a copy of the work to enable viewing, or 'mirror' sites that copy work to enable more swift viewing, could be considered unauthorized use in a national context.[54]

Under a system of national treatment there can be many differences in the way in which the general principles of a treaty are interpreted and applied. Even legal systems as close as the British and American

---

[52] Article 14(1), 'Provisions on enforcement of rights', *WIPO Copyright Treaty*, ibid.

[53] Article 10, 'Limitations and exceptions', *WIPO Copyright Treaty*, ibid.

[54] See, for instance, Dominic Bencivenga, 'Corporate update: global copyright pacts – treaties address works transmitted on Internet', *New York Law Journal*, 9 January 1997. Available: www.ljx.com/internet/0109wipo.html

vary on the essential features of copyright. For instance, while the UK Copyright Designs and Patents Act of 1988 recognizes the labour invested in selecting and arranging material for a compilation, the US Supreme Court held that such a work shall not be protected if it is the result of effort only, which requires no skill or judgement.[55] The lack of uniformity in law can raise problems of uncertainty. Thus while databases are in principle protected under international treaty, the definition of a database is open to interpretation in the national context. Prior to the WIPO treaty, Charles Meyer pointed out that the Berne Convention permits 'Member States to make variations in defining what is required for fixation, the standard of originality, special cases for reproduction, the remedies available for infringement, and other specifics in implementing convention provisions'.[56] It is difficult to see how the WIPO treaty in any way addresses this minutia of the law through statements of general principle, and it is precisely this minutia that is important, for remedies for copyright infringement under a national treatment system must be sought in the courts of the state in which the infringement takes place. The national treatment approach thus risks preserving 'laxity' in some states.[57]

Another problem with the national treatment approach is the difficulty of enforcement. Enforcement is up to the individual, not to the signatory government. Thus, a national treatment regime can involve high costs to a copyright owner wishing to enforce his or her rights internationally, as the rights holder is required to take legal counsel in each of the infringing states as local lawyers would be familiar with local practice in each state. This is in addition to the fact that the foreign national could have his or her rights recognized only to the extent that national law accords rights for intellectual property. Having said that, the Convention permits a signatory to deny recognition of the rights of nationals of a Member State that does not recognize the rights of that state. The Additional Protocol to the Berne Convention of 1914 accords a signatory the right to deny protection of intellectual property of nationals of a state that is not signatory to the Convention if the latter does not recognize the rights of that state's nationals. The Berne Convention also authorizes a Member State to

---

[55] *Feist v. Rural Telephone*. See Bainbridge, op. cit., p. 40.

[56] Charles J. Meyer, 'National and international copyright liability for electronic system operators', *Indiana Journal of Global Legal Issues*, vol. 2, no. 2, 1995, p. 9. Available www.law.indiana.edu/glsj/vol2/no2/meyer.html

[57] Without a standard, suggestions of 'laxity' raise the problem of relativism, which is addressed in the following chapter.

seize copied works that are subject to seizure in any other Member State, but it does not require the state to do so.[58]

ADAPTING LEGISLATION IN THE UNITED STATES AND EUROPEAN UNION

A debate has been raging in the United States and the European Union about how to adapt copyright legislation to the new digital environment. As seen above, both the US government and the European Union have recognized that copyright laws should be amended to keep pace with new digital technologies and computer-mediated communication, and these efforts pre-date the conclusion of the WIPO treaty. Though much of the legislation at the time of this writing is in the drafting or reporting stage, there is a sufficient body of work on which to make an assessment of the similarities between the proposed laws in the US and the EU.

Adaptation in the United States

Very early in the development of the Internet, the US Congress Office of Technology Assessment recognized the extent to which digital communications challenged existing laws. It stated,

> Although Congress has always had to reckon with technological change, the new information and communications technologies available today are challenging the intellectual property system in ways that may only be resolvable with substantial changes in the system or with new mechanisms to allocate both rights and rewards.[59]

The reference to 'new mechanisms' is illustrative of a twofold process for protecting copyrights in the digital age: one is through legislative adaptation; the other is through encryption and other technological devices for the protection of copyrighted information.

---

[58] Theoretically, an issue of copyright infringement could be brought by a government against another government, but remedies would have to be sought at the extreme by taking a case to the International Court of Justice, and a judgement (which has never happened, since no copyright issue had ever been taken to the ICJ) could be enforced only by a resolution of the United Nations Security Council. See David Nimmer, 'The end of copyright', *Vanderbilt Law Review*, vol. 48, 1995, p. 356.

[59] US Congress, Office of Technology Assessment, *Intellectual Property Rights in an Age of Electronic Information* 7 (1986).

By virtue of technological advances, it is possible to make on-line information available on condition of payment, much like the purchase of a book or journal. Individuals could be charged commensurate to their usage of information on the Internet, and this system could be administered at the site storing the information regardless of where the individual using it is located. In fact, this 'technological fix' was built into the High Performance Computing Act. Section 102 of the Act states that the NII shall:

> (5) be designed and operated so as to ensure the continued application of laws that provide network and information resources security measures, including those that protect copyright and other intellectual property rights, and those that control access to data bases and protect national security;
> (6) have accounting mechanisms which allow users or groups of users to be charged for their usage of copyrighted materials available over the Network and, where appropriate and technologically feasible, for their usage of the Network.[60]

There is no good reason why digital technologies should serve the interests of the public by granting access to knowledge but not protect copyright holders against the wanton infringement of their rights. In fact, the very digital technology that raises the problem of infringement also contains the potential for arresting unauthorized copying. As Richard Pearse argued:

> The photocopier is not designed to track what is being copied, only the number of copies. Tangible copies have no mechanism to record whether they have been used, read, or copied. On the other hand, the use of a computer to access data can be traced and controlled.[61]

The same technology that threatens to turn potentially everyone into an infringer can be used to identify the users, or to assert proprietary ownership of material to an extent that denies individuals access unless appropriate compensation is paid. For instance, Digimark embeds information, such as electronic signatures and serial numbers, directly within photographs, video and audio. This can identify ownership without blocking access as does encryption, or damaging files as does

---

[60] United States Congress, 'High Performance Computing and High Speed Networking Applications Act of 1993', US Cong. H.R. 1757, Washington DC: Government Printing Office, 1993.

[61] Richard Pearse, 'Library open-distribution systems and copyright infringement in Canada and the United States', *Law Library Journal*, vol. 86, Summer 1994, pp. 399–443, at p. 443.

'watermarking'.[62] There have also been many developments in secure on-line payment systems which would enable orders and secure payment to be made on the network for the use of copyrighted materials on a pay-for-use basis.[63]

Pay-per-use facilities are already in use in electronic networks. Legal databases, such as Lexis/Nexis and WestLaw, and other full-text retrieval systems of journal articles, such as EBSCO Masterfile, offer researchers the ability to search for information using keywords, to scan the information available, and to download the full text of journal articles and newsprint. They do so either for an annual subscription fee, or for the amount of time that users are on-line. This is, after all, an extension of the reasoning that underlay the elaboration of the principle of Pay for Use, otherwise known as the Public Lending Right (PLR) which was expressed in the United Kingdom in the Public Lending Rights Act, 1979. The PLR is a method of balancing society's interest in free access to information, in the form of the public library, and the rights of copyright holders who should be compensated for lost sales of their works. There are two systems of public lending rights. One is to pay the copyright holders a flat fee for every copy of their book held in the stock of selected public libraries and the other is to pay authors a fee every time a book is loaned out.[64] The latter could be fairer, since society's demand for a good book should equate to the royalty received by the copyright holder. The former scheme has been extended to the reproduction of journal articles in the United States, which operates in the form of the Copyright Clearance Center (CCC). The CCC collects royalties from member libraries to distribute to publishers; the amount is calculated on the basis of the number of photocopies made in the building.

These systems were devised in response to the advent of public libraries – placing works in which private rights subsist in the public domain without requiring that each member purchase the work – and in response to the proliferation of copying technologies – the photocopy machine. 'Virtual libraries' promise both to put more

---

[62] 'Digimarc Corp. announces new copyright protection technology: irremovable signatures protect creative property in the digital age', *Business Wire*, 28 June 1995. Available: www.digimarc.com.

[63] 'Secure electronic VISA purchases begin', available URL: http://www.visa.com/gci-bin/vee/vw/news/PRelco042997.htm; 'VISA delays "SET" rollout while MasterCard completes first transaction', *Report on Electronic Commerce*, 14 January 1997, available URL: http://brp.com/netline/netline.html

[64] See Cornish, op. cit., pp. 361–5.

information into the public domain and to ease copying at the same time. It seems reasonable, therefore, that Congress was considering a twofold approach that would use technology and an adaptation in the law to redefine lending rights in addition to copyrights. It could be that the National Information Infrastructure Task Force expected the nature of 'text' to change so profoundly that the copying of information would be less important than the temporary access, or use, of the information. Hence the reference to new mechanisms to balance rights and rewards, and hence also the inclusion of a reference to such technologies in the WIPO treaty. Thus, the emerging technologies have the potential to overcome the most pressing problems that even *pre-date* the Internet: preventing infringement and receiving compensation. By comparison, copyright law alone seems to be a sub-optimal solution.[65]

The Intellectual Property Rights Working Group of the NIITF was charged with the task of making proposals for the amendment of copyright legislation. It issued a Green Paper in July 1994 outlining that US copyright laws should be amended in the electronic age. It recommended that: 'It may be necessary to harmonise levels of protection under disparate systems of copyright, author's rights, and neighbouring rights, and consideration should be given to ways to bridge the gap among these systems.'[66] The final White Paper published in 1995 proposed several legislative changes that were introduced as the NII Copyright Protection Act of 1995, the stated purpose of which was to 'adapt the copyright law to the digital, networked environment of the national information infrastructure'.[67]

Given the fanfare that led up to the publication of the Act, particularly through statements of the Working Group about the wide-ranging changes that would be required, and the issuance of the White Paper regarding the liability of system operators while court cases

---

[65] Of course, while such technological fixes can apply to most material published on the Internet, it cannot be extended to every piece of information, such as email messages uploaded to bulletin boards. But then, individuals always run the risk of copying if they choose to express their ideas in public, and this is not peculiar to the Internet.

[66] The Working Group on Intellectual Property Rights, National Information Infrastructure Task Force, 'Intellectual property and the National Information Infrastructure: a preliminary draft of the Report of the Working Group on Intellectual Property Rights', 1994. See also, 'EU-US: Commission plans renewal of transatlantic relations', *European Information Service: European Report*, 29 June 1995.

[67] NII Copyright Protection Act of 1995 (H.R.2441 and S.1284). Available at www.thomas.loc.gov.

were proliferating, the Act was notable in its minimalism. At only four pages in length, it was limited mainly to amending title 17 of the US code through the insertion of 'by transmission' as a means of distribution and importation, and the addition of the word 'digital'. However, several sections of the Act proved very contentious; so contentious, in fact, that the Act failed achieve sufficient support in Congress to become law.

One provision related to 'copyright protection and management systems'. Section 1201 stated:

> No person shall import, manufacture, or distribute any device, product, or component incorporated into a device or product, or offer or perform any service, the primary purpose or effect of which is to avoid, bypass, remove, deactivate, or otherwise circumvent, without the authority of the copyright owner or the law, any process, treatment, mechanism, or system which prevents or inhibits the violation of any of the exclusive rights of the copyright owner.[68]

The intent of this provision was to prevent persons from circumventing the electronic anti-copying devices that could be attached to digitized material, such as electronic signatures or encryption systems, and thereby circumventing pay-for-use. But what is a 'primary purpose'? A variety of associations, ranging from the computer and software industries to telephone and electronics companies and consumer and technology organizations lobbied vociferously to have the bill delayed, citing such legitimate uses of the technology as back-engineering software for the benefit and progress of science.[69]

Other voices of discontent came from the educational and cultural communities which were concerned that the Act did not reaffirm 'fair use' in the digital environment.[70] Although the Act made reference to limitations on the exclusive rights of copyright holders for non-profit organizations to distribute to the visually impaired, it did not stipulate how 'fair use' would be defined in other environments. It is generally recognized in most states' copyright laws and by the Berne Convention that there should be exceptions to the prohibition against

---

[68] NII Copyright Protection Act of 1995, ibid., Sec.1201.

[69] It is established that copying devices themselves, such as VCRs, are not illegal since there are many legitimate uses of the device (even for recording a broadcast to view at a later time). The difficulty with this portion of the Act was that the technology itself would become illegal, not the specific use of the technology.

[70] The campaign of the National Initiative for a Networked Cultural Heritage (ninch) was most impressive (www-ninch.cni.org) as was that of the Digital Future Coalition (www.ari.net/dfc).

copying for such purposes as teaching, research and scholarship. How are the interests of students in less fortunate university departments which cannot afford fees for access in a fully commercialized pay-per-use system to be addressed in a balanced way? This could run the danger of creating knowledge-rich and knowledge-poor on the sole criterion of wealth.[71]

Finally, on-line service providers – and libraries and schools which maintain local area network services – were not satisfied that the Act limited sufficiently their liability for copyright infringements that could occur on their networks. The Act made specific provision that 'no person shall knowingly provide copyright management information that is false, or knowingly distribute or import for public distribution copyright management information that is false', and that 'no person shall, without authority of the copyright owner or the law knowingly distribute or import for distribution copyright management information that has been altered without authority of the copyright owner or the law'.[72] However, the Act did not stipulate what constitutes 'knowledge' (scienter) or the reasonable endeavours that would satisfy due diligence in seeking knowledge.

Primarily for these reasons, the NII Copyright Protection Act of 1995 was not passed. However, many of its provisions resurfaced in the WIPO Copyright Treaty of 1996, which led some critics in the United States to charge that WIPO had been used as a mechanism to circumvent domestic law-making. Not surprisingly, there followed strong dissent of the provisions of the WIPO treaty. The American Library Association was concerned that the treaty could undermine the 'fair use' doctrine,[73] and the Ad Hoc Alliance for a Digital Future worried that the temporary copies made in the cache system, or

---

[71] Note, however, that many writers have suggested that encryption technologies could be used either to inhibit alteration of a work once it has been downloaded, or to self-erase a document after a period of time (i.e., for students at the end of term). It has also been suggested that various levels of password could be devised. Students and academics may have an access code that permits unlimited on-line reading and copying up to a point, after which they would be charged a fee. See Georgini, op. cit.; and R. J. Linn, 'Copyright and information services in the context of the national research and education network'. Available: gopher.wiretap.spies.com.

[72] NII Copyright Protection Act of 1995, op. cit., Sec.1202(a) and (b).

[73] See American Library Association, 'America's libraries call for caution as international copyright negotiations for the digital age commence', press release, 29 November 1996. Available www.dfc.org/dfc/docs/libpr.htm. The principle of 'fair use' permits copies to be made of a work for non-profit purposes, such as education and research.

'buffer', of a computer automatically when it accesses a document on-line could be considered a violation of copyright under the treaty.[74] There also followed a veritable flurry of proposed legislation in the United States.

Among the proposals was the 'No Electronic Theft (NET) Act', introduced to the House of Representatives on 7 January 1997.[75] This was an anti-piracy bill which mandated criminal penalties for anyone inside the United States distributing for profit over the Internet copyrighted material of a total retail value of more than US$1,000. Another was the 'On-Line Copyright Liability Limitation Act', introduced to the House on 17 July 1997, another version of which was presented on 12 February 1998.[76] Essentially, this was a proposal to limit the liability of system operators by providing exemptions for liability for copyright infringements on-line if a person is not responsible for placing the material on-line or determining the recipients of the material. It also provided for protection from civil claims if the system operator were to block access to material that it suspected of infringing copyright.

Among the more comprehensive proposals were the 'WIPO Copyright Treaties Implementation Act' (hereafter Implementation Act), introduced to the House on 29 July 1997[77] and the competing 'Digital Era Copyright Enhancement Act' (hereafter Enhancement Act), introduced to the House on 13 November 1997.[78] Both of these were designed primarily as implementing legislation for the WIPO treaty. Both also contained additional provisions relating to copyright protection systems, and the integrity of copyright management information. The essential difference between them is that the Implementation Act concentrated on technical devices, while the

---

[74] Ad Hoc Alliance for a Digital Future, 'Industry coalition warns of WIPO threat to information society', press release, 28 November 1996. Available at www.dfc.org/docs/adhocpr.html

[75] 'No Electronic Theft (NET) Act', H.R.2265, 105th C. Enrolled Bill sent to the President. Available: thomas.loc.gov/

[76] 'On-Line Copyright Liability Limitation Act', H.R.2180, 105th.C., 17 July 1997; and H.R.3209, 105th.C., 12 February 1998. Both available: thomas.loc.gov/

[77] 'WIPO Copyright Treaties Implementation Act', H.R.2281, 105th.C., 29 July 1997. This was first introduced in the Senate as the 'Digital Millennium Copyright Act of 1998', S.2037, 12 May 1998, which was passed by the Senate. Both available at www.thomas.loc.gov/. For the sake of clarity the following discussion concentrates on the House version.

[78] 'Digital Era Copyright Enhancement Act', H.R.3048, 105th.C., 13 November 1997. Available at www.thomas.loc.gov

Enhancement Act concentrated on conduct. That is, the Implementation Act reincorporated, though in a much more qualified formulation, a prohibition (including the manufacture, importation, or sale) of technology, the primary purpose of which is to circumvent technological protection measures that control access to a copyrighted work or that interferes with copyright information contained in the work. The Enhancement Act, on the other hand, prohibited the act of circumvention or interference with the copyright information. Both Acts contained provisions regarding civil remedies in the case of an infringement of copyright, and the Implementation Act in addition contained criminal penalties. Additional provisions of the Enhancement Act not contained in the Implementation Act related to outlining fair use, distance learning, and limitations on exclusive rights. This applied explicitly fair use doctrine for educational and scientific purposes by ensuring that libraries, for instance, would be able to make electronic copies for archive purposes, and, importantly, it would prohibit on-line shrinkwrap licences. The absence of these measures in the Implementation Act prompted many lobby groups, such as the Digital Future Coalition, to argue very strongly against it.[79]

However, a later, amended, and truly mammoth version of the Implementation Act emerged, which, unlike its predecessor, had the aura of a potential law due both to its comprehensiveness and careful balance.[80] This version of the Implementation Act kept the general prohibition of technologies that would permit the circumvention of technological protection measures, though it incorporated many of the additional provisions of the Enhancement Act regarding fair use for educational (including distance education), scientific, and archival purposes. In addition, it now contained provisions that would permit the use of circumvention technology for back-engineering encryption devices for the purpose of research, and stipulated a host of permissible related acts. The Act also maintained both civil and criminal remedies in the case of infringement. To monitor progress in all areas, the Act provided for periodic reports to Congress by the Secretary of Commerce in order to review the impact of the legislation.

The provisions relating to system operators are worth discussing in some detail, as numerous exemptions for liability may, at first sight, seem to run counter to the logic of *localizing* and *privatizing* the

---

[79] See Digital Future Coalition, 'Real world problems created by H.R.2281, as reported to the Judiciary Committee', 3 June 1998. Available: www.ari.net/dfc/issues/wipo/realwrd/realwrd.html

[80] H.R.2281. Available: thomas.loc.gov

policing of the system discussed earlier in this chapter. In very strong terms, the Act prohibited the interference of copyright management information, or the distribution of material that had been interfered with, with the important qualification 'knowingly' to safeguard system operators. Indeed, this version of the Implementation Act also contained some of the provisions of the On-Line Copyright Liability Limitation Act to stipulate exemptions for liability of system operators. Section 512(A) provides that the system operator will not be liable for the storage or transmission of copyright infringing material if:

> (1) it was initiated by or at the direction of a person other than the service provider;
> (2) it is carried out through an automatic technical process without selection of such material by the service provider;
> (3) the service provider does not select the recipients of such material except as an automatic response to the request of another;
> (4) no such copy of such material made by the service provider is maintained on the system or network in a manner ordinarily accessible to anyone other than anticipated recipients, and no such copy is maintained on the system or network in a manner ordinarily accessible to the anticipated recipients for a longer period than is reasonable necessary for the communication; and
> (5) the material is transmitted without modification to its content.[81]

Notably, Section 512(B) included an exemption of liability for transient copies related to computer memory system caching. Finally, the Act provides that the system operator will not be liable for copyright infringing material stored on its network if it does not have 'actual knowledge' that the material is infringing, and takes immediate action to disable access to the material once it does know about it. Instead of holding the system operator liable, the provision relating to the identification of the direct infringer, Section 512(G), requires the system operator to provide the identity of the person who infringed the copyright.

This Act has yet to become law at the time of writing, but it seems unlikely that legislators will reverse five years of progress in honing their approach in favour of a radically different model. Thus the question needs to be asked: were this Act to become law, would the exemptions for system operators be contrary to the logic of domestication, localization and privatization of this deregulated and liberalized system? One could argue that providing such exemptions to

---

[81] H.R.2281. Sec.512(A). ibid.

system operators could make them act in a less proactive policing role than banks, for instance, which are required, under pain of criminal charges, to police the financial system for money laundering. Yet, the nature of a system operator's business is more akin to a library and a postal service than to a bank. If system operators could be held liable for contributory (innocent) infringement on a massive scale, their execution of due diligence potentially could impair the development of the information superhighway, i.e., reduce the amount of information available, for instance if they were to err on the side of caution and decline to store or transmit more material than they accept. It is very unlikely that a bank, in the execution of due diligence, could reduce the money supply; rather, banks simply clog up administrative reporting channels.[82] Moreover, by requiring system operators to divulge the identity of the direct infringer in the event of a claim requires that the system operator implement some procedure akin to the 'Know Your Customer' rule. It would seem, therefore, that the US approach to the issue of copyrights on the Internet is consistent with the general logic of governance outlined in this book. The extent to which the European Commission is entertaining a similar approach is the subject of the following section.

Adaptation in the European Union

In comparison with the speed with which legislation was drafted in the United States, movement in the European Union has been painfully slow. As a result, the European Union is not nearly as close to finalization of a comprehensive Directive at the time of this writing as the US seems close to finalization of legislation. Notwithstanding, it is possible to identify the manner in which the European approach is evolving in order to make reasonable comparisons with the United States.

The comparative slowness of the European Union is due in part to the fact that the politics of the European Commission are more complex than the politics of the US Congress. While navigating legislation through pluralist democratic processes in the United States can be cumbersome at times, the legislative process there is animated by private interests. In the EU, by contrast, the process of adaptation

---

[82] And make interest on the money that they freeze while making investigations to satisfy themselves of the *bona fide* nature of the money.

to change involves steering to a common position fifteen sovereign states, each with their own traditions and legal systems. The slowness is also due in part to the fact that the project of adapting legal systems in Europe to meet the challenges of the digital environment requires, *a priori*, the harmonization of intellectual property systems within the EU. Despite progress in harmonizing and approximating laws in many areas of the internal market, often wide discrepancies in the area of intellectual property law remain, which, according to the Commission, hinder the further development of the internal market.[83] The European Commission therefore has pursued a two-pronged approach to the protection of intellectual property in the EU. One certainly was oriented directly to the information society, on the question of which the Commission's Legal Advisory Board (LAB) was active. However, the Commission and the LAB also worked towards the harmonization of national systems of intellectual property protection in Europe generally.

The issue of a common standard of protection for digitized material on the Internet proceeded within the wider context of regional harmonization of intellectual property regimes. For instance, while the European Union, like the United States, spent considerable time deciding whether an on-line text on an Internet site is considered a broadcast, performance, or 'text', the issue became bound up in a Commission proposal for a harmonized right of communication to the public. Certainly there was a dynamic relationship between harmonization for the sake of the further development of the internal market and the specific provisions for digitized material. However, this section is concerned only with the measures most directly related to the Internet,[84] and in particular with the two issues explored above in the context of legislative adaptation in the United States: that of electronic means of protection, and the liability for systems operators.

Like the US government, the Commission recognized early, in the late 1980s, the need to adapt frameworks for the protection of

---

[83] See, for instance, European Commission, *The Completion of the Internal Market: White Paper of the Commission to the Attention of the European Council*, COM(85) 310(final), 14 June 1985, which refers, in familiar 'Euro-speak' to the necessity of harmonizing systems of intellectual property protection in the EU for the 'proper functioning of the Single Market'. On the internal project of the EU, see A. David Demiray, 'Intellectual property and the external power of the European Community', *Michigan Journal of International Law*, vol. 16, Fall 1994, pp. 187–237.

[84] There were various Directives, including: Directive 96/9/EC of the European Parliament and of the Council of 11 March 1996 on the Legal Protection of

intellectual property in the digital environment.[85] Work had been progressing on the Information Society since the early 1990s, and culminated in *Europe and the Information Society,* otherwise known as the 'Bangemann Report', in 1994, which identified as a high priority the establishment of an effective legal framework.[86] This led to a European Commission Communication, *Europe's Way to the Information Society: An Action Plan* that dealt in some detail with the regulatory and legal framework. It acknowledged that 'the globalisation of the electronic information market' would raise problems in 'identifying intellectual property rights holders, monitoring the use of information products enjoying intellectual property protection and ensuring the management of these rights'.[87] The Action Plan led to the Commission's Communication *Copyright and Related Rights in the Information Society* in July 1995[88] and to a further Communication in November 1996, the *Follow-up to the Green Paper on Copyright and Related Rights in the Information Society,*[89] which culminated in a December 1997 *Proposal for a Directive on Copyright and Related Rights in the Information Society.*[90]

Like the US legislators, the European Commission did not entertain seriously the 'end of copyright' thesis expounded by many. Although the Commission recognized that 'the problems of identifying

---

contd.
Databases; Council Directive 93/98/EEC of 29 October 1993 to harmonize the Term of Protection of Copyright and Certain Related Rights; Council Directive 93/83/EEC of 27 September 1993 on The Coordination of Certain Rules Concerning Copyright and Rights Related to Copyright Applicable to Satellite Broadcasting and Cable Retransmission; and Council Directive 91/250/EEC of 14 May 1991 on the Legal Protection of Computer Programs. These are available at: www./europa.eu.int.

85 European Commission, 'Copyright and the new technologies', *Green Paper on Copyright and the Challenge of Technology: Problems in Copyright Calling for Immediate Action,* COM(88) 172(final) 17 June 1988; European Commission, *Working Programme of the Commission in the Field of Copyright and Neighbouring Rights: Follow-up to the Green Paper,* COM(90) 584(final) 17 January 1991.

86 *Europe and the Global Information Society: Recommendations of the High Level Group on the Information Society to the Corfu European Council,* 26 May 1994.

87 European Commission, *Europe's Way to the Information Society: An Action Plan, Communication from the Commission,* Brussels, 19 July 1994, COM(94)347 final.

88 European Commission, *Copyright and Related Rights in the Information Society,* COM(95) 382 Final, 19 July 1995.

89 European Commission, *Follow-up to the Green Paper on Copyright and Related Rights in the Information Society,* COM(96) 586 Final, 20 November 1996.

90 *Copyright and Related Rights in the Information Society: Proposal for Directive/ Background,* 10 December 1997. Available: http://europa.eu.int/comm/dg15/en/ intprop/intprop/1100.htm

intellectual property right holders, monitoring the use of information products enjoying intellectual property protection and ensuring the management of these rights will increase considerably',[91] it chose adaptation as opposed to wholesale change of copyright systems. It stated:

> New legislative action at Community level must meet the needs and practices of copyright markets and be consistent with, and accommodate, existing concepts and traditions. Such action should not imply radical changes ... It is the environment in which works and other protected matter will be created and exploited that has changed, not the basic copyright concepts.[92]

The Commission realized that the trans-border nature of the Internet raised serious questions of territoriality, including issues of the applicable law, jurisdiction and enforcement of rights, particularly since infringements can take place in jurisdictions which take a more lax approach to protecting copyright holders. A great deal of study pointed early, in 1995, to the need to *localize* infringements, particularly given the 'difficulties of specifying one single place where the transmission originates'.[93] One option that was considered, but set aside, was to apply a 'country of origin' rule where the infringement of copyrights would be deemed to take place in the country where the information was stored. Failing a totally harmonized international copyright, this approach would raise issues of extraterritoriality and it was therefore discounted in favour of an approach similar to that of the United States, which would require tackling 'the scope and limits of the responsibility of on-line service providers'.[94] This could refer to a system outlined above, namely that of placing some responsibility on system operators to police the system for copyright infringements which would both localize and privatize governance in this area.

A corollary of this would be forcing system operators through some mechanism to make private contracts with users in the European Union. The Commission reported that 'the majority of interested parties' who were asked for their views in drafting the Directive 'appear to take the view that the problems that might be created by the

---

[91] *IMPACT* 2. Section III, Action Line 2: 'Removing legal and administrative barriers'. See also the Commission Communication *Europe and the Information Society: The Way Forward: An Action Plan* (COM(94)347).

[92] *Communication on Copyright and Related Rights in the Information Society*, COM(95) 382(final), 19 July 1995.

[93] Ibid., p. 3.

[94] Ibid.

transfrontier nature of acts of digital transmission ... can appropriately be taken care of through contractual freedom and the application of existing private international law'.[95] Through private international law rules, the contract between the system operator and the Internet user could be governed by the law of the state with the closest connection with the performance of the contract, that is, the law of the state where the service provider is situated.

The draft Proposal for a Directive published on 10 December 1997 did not include provisions relating to the liability of on-line service providers. It seems the Commission will consider a wide range of liabilities for system operators, including copyright infringements, defamation, privacy, and pornography, in a special Directive that is forthcoming some time in 1998. The early indications, however, are that a model for copyright similar to that of the United States is being considered.

As regards technical measures to protect anti-copying devices, the Commission sponsored a number of projects to ensure technical standardization across the Union of encryption and other technologies to protect rights management systems such as watermarking.[96] The Commission had stated that such technical mechanisms are an effective way to combat piracy and to ensure the integrity of copyright management information, and was considering making illegal the use of technology 'whose primary purpose or effect is to bypass, remove, de-activate or otherwise circumvent the copyright protection system'[97] while allowing sufficient scope to obtain the technology for permissible acts, as in the US Implementation Act. Interestingly, the related issue of pay-per-use seemed not to attract as much attention as it did in the United States, although the Commission noted that a 'minority of respondents' to its requests for comments and consultation expressed concern that 'widespread use of such devices might result in a *de facto* creation of new information monopolies'.[98] Nevertheless, the

---

[95] *Follow-Up to the Green Paper*, Com(96)586 final, op. cit., p. 18.

[96] These included 'COPEARMS' (Coordinating Project for Electronic Author's Rights Management Systems); 'CITED' (Copyright in Transmitted Electronic Document); 'COPICAT' (Copyright Ownership Protection in Computer Assisted Training); 'OSPREY' (Open Structure for Protecting Rights Electronically); 'AMIDE' (Advanced Multimedia Information Dissemination Environment); and 'TALISMAN' (Tracing Authors Rights by Labelling Image Services and Monitoring Access Network). Information on each is available at: http://ww2.echo.lu/.

[97] *Follow-Up to the Green Paper*, Com(96)586 final, op. cit., p. 12.

[98] Ibid.

Proposal for a Directive in December 1997 provided for legal remedies against persons who manufacture and distribute such technology, without any mention of permissible acts for the purposes of research, and without any mention of exceptions for educational and other 'fair use'.[99]

CONCLUSION?

Information is becoming increasingly global. Technology is compressing territory to the extent that the Internet eases access to information located across borders. As a result, the problem of infringement of intellectual property is now greater than ever before. This chapter has shown that the problem of copyright was considered in the United States and Europe due to the fact that both the US government and the European Commission have been pursuing the further development of networked information technology systems for a host of public policy reasons. The protection of copyrights on the Internet is a significant issue, because it is feared that without a suitable legislative framework individuals will decline to place their material on the Internet and thereby frustrate efforts to develop a privatized market-based system.

The rationale of governance in both the United States and the European Union has been to gravitate towards adaptation of extant systems of protection for intellectual property rights rather than accept the arguments of many commentators that the transborder nature of information mandates an entirely new approach. Some, like Dan L. Burk, have gone so far as to suggest that 'the concept of political boundaries is rapidly becoming obsolete and requires reappraisal. The nation–state may have been the political organization best suited to the industrial age, but it is not necessarily suited to an informatics age.'[100] However, this chapter has shown that adaptation has taken the form of proposals for domestic legislation in the United States and proposals for a Directive in the European Union that will create municipal law to deal with the problems posed by the new digital environment. Interestingly, the approach favoured in both the US and the EU seems to be a mixture of 'old' ways of dealing with copyright, as well as new forms of encryption and copyright management technology that offer the potential for even greater protection of

[99] *Proposal for a Directive,* op. cit., p. 4.

[100] Burk, op. cit., p. 50.

copyrights than in the past. The nation–state is hardly going to stand by and watch the globalization of information undermine its efforts to develop information societies.

It is also interesting that domestication has been accompanied in this case by an attempt at localization of copyright infringement on the territory of the state in the United States, which has also meant a privatization of the function of policing the system for copyright infringements. Given that the US legislation has not yet come into force, and one is yet to see a document relating to the liability of on-line service providers in the EU, it is too early to draw substantive conclusions. However, it has been shown that the trend towards localization and privatization in both the US and the EU has been in proposals to place liability on system operators. The early response in the United States was to rush to place a strict liability on them. A later, tempered, approach placed the onus on the system operators to hold sufficient information about their users to enable a copyright holder to obtain from the system operator the information (presumably where the copyright infringing user is located on the territory of the state), or to sue the system operator who would be able to reclaim damages from the user through a private contract. The trend in the European Union appears also to be gravitating towards placing some kind of liability on system operators which will emerge in a Directive covering a range of other issues. Thus, it is not too early to point to visible trends in the rationale of governance which is to legislate a new problem through known means, to localize a global risk, to privatize the function of governance, and to harmonize municipal laws.

CHAPTER 6

THE EFFICACY OF HARMONIZATION AND PRESSURES FOR 'HARMONIZATION SPREAD'

This chapter is concerned with the question of efficacy. Is the harmonization pursued in the transatlantic area which has resulted in a geographically limited system of governance sufficient to deal with the problems that are more global in nature? The strategy of harmonization must be problematized. Up to this point the analysis has been confined to strategies of the transatlantic community in meeting the challenges of globalization. Yet the domestication of transnational risks and the harmonization of laws limited to the transatlantic area cannot deal effectively with problems that are by nature spread wider geographically than the Atlantic community. For transnational risks to be controlled effectively would require all states to adopt the same laws.

However, the global spread of harmonization is limited by the very things that have promoted differentiated legal systems: the fact that states have different national priorities, administrative and political cultures, value systems and social mores. Indeed, the suggestion that harmonization could spread beyond the Atlantic community to states with very different traditions and values raises the difficult problem of relativism. This chapter investigates these impediments. However, it is noted that there appear to be many incentives for harmonization to spread to other states, and that these derive, in large part, from a mixture of coercion and consent.

THE SUPERVISION OF INTERNATIONAL BANKS

The efficacy of transatlantic harmonization in protecting the United States and the European Union from shocks in the international financial system is open to question. Unless all states supervise their banks to the same extent as the US and the EU do, contagion risks could continue to cross their borders. The fact that banks are adequately supervised in the transatlantic community will not stop banks elsewhere from collapsing and sparking a crisis in the payment systems of both the United States and European Union.

However, there are coercive mechanisms built into the US Foreign Bank Supervision Enhancement Act and the EU Consolidated Supervision Directive taken in conformity with the Basle Committee's Minimum Standards that could compel other states to adopt similar prudential supervisory practices. This refers to the 'lock out' provisions raised in Chapter 3. That is, if foreign banks wish to operate in countries that have endorsed the Minimum Standards, they are required to be supervised by their home banking authority to the satisfaction of the host country regulators. Since the G10 countries comprise almost 80 per cent of the world's banking market, their market power could drive regulation elsewhere. If this does not occur, there are strong incentives for banks that wish to operate in the G10 to shun states that are not considered to be supervised adequately.

These powers of a host state regulator to 'lock out' a foreign banking establishment already has given rise to a good deal of controversy. Some have argued that this provision which is designed to be *protective* may become in practice a *protectionist* device to enable bank regulators to close their financial services market to foreign competitors. McInerney stated that this 'welcomed step may unfortunately entail the concomitant vice of creating a "fortress West" shielded from potentially more dangerous activities occurring in the rest of the world'.[1] Todd Gibson expressed a similar sentiment when he stated flatly,

> The international banking community will become polarised. Those banks who have consolidated supervision will be able to enter any and all banking markets, while those banks hailing from countries that lack consolidated comprehensive supervision will be effectively blocked from the major marketplaces [i.e. G-10 markets]. Over time 'in' lists and 'out' lists will develop.[2]

---

[1] Thomas F. McInerney III, 'Towards the next phase in international banking regulation', *DePaul Business Law Journal*, vol. 7, 1994, p. 163.

[2] Todd L. Gibson, 'The Foreign Bank Supervision Enhancement Act of 1991: short run consequences en route to the long term goal', *Case Western Reserve Journal of International Law*, vol. 27, 1995, p. 137.

That host-country regulators can prohibit the establishment of a branch of a foreign bank in their jurisdiction if they are not satisfied with the level of supervision of the bank's home supervisory authorities could be a concern. On this point, Gerald Corrigan, the Chairman of the Basle Committee, stated that he 'did not expect the minimum standards to create a system to blacklist countries and rejected the possibility that they would be used as a tool of protectionism'.[3] Indeed, it remains the case that the Minimum Standards do not have the force of law; they are voluntary. However, to be truly effective, either the Minimum Standards must be adopted by all states or there must be a mechanism within the Concordat which permits regulators to shut out banks from those states. Since all states have not adopted the Minimum Standards, it seems reasonable that the second option should pertain.

However, that it is possible – even in theory – that the Minimum Standards could be used as an element of protectionism is a matter of concern. That this may conflict with the pursuit of greater liberalization of financial services through the World Trade Organization – which also has been a policy of the US and the EU – is of utmost relevance to the final shape of the liberal, globalized banking regime.

Indeed, one could argue – erroneously, but one could make the case none the less – that the provisions of the Basle Committee's Minimum Standards and the national legislations adopted in conformity with them may be antithetical to the other goal of the industrialized states, which is the liberalization of market-access for financial services industries. Trade in services, including trade in financial services, was included on the agenda of the Uruguay Round of multilateral trade negotiations (MTN) of the GATT due to the strong insistence of the United States to develop a system of non-discriminatory treatment of providers of financial services, such as banking. The question that becomes immediately apparent is to what extent the insistence on adequate consolidated supervision by home state regulators conflicts with the goal of promoting non-discriminatory treatment in the General Agreement on Trade in Services (GATS).

However, liberalization in the context of GATS does not entail the same commitments to unconditional most-favoured nation (MFN) treatment as did the GATT. In the services negotiations of the GATT,

---

[3] Bruce Zagaris and Scott B. MacDonald, 'Money laundering, financial fraud, and technology: the perils of an instantaneous economy', *George Washington Journal of International Law and Economics*, vol. 26, 1992, p. 93.

a number of 'impediments' to the free trade of financial services were enumerated. These include national laws barring foreign establishments from offering certain services; national laws separating securities and commercial banking activities; and requirements for a percentage of ownership of the foreign affiliate.[4] For instance, foreign branches in Mexico cannot offer a full range of services and foreigners are restricted to a maximum participation of 30 per cent ownership of Mexican banks, with individual investors limited to 5 per cent.[5]

The Uruguay Round Agreement on trade-related aspects of services provided only for 'national treatment', that is, Article XVII requires that each Contracting Party 'shall accord to services and service providers of any other Party, in respect of all measures affecting the supply of services, treatment no less favourable than it accords to its own like services and service providers'.[6] Paragraph 5 of the Decision on Financial Services[7] states that 'Each Member shall grant financial service suppliers of any other Member the right to establish or expand within its territory, including through the acquisition of existing enterprises, a commercial presence.' However, the principle of national treatment requires that foreign establishments are treated no less favourably than domestic establishments. For instance, US banks in Canada benefit from the power to establish a national system of branches and to participate in securities activities, whereas Canadian banks in the United States are limited in these respects due to the Glass-Steagal Act.

More importantly, differences in national regulation of financial services were recognized, and permitted to subsist in order to protect the safety and soundness of the national financial system. Paragraph 5 is qualified by paragraph 6 which states that 'A Member may impose terms, conditions and procedures for authorisation of the establishment and expansion of a commercial presence in so far as they do not

---

4 See *Industry and Trade Summary: Commercial Banking*, USITC Publication 2638 (SV-4), June 1993, pp. 27–30.

5 'Three for free trade: North American Free Trade Agreement', *Canadian Banker*, vol. 99, no. 2, 1992, p. 6.

6 See Matthew Kennedy, 'Services join the GATT: an analysis of the General Agreement on Trade in Services', *International Trade Law and Regulation*, vol. 1, no. 2, March/April 1995, pp. 11–20; and Yi Wang, 'Most-favoured nation treatment under the General Agreement on Trade in Services – and its application in financial services', *Journal of World Trade*, vol. 30, no. 1, February 1996, pp. 92–124.

7 Decision on Financial Services, Final Act Embodying the Results of the Uruguay Round, MTN/FA, 15 December 1993 (UR-93-0246).

circumvent the Member's obligation under paragraph 5 and they are consistent with the obligations of this Agreement.' This raises the question of whether the stringent requirements under the FBSEA or the EU Directive are 'protectionist' in the sense of representing a non-tariff barrier to trade (NTB). What constitutes an actual non-tariff barrier to trade, as opposed to a *bona fide* government policy, is inherently difficult to determine and has been debated endlessly in the GATT.

Conflicts have already arisen in connection with the FBSEA and Mexican banks. The North American Free Trade Agreement (NAFTA) contains provisions for market access for financial services industries of members of NAFTA similar to those in the Uruguay Round Agreement.[8] However, the Federal Reserve Board determined that Mexican banks were not supervised on a consolidated basis and therefore refused entry of Mexican banks into the US.[9] And, from the passage of the FBSEA in 1991 to 1995, only one Latin American bank was authorized to conduct business in the United States.[10]

Developing countries could take the view that the United States and the European Union may trumpet non-discrimination in market access opportunities from their high horse since they do accord national treatment. Indeed, they benefit from increased liquidity in their markets, and from the benefits of competition in that sector. Yet, at the same time, they fall back upon the requirement for prudential supervision to which only few states have adhered to shelter their markets.

This would not be uncharacteristic. Opponents of liberalization have always regarded liberalism as the tool of the great powers. As Winfried Ruigrok aptly summarized, 'free trade doctrine has always been operating as the protectionism of the strong.'[11] The Mercantilists of the mid-1800s rejected liberalization on the grounds that the established industrial states could decimate weaker economies. The ideological justifications of liberalism – that is, of market efficiency, the 'invisible hand' of the market to guide resources optimally for all, and of a natural harmony of interest among states – were criticized as an ideological tool to serve the interests of the strong. As E.H. Carr stated, such an idea 'serves as an ingenious moral device invoked, in

---

[8] North American Free Trade Agreement, US Government Printing Office, 1992-330-817/70635, especially Chapter 14 relating to financial services.

[9] Reported by Gibson, op. cit., p. 131.

[10] Ibid., p. 139.

[11] Winfried Ruigrok, 'Paradigm crisis in international trade theory', *Journal of World Trade*, vol. 25, no. 1, 1991, p. 88.

perfect sincerity, by privileged groups in order to justify and maintain their dominant position'.[12] But one could argue that *any* institutionalized liberal system must maintain safeguards. The liberal international trade system has never been completely liberal, as the GATT was peppered with exceptions from the general norm of liberalization through escape clauses and other safeguard measures. Similarly, the IMF, though designed as an institution to uphold a liberal international economy, contained in-built capital controls to safeguard domestic economies – particularly the goal of full employment – from large speculative movements of capital. Although the Bretton Woods system was designed to facilitate the rise of a liberal international economy, the undesirable aspects of unbridled liberalism were tempered. It has been said that the post-war institutionalized economy, unlike previous liberal systems, was one guided by 'embedded liberalism', in the sense that its primary objective was stability for domestic economies.[13] In many respects, it was far from liberal.

Thus, there certainly is a precedent for establishing safeguard mechanisms within a system whose goal is otherwise to promote liberalism. No doubt, the present arrangements differ markedly from the institutionalization under Bretton Woods. The Basle Concordats are not institutions, they are non-binding, and they do not contain sanction mechanisms for non-compliance as do the Bretton Woods institutions.[14] The present regulatory regime is more diffuse than that which characterized the highly institutionalized system under Bretton Woods. While the liberalization efforts are taking place under the GATT/WTO, the protective measures are formulated through the work of the Basle Committee and given expression in national law.

Yet, if the work of the Basle Committee and the rules expressed through the WTO are together to create a regime for the governance of international banking in the new globalized erà, this does not alter the fact that there *must* be mechanisms to prevent 'free-riding'. Free-riding behaviour is characteristic in systems where a public good is

---

[12] E. H. Carr, *The Twenty Years' Crisis*, London: Macmillan, 1939, pp. 80–1.

[13] See John Gerrard Ruggie, 'International regimes, transactions and change: embedded liberalism in the postwar international economic order', in Stephen Krasner (ed.), *International Regimes*, New York: Cornell University Press, 1983.

[14] The IMF had the power to sanction governments for failing to adhere to the Articles of Agreement, and the GATT enforcement mechanisms were enshrined in Article XXXI.

provided.[15] The gold standard is a classic example of a public good: one state with an overriding interest in monetary stability, historically the largest trading nation (such as Britain and the United States) adopted a governance function in the international monetary system to provide a stable international currency which all states could use. Britain and the United States (while enjoying rights of seigniorage, of course) absorbed the costs of maintaining the international public good which other states enjoyed without bearing the costs.

The present international financial system is a diffuse one where international liquidity is provided by private lending. The public good is not now the maintenance of sufficient liquidity – if anything, there is excess liquidity. However, the public good remains *stability*, as indeed it always has been. For what was the purpose of the gold standard if not to inject some stability into the international financial system? Stability in a diffuse system of private lending takes the form of prudential supervision of private banks.

All public goods, by definition, invite free-riding. It is for this reason that the IMF and the GATT included coercive enforcement mechanisms to prevent free-riding (enjoying the access to a liberal market of a state which maintained low tariffs while retaining higher ones.) In this light, the qualification of the Minimum Standards which permit host-state regulators to refuse the entry of an establishment from a state which retains a lax regulatory system can be seen as a sanctioning function which is essential to the maintenance of a sound international regime: it provides stability.

Therefore, the qualification in the Basle Committee's Minimum Standards that permits host states to refuse the establishment of a foreign bank in their jurisdictions could be seen as a necessary element to accompany a liberal banking regime which is protective in nature, rather than protectionist. Indeed, this is the reasoning of Gerald Corrigan, which, in the words of Zagaris and MacDonald, is that the 'minimum standards are intended ... to encourage *a system whereby the countries with stronger enforcement systems help other countries improve their enforcement systems*'.[16] If sheer market power and incentives for market access into highly regulated areas lead to a spread of prudential

---

[15] Public goods are defined as goods to the international community which are non-exclusive, in the sense that no one can be excluded from enjoying their benefit, and non-rival, in the sense that the consumption of the good by one party does not decrease the amount of the good available to another. See James Buchanan, *The Demand and Supply of Public Goods*, Chicago: Rand McNally & Company, 1968.

[16] Zagaris and MacDonald, op. cit., p. 93. Emphasis added.

supervision, it will only serve the public good of stability. And it would not be the first time that international systems of governance reflect the domestic priorities of the largest states in the system. Although it could be the first time that ensuring the international public good depends not on coordinated international action at the level of public policy, but on harmonized systems of municipal law.

MONEY LAUNDERING

There are many problems with the philosophy of controlling money laundering at the placement stage. Some of these have been noted, such as the fact that it is difficult for a bank to distinguish a paper company (such as an off-shore trust) from a *bona fide* commercial enterprise, and the fact that such uncertainty coupled with the threat of criminal charges have caused administrative overload in reporting channels. Another problem is that criminals likely will anticipate reporting and investigations and thus may not continue to use the same bank accounts for very long.

However, the main problem is that to stamp out money laundering effectively at the placement stage requires that all states adopt the same laws. As the case of BCCI illustrated, it was relatively easy to structure the corporate matrix of the bank so that its headquarters was a holding company incorporated in Luxemburg, with its principal operations in Luxemburg and the Cayman Islands, two states which had relatively strong bank secrecy requirements. To be truly effective, controls at the placement stage must be implemented on a global scale, lest some states remain 'havens' for illicit activity.

However, not everyone is as committed as the United States and the European Union to the fight against money laundering, nor do all states possess the same administrative capacities. Some developing states have enacted bank secrecy laws for the purpose of encouraging much-needed investment, and have advertised in major US newspapers their welcoming of capital with 'no questions asked about the source of the funds'.[17] As Barry Rider commented, the competition to attract capital is such that 'some jurisdictions have been encouraged to prostitute their national integrity and sovereignty by providing a

---

[17] Scott B. MacDonald, 'Money laundering and the Asia/Pacific region', *Butterworths Journal of International Banking and Finance Law*, June 1993, pp. 271–4, referring to the advertisement by the Pakistani government of the sale of its interest-bearing bonds.

laundry for the most undesirable aspects of criminal and subversive activity'.[18] In this context, however, it should be pointed out that most 'dirty' money from the sale of drugs and 'hot' money from crime and commercial fraud originates in the OECD countries, and must be laundered *out* of these states.

Not only are there differing national priorities, but to expect all states to enact the same laws raises problems of relativism, as the criminalization of money laundering extends deeper into what states define as a 'crime'. To criminalize the movement of money derived from 'illegal' activities requires that all states criminalize the same things, otherwise definitions of what constitutes 'dirty' and 'hot' money will also vary. It may indeed be hypocritical to suggest that states should conform to what is effectively a global moral standard. After all, it was not until Criminal Justice Act 1993 that laundering of all monies derived from illegal activities was criminalized in the United Kingdom, and this is one of the oldest commercial nations of the world. Some states may genuinely resist the adoption of what are essentially Western norms, and the states that wish to continue to maintain strict bank secrecy laws can evoke relativism and hegemonial Western norms as an argument against conformity.

However, there are pressures which could force more states to adopt the same kind of approach to deal with the problem of money laundering as already has been adopted by the US and the EU. The first is normative pressure. The second may be termed the 'balloon theory'. This refers to the effects of squeezing a balloon; the more one squeezes one part of an inflated balloon, the more the air is displaced to other parts. By analogy, the more regulations tighten, for instance in controlling money laundering, the more money laundering activity is displaced to other states rendering it more visible. The third pressure, which follows directly from this, relates to the pressure that the United States is exerting on other states with lax regulations to amend their laws to become more like US laws. There is here a kind of structural power, in which one state is able to impose a framework that determines the method of managing pressures that will be adopted by other states.[19]

---

[18] Barry Rider, 'The financial world at risk: the dangers of organized crime, money laundering and corruption', *Managerial Auditing Journal*, vol. 8, no. 7, 1993, p. 8.

[19] This definition is that of Susan Strange in *States and Markets: An Introduction to International Political Economy*, London: Pinter Publishers, 1988; and Stephen Gill and David Law, 'Global hegemony and the structural power of capital', *International Studies Quarterly*, vol. 33, no. 4, 1989, pp. 475–99.

Normative pressure is evident in the emerging international consensus on the way forward as expressed in the United Nations, the Basle Committee and the Financial Action Task Force of the G7. It is true that not all states have become signatories to the relevant UN Conventions, that the Basle Committee is an exclusive club of Western bank regulators, and that the G7 is even more exclusive. It is also true that none of the measures taken in these fora have the backing of coercive force among their members, let alone those who are not members. However, such international agreements lay the framework for normative 'regimes'[20] – particularly those as widely accepted as the UN Convention – in the sense that they express a consensus on norms and principles which prescribe certain actions and proscribe others.

Of course, it is unlikely that normative pressure alone is sufficient to compel a state to change its banking laws. However, such expressions of consensus can legitimate the demands of states that have conformed with these principles in attempting to coerce those that have not.[21] Such 'regimes' can provide not only an impetus to and the framework for the adoption of national legislation, but moral leverage to legitimate certain actions and to proscribe others. The states that do shoulder the burden of trying to ensure the cleanliness of money entering the global financial system from within their jurisdictions could have recourse to this instrument to coerce and cajole other states to do likewise.

There are indications that the United States is doing so. The requirement to 'Know Your Customer' and particularly to institute internal information gathering and record keeping has placed considerable financial burdens on banks in executing their legal obligations. The United States has argued that this unfairly penalizes banks in the states that have conformed with international principles while leaving banks operating elsewhere free from the financial and administrative costs. Moreover, the United States and others that have adopted anti-money-laundering legislation are facing administrative strains on their government bureaucracies. Thus, the second force for policy convergence is coercion for 'burden sharing'.

---

[20] Stephen Krasner, 'Structural causes and regime consequences: regimes as intervening variables', in Krasner (ed.) *International Regimes*, op. cit.

[21] For an example of the way in which such mechanisms of legitimation were employed in the Uruguay Round of the GATT in areas in which there were no formal agreements, see J. Wiener, *Making Rules in the Uruguay Round of the GATT: a study of international leadership*, Aldershot: Dartmouth, 1995, pp. 20–54 for the theoretical argument, and pp. 152–7 for an illustration.

The United States has been monitoring closely states that permit money laundering. Since the issue of money laundering was 'securitized' in the Reagan administration's 'war on drugs', the Clinton administration has drawn up a list of states 'to watch', namely Thailand, Austria and the Cayman Islands, in an effort to persuade them to amend their bank secrecy laws.[22] As Frank C. Razzano argued, citing the example of the United States freezing the assets of Banco de Occidente, a Colombian bank with no operations based in the United States, 'the United States' Money Laundering Control Act was specifically intended to be applied extraterritorially and to cover activity that occurs outside of the US'.[23]

This pressure seems to have prompted other states to adopt anti-money-laundering legislation, such as Colombia, Ecuador, Mexico, Peru, Switzerland and Venezuela. The case of Switzerland illustrates the 'balloon theory' outlined above, and the diplomatic pressure exerted by the United States. For many years, Swiss law prohibited the disclosure of customers' financial details without the express consent of the customer, and maintained an additional layer of secrecy by operating 'Form B' accounts ('anonymous', or numbered accounts) which concealed the identity of the beneficial owner of the funds in the account. While banks were required to be vigilant to learn the source of the funds to ensure that they did not originate from criminal activities, the Form B account permitted the nature of the assets effectively to be disregarded. However, it was estimated by the Swiss National Bank that transfers of funds of suspect origin from Eastern Europe alone rose from US$2 billion in late 1992 to US$3.9 billion in 1994.[24] The United States began to pressure Switzerland to change its laws. In reaction to these pressures, Switzerland amended its legislation (namely, Articles 305 bis and 305 ter of Swiss Penal Code). On 25 April 1991, the Swiss Federal Banking Commission abolished the Form

---

[22] 'USA apparently pushing Thailand to adopt money-laundering law', *BBC Summary of World Broadcasts*, 26 October 1995. It has even been suggested that states should use trade sanctions against states that turn a blind eye to money laundering, and could justify doing so under the public moral exception of the GATT, for instance. See M.B. Comstock, 'GATT and GATS: a public morals attack on money laundering', *Journal of International Law and Business*, vol. 15, Fall 1994, pp. 139–77.

[23] See Frank C. Razzano, 'American money laundering statutes: the case for a worldwide system of banking compliance programs', *Detroit College of Law Journal of International Law and Practice*, vol. 3, 1994, pp. 277–307.

[24] 'Swiss experts say Eastern crime money a threat', *The Reuters European Business Report*, 24 October 1995.

B account. Swiss banks are now required to be certain of the identity of non-resident depositors and to disclose it to the authorities.[25]

This change in Swiss law has enabled the United States and Switzerland to conclude a treaty of mutual assistance. The US–Switzerland Treaty on Mutual Assistance,[26] like the US–UK Treaty on Mutual Assistance in Criminal Matters,[27] provides for mutual assistance in the freezing, seizure and forfeiture of proceeds from crime. It also provides for assistance in criminal proceedings, such as in taking testimony, documents, records and evidence, serving documents, locating or identifying persons, and transferring persons in custody. The treaty contains certain caveats which permit either state to decline cooperation if they deem that a request is extraterritorial in nature and objectionable, or if cooperation would place undue burdens on the state's public policy. Also, the US–Switzerland treaty may compel the disclosure of financial details only on the basis of 'dual criminality', that is, only if the offence to be punished in the United States is also punishable in Switzerland. Moreover, Switzerland may deny a request for information if it prejudices Swiss 'essential interests' defined as 'serious harm to the Swiss economy'. Nevertheless, cooperation between the United States and Switzerland recently has been constructive under the treaty.[28]

The United States has negotiated similar bilateral treaties with seventeen states, among which are Venezuela, Peru, Colombia and Panama. It is still more difficult for law enforcement agencies to coordinate and share information than for the criminals. However, the point here is that harmonization spread is not only possible, but that it is occurring. No doubt, optimists would view this as a positive development.

However, it must be pointed out that there is a point at which such optimism must be tempered by the complexity of the harmonization

---

[25] See Rebecca G. Peters, 'Money laundering and its current status in Switzerland: new disincentives for financial tourism', *Journal of International Law and Business*, vol. 11, Spring 1990, pp. 104–39; Kanwar M. Singh, 'Nowhere to hide: judicial assistance in piercing the veil of Swiss banking secrecy', *Boston University Law Review*, vol. 71, November 1991, pp. 847–61; Economics Intelligence Unit, *EIU Country Forecasts*, 1 May 1994; and 'Financing foreign operations: Switzerland', *Economist Intelligence Unit*, 1 October 1995.

[26] This has been in force since May 1973, although the recent change to Swiss law has made its operation significantly more effective.

[27] See Marian Nash, 'US–UK treaty on mutual legal assistance in criminal matters', *The American Journal of International Law*, July 1995, vol. 89, pp. 589–96.

[28] See Singh, op. cit., esp. p. 850 and p. 858.

process. It was seen that not only must the laws relating to banking practice and crime be harmonized, but a host of related laws as well, for instance in the civil liability of banks arising out of the banker–customer relationship. The case of Switzerland illustrates the difficulties that can be encountered by systems that do not follow the common law tradition of bank secrecy as do the United States and the United Kingdom. The changes to the law in Switzerland have created tensions between the criminalization of money laundering and the obligation of the bank to its customer under civil law. Swiss law utilizes the same *mens rea* requirement as the US and UK in that it encompasses wilful blindness as well as actual constructive knowledge. Bankers who do not take precautions to ensure that the funds are derived from legitimate commercial activities can be charged with assisting money laundering. Proposals to change the Swiss Banking Act to *require* them (as opposed to merely being allowed) to report money of suspicious origin were sent back for revision as this conflicted with the civil requirement of banking secrecy. Optimists, no doubt, would argue that this is an indication of the pressure for 'harmonization creep' into other areas, for instance, for similar immunities to be adopted as in the United States and United Kingdom.

COPYRIGHTS ON THE INTERNET

There are many practical problems with the attempt to stop infringements of copyright by passing national laws. The major one is that persons outside of the state who reach into a computer network with a modem are not governed by those laws. Even if a system operator, as in the United States, were required to provide the identity of the person who is alleged to have infringed a copyright, the law is of little use if that person were located outside of the state. The copyright holder would be required to fight his case in the national courts of the state where the infringement took place. Again, the only really effective method of ensuring that strategies of domestication actually work is if they are accompanied by global harmonization.

And again, there are many impediments to harmonization on a global scale. For instance, many developing countries' attitudes towards intellectual property protection are not as strict as those which grew out of the industrial revolution in developed countries. Indeed, many developing countries explicitly rejected the idea of proprietary knowledge when economic development was at stake. Intellectual property protection has been the topic of heated discussion between developed and developing countries for many years. Ten years of acrimonious discussions took place in the 1970s in the United Nations Conference on Trade and Development (UNCTAD) where developing countries demanded a transfer of technology from the developed countries which ended in a lack of agreement.[29] The protection accorded to intellectual property also depends as much on the underlying cultural and philosophical traditions of a society as it does on economic considerations.[30]

To be sure, there has been coercion in this area as well. In the absence of effective internationally agreed coercive apparatuses, the United States has pursued various measures of self-help, for instance by linking inadequate protection of intellectual property rights to the extension of the Generalized System of Preferences in the 1984 US Trade Act, and the US began to target 'offending' states with trade retaliation under 'Super 301' of the 1988 Omnibus Trade and Competitiveness Act.[31] The United States also pursued a multilateral strategy by linking intellectual property to international trade. The US introduced the issue of intellectual property to the General Agreement on Tariffs and Trade following the Tokyo round which concluded in 1979. At that time, the United States initiated negotiations on an Agreement on Measures to Discourage the Importation of Counterfeit Goods, which allows for the confiscation of counterfeit goods at the border.[32] Following this first formal linkage between trade and

---

[29] See Harvey J. Winter, 'the role of the United States Government in improving intellectual property protection', *Journal of Law and Technology*, vol. 2, Fall 1987.

[30] For instance, copying a work in traditional Korean society is an expression of honour. The Indian and Brazilian positions in the Uruguay Round, discussed below, on the patentability of pharmaceutical products can be seen to be based as much on ideas of social and economic justice as on balance-of-payments considerations.

[31] On linking US aid to IPR protection, see the Caribbean Basin Economic Recovery Act of 1983, 26 USCA, S.6015 (repealed). The renewal of GSP was linked to the protection of IPR in the Trade and Tariff Act of 1984, 19 USCA, S.1654. 'Super 301' incorporated Sections 301–310 of the Omnibus Trade and Competitiveness Act of 1988, Pub. L. No.100–418, 102 Stat. 1107, the latter of which related to intellectual property issues. On the coercive tactics of the US, see Jagdish Bhagwati and Hugh T. Patrick (eds), *Aggressive Unilateralism: America's 301 Trade Policy and the World Trading System*, Ann Arbor: University of Michigan Press, 1991. It is worth noting that both the United States and China are members of the Berne Convention.

[32] This drew its inspiration from Section 337 of the 1930 US Trade Act (19 USC, S.1526). See GATT Doc. L/5382, 18 October 1982. Further information on the anti-counterfeiting code of the Tokyo Round can be found in William N. Walker, 'Private initiative to thwart the trade in counterfeit goods', *World Economy*, vol. 29, no. 4, 1981. On the history of intellectual property in the international trade regime, see

intellectual property in the early 1980s, the US government was pressured to seek a comprehensive international agreement for the protection of intellectual property by several special interest groups, as well as by the government's own estimates that inadequate protection in other states has resulted in a loss for US industries of between US$43 billion and US$61 billion in 1986 alone.[33]

Negotiations on Trade-Related Aspects of Intellectual Property Rights (TRIPS) were included on the agenda of the Uruguay Round of the General Agreement on Tariffs and Trade. In presenting the US negotiating position, former US Trade Representative Clayton Yeutter argued that 'inadequate and ineffective protection for intellectual property ... is a severe and growing problem ... [increased protection] increases the confidence of companies that engage in research and development and other intellectual creativity'.[34] The differing attitudes towards intellectual property between developed and developing states resurfaced in the GATT negotiations. Many developing countries, led by Brazil and India, argued vehemently against the 'monopoly-profit incentive' theory that guided the US and EU positions by insisting that ideas, expressions, and industrial patents should exist in the 'domain of mankind' for the 'international public good'.[35]

Notwithstanding such arguments, the result of the TRIPS Agreement is a more harmonized system of patent and copyright protection

---

contd.
Marshall A. Leaffer, 'Protecting United States intellectual property abroad: toward a new multilateralism', *Iowa Law Review*, vol. 76, January 1991.

[33] These figures were cited in the first comprehensive study done by the US International Trade Commission. See USITC, *Foreign Protection of Intellectual Property Rights and the Effects on US Industry and Trade*, Publication No. 2065, 1988. See also, 'US fury over piracy by Taiwan companies', *Financial Times*, 1 April 1993, p. 7; 'Intellectual piracy captures the attention of the President and Congress', *National Journal*, 22 February 1986, pp. 443–5.

[34] 'US intellectual property proposal is unveiled before GATT negotiating group', *International Trade Reporter*, vol. 4, no. 43, 4 November 1987, p. 1347.

[35] See the statements by developing country negotiators in 'GATT: intellectual property: who should own it?', *Inter Press Service*, 23 November 1990; 'Preying mantra', *The Guardian*, 12 November 1993, p. 15; and Kevin Watkins, 'Agenda: the great trade robbery', *The Guardian*, 3 December 1993, p. 15. See also Desai, 'India and the Uruguay Round', *Journal of World Trade Law*, vol. 33, 1989, esp. p. 47; and Keith E. Mascus, 'Normative concerns in the international protection of intellectual property rights', *World Economy*, vol. 13, pp. 387–8.

with coercive measures of enforcement.[36] As regards copyrights, the TRIPS Agreement requires signatories to adhere to the Berne Convention, and in addition it established minimum standards, for instance in defining patentable and copyrightable material and the duration of protection. Moreover, the TRIPS system is coercive, to the extent that intellectual property issues, including copyrights, could fall to be arbitrated under the dispute settlement procedures of the World Trade Organization (WTO) which provide for coercive remedies in some circumstances, such as the suspension of trade concessions.[37] However, the TRIPS Agreement does not deal specifically with copyright law in electronic media such as the Internet, although it did clarify the protection of computer programs and databases which can be directly relevant to the Internet.[38]

CONCLUSION

This chapter has acknowledged the limitations of a system of transnational harmonization that is limited in geographical scope to meet the challenges of globalization that are more widely dispersed. However, it has pointed to several mechanisms – normative pressure,

---

[36] 'Agreement on Trade-Related Aspects of Intellectual Property Rights, including trade in counterfeit goods' (Annex III) GATT Doc. MTN/FAIIAIC (1994), available www.wto.org. For discussion, see John G. Byrne, 'Changes on the frontier of intellectual property law: an overview of the changes required by GATT', *Dusquesne Law Review*, vol. 34, Fall 1995; Rajan Danjee and Lawrence Boisson de Chazournes, 'Trade-Related Aspects of Intellectual Property Rights (TRIPS): objectives, approaches and basic principles of the GATT intellectual property conventions', *Journal of World Trade*, vol. 24, no. 5, 1990; and J. H. Reichman, 'Universal minimum standards of intellectual property protection under the TRIPS component of the WTO agreement', *International Lawyer*, vol. 29, 1995.

[37] Part V of the TRIPS Agreement establishes a dispute settlement procedure that incorporates Articles XXII and XXIII of GATT. For the revised dispute settlement procedures of the WTO, see the Understanding on Rules and Procedures Governing the Settlement of Disputes, Uruguay Round Final Act, Art.3.1, GATT MTN/FA III. For commentary, see Thomas J. Dillon, Jr., 'The World Trade Organisation: a new legal order for world trade?', *Michigan Journal of International Law*, vol. 16, Winter 1995, pp. 349–401. With specific reference to TRIPS, see Paul Edward Geller, 'Intellectual property in the global marketplace: impact of TRIPS dispute settlements?', *International Lawyer*, vol. 29, 1995. Civil and administrative remedies are also provided for under Section 2 Part III of the Agreement.

[38] Although under Article 9(1) of the Berne Convention the copying and storage of works in a computer can be considered copying.

the 'balloon theory', diplomatic coercion, and market power – that could pressure other states to conform to the standards emerging across the Atlantic. Interestingly, structural power, particularly of the US, seems to be promoting the international public good of stability in some issue areas. And notably, this structural power differs from traditional conceptions of 'hegemony' in International Relations, the traditional focus of which has been conformity in matters of government policy that are exercised in the international arena, such as trade and monetary policy. Structural power here appears to be oriented towards pressuring governments to change their municipal laws that govern civil society actors.

The following chapter introduces an area in which harmonization has spread more globally. It considers the case of international trade, the oldest activity in the international economy, and examines the way in which high degrees of integration between states of various legal traditions into the liberal trade system have promoted the adoption more globally of harmonized private international commercial rules.

CHAPTER 7

THE HARMONIZATION OF PRIVATE INTERNATIONAL COMMERCIAL LAW

The *Lex Mercatoria*

The purpose of this chapter is to outline the harmonization of laws that has taken place in the oldest activity in the international economy, trade. This is for several reasons. The first is to develop the argument that the harmonization of national laws among states with diverse administrative and political, legal and administrative cultures is not only possible, but is a fact. It suggests that there are integrative tendencies inherent in a liberal system that promote the harmonization of national laws. Specifically, harmonization is found in circumstances where there are high degrees of integration into a system; where the benefits of integration outweigh the costs; and where the desire to streamline the operation of the liberal system by reducing government interference extends to proactive government policies to promote harmonization.

Whereas the deregulated financial system is only twenty years old, and the commercialized Internet is still in its infancy, the post-war liberal trade system is fifty years old at the time of writing. Many of the modern laws, rules, customs and usages for trade have been harmonized through intergovernmental institutions, such as the Hague Conference on Private International Law; the International Institute for the Unification of Private Law (Unidroit), and the United Nations Centre for International Trade Law (UNCITRAL), whose model laws have been transposed into municipal law. There also are a number of international professional associations, such as the International Law Association, and the International Chamber of Commerce (ICC). The ICC's INCOTERMS define the meaning of such standard terms as f.o.b. (free-on-board) and c.i.f. (cost-insurance-freight) which are recognized by commercial states.

Some scholars have argued that the international commercial

community utilizes terms, usages and customs so cosmopolitan in nature as to give them a special 'anational' character. This strong thesis argues that international commercial law is autonomous law since the standardization and harmonization of principles, terms and usages of the international commercial community are such that they do not derive from, or depend on, the laws of states. There is also a positivist description of the harmonization of private commercial law, which is sufficient to make the case developed here that a highly integrated (globalized) system in the international economy has promoted the harmonization of the national laws of states with diverse cultural and legal systems.

'TRADITIONAL' INTERNATIONAL TRADE LAW: THE CONFLICT OF LAWS

The 'traditional' view of private international commercial law, as expressed by the Permanent Court of International Justice in the *Serbian Loans* case, is that: 'Any contract that is not a contract between states in their capacity as subjects of international law is based on the municipal law of some country.'[1] The task of the court, or arbitral tribunal, under this framework is to give effect to the expressed choice of law of the parties to a contract, and in absence of such an expressed choice, to determine the 'proper' law of the contract through conflict of laws rules. The presumption is that a contract may not 'float' independent of any municipal system of law; rights can be acquired only under a particular municipal system of law, and therefore must be enforced with reference to that system.[2]

Under this traditional view, an international commercial contract must have a governing law, or *lex causae,* for three principal reasons. First, a contract cannot 'float', but must exist by virtue of some legal system to give it life.[3] Second, rights acquired by persons should be

---

[1] Quoted in P. M. North and J. J. Fawcett, *Cheshire & North's Private International Law,* 11th edn, London: Butterworths, 1987, p. 485.

[2] See G. C. Cheshire, *Private International Law,* London: Butterworths, 1965, p. 36; Dicey, *Conflict of Laws,* London: Stevens, 1958, General Principle 5.

[3] As stated in the *Amin Rasheed Shipping Corpn. v. Kuwait Insurance Co.,* 'contracts are incapable of existing in a vacuum'. Quoted in Peter North, *Private International Law Problems in Common Law Jurisdictions,* London: Martinus Nijhoff, 1990, p. 108. See also F. A. Mann, 'England rejects "delocalised" contracts and arbitration', *International Commercial Law Quarterly,* vol. 33, 1984, pp. 193–8.

'recognised and protected by the courts of all civilised countries'.[4] Finally, to reach a just solution, a right that is acquired under a particular system of law must be judged 'in accordance with the law under which the right is acquired'.[5]

It is established in the English rules of private international law that party autonomy to determine the proper law of their contractual relationship will be respected.[6] Lord Atkin stated in *R. v. International Trustee for the Protection of Bondholders Aktiengesellschaft* that 'the legal principles which are to govern an English court on the question of the proper law of the contract are now settled. It is the law which the parties intended to apply.'[7] The system that is chosen by contracting parties can have serious implications relating to their responsibilities with regard to the performance of the contract, and indeed with regard to the very validity of the contract itself.[8] Thus parties to a contract should have absolute freedom (with certain qualifications) to determine the governing law of their contract.

In what is considered to be the lead case on this principle of freedom of choice, Lord Wright ruled in *Vita Food Products Inc. v Unus Shipping Co.* that even though both parties to a contract were not English, but expressed that English law would govern their contract, English law should apply. He stated, 'Where the English rule that intention is the test applies, and where there is an express statement by the parties of their intention to select the law of the contract, it is difficult to see what qualifications are possible.'[9] Dicey formulated this into Rule 127, sub-rule 1, which reads as follows: 'When the intention of the parties to a contract, as to the law governing the contract, is expressed in words, this expressed intention, in general, determines the proper law of the contract.'[10]

---

[4] Clive M. Schmitthoff, *The English Conflict of Laws*, 3rd edn, 1954, p. 3. Dicey, op. cit., General Principle 1.

[5] Cheshire, op. cit., p.36. Dicey, op. cit., General Principle 5.

[6] See R. H. Graveson, *Comparative Conflict of Laws: Selected Essays*, vol. I, Oxford: North-Holland Publishing, 1977, pp. 34–83; J. H. C. Morris, *The Conflict of Laws*, 3rd edn, London: Stevens & Sons, 1984, pp. 270–373; and North and Fawcett, op. cit., pp. 447–50.

[7] Cited in J. G. Castel, *Conflict of Laws: Cases, Notes, and Materials*, 2nd edn, Toronto: Butterworths, 1968, p. 810.

[8] The concept of the 'proper law' is detailed by R. H. Graveson, op. cit., p. 289.

[9] For the facts of the case see J. H. C Morris and P. M. North, *Cases and Materials on Private International Law*, London: Butterworths, 1984, pp. 443–9. For commentary, see Castel, op. cit., p. 804.

[10] Dicey, op. cit.

Lord Wright nevertheless made two important qualifications to the freedom of choice: 'provided the intention expressed is bona fide and legal, and provided that there is no reason for avoiding the choice on the ground of public policy'.[11] That an intention should be bona fide and legal relates to the question of evasion. *Dépeçage*, or the application of different laws to different provisions of a contract, is permitted in English law. As Upjohn J. remarked, 'the parties may well contemplate that different parts of their contract shall be governed by different laws'.[12] Parties may even stipulate that in certain eventualities, or contingencies, a particular law should apply. In fact, it may be prudent to do so.[13] However, parties cannot subject a particular part of a contract to evade the law of a country, according to the doctrine of 'fraus legis'. For instance, contracting parties are not permitted to agree that US law should apply to their entire contract, with the exception of a provision restraining trade in order to evade US anti-trust legislation. Nor can parties choose a law to validate their contract that would be illegal under the laws ordinarily more closely connected with them. Thus, to avoid what is known as 'forum shopping', the choice of law has to be for a bona fide purpose, and not for the purposes of evasion. This was held in the lead case of *Golden Acres Ltd. v. Queensland Estates Ltd.* wherein a real estate agent in Queensland used Hong Kong law in a contract otherwise connected with Queensland to evade a Queensland law limiting the commission of the estate agent.[14]

The second qualification relating to avoiding a public policy relates to mandatory public laws. Mandatory public law rules have been defined by A. M. F. Maniruzzaman as a 'category of rules [that] is considered to be outside the scope of the will and agreement of the contracting parties with regard to the proper law of the contract'.[15] A. J. E. Jaffey defined these as rules that are 'applicable irrespective of

---

[11] In *Vita Food Products Inc. v. Unus Shipping Co.*, in Morris and North, op. cit.

[12] *Re Helbet Wagg*, cited in A. J. E. Jaffey, 'Essential validity of contracts in the English conflict of laws', *International and Commercial Law Quarterly*, vol. 23, 1974, pp. 1–29, at p. 7.

[13] See North and Fawcett, op. cit., p. 448; Clive M. Schmitthoff, *Schmitthoff's Export Trade: The Law and Practice of International Trade*, 9th edn, London: Stevens & Sons, 1990, p. 210.

[14] Quoted in Philip Wood, *Law and Practice of International Finance*, London: Sweet & Maxwell, 1980, pp. 10–11.

[15] A. M. F. Maniruzzaman, 'International arbitrator and mandatory public law rules in the context of state contracts: an overview', *Journal of International Arbitration*, vol. 7, no. 3, 1990, p. 54.

the agreement or intention of the parties'.[16] Mandatory rules are of a type that fall within the category of an 'ordre public', or 'subject to the exigencies of public policy'.[17] For instance, the Unfair Contract Terms Act 1977 is mandatory in the sense that contracting parties cannot contract out of its provisions.[18] In the lead case of *Boissevain v. Weil*, a British subject borrowed French francs from a Dutchman in Monaco and promised to repay sterling as soon as English law would permit. The House of Lords held that in borrowing foreign currency the British subject, notwithstanding her residence at the time, contravened the Defence (Finance) Regulations 1939, as read in conjunction with Section 3(1) of the Emergency Powers (Defence) Act, 1939, thus rendering the contract illegal and void.[19]

In the event that no governing law is stipulated in a contract, it is the duty of the court to ascertain the proper law. Private international law, otherwise referred to as the 'conflict of laws', is the technique through which the courts, or arbitral tribunals, determine the proper law governing an international contract.[20] However, making this determination can be complicated, given the range of factors that can be taken into consideration. Should the courts, subjectively, attempt to impute the intention of the parties after the fact, or should the court take into account objective factors that have a close connection with the case at hand? If the latter, what factors should be considered? Is the proper law to be determined by the place of contracting, the place of performance, the domicile of the seller, or the domicile of the buyer? According to Professor Yntema, the debate over such factors has complicated this area so that 'the natural processes of common understanding [have been] clogged by artificial manipulations of suppositious hypothesis and betimes obfuscated by the spurious vibrations of allegedly dynamic theories of uncharted chaos'.[21]

In the absence of an expressed choice of law in a contract, there are two methods through which to determine its proper law. The subjective method attempts to impute an intention by asking what

---

[16] Jaffey, op. cit., p. 1.

[17] Schmitthoff, *The English Conflict of Laws*, op. cit., p. 3.

[18] P. B. Carter, 'Contracts in English private international law', *British Yearbook of International Law*, vol. 57, 1986, pp. 1–32, at pp. 10–11.

[19] See Morris, op. cit., p. 279. See also North and Fawcett, op. cit., pp. 453–4, and 483–5; and particularly Jaffey, op. cit., p. 21.

[20] Castel, op. cit., p. 1; Morris and North, op. cit., p. 259.

[21] Hessel E. Yntema, 'The historic bases of private international law', in Castel, op. cit., p. 23.

reasonable persons would have chosen. The objective method purports to take a more detached view, to ascertain to which system of law the contract has its closest and most real connection.

Under the subjective method, or the 'delocalization theory', the court will attempt to ascertain what the parties would have chosen if they had thought about the matter. Lord Atkin in *R. v. International Trustee for the Protection of Bondholders Aktiengesellschaft* stated that 'if no intention is expressed, the intention will be presumed by the court from the terms of the contract and the relevant surrounding circumstances'.[22] According to Lord Wright, 'The court has to impute an intention, or to determine for the parties what law is the proper law which, as just and reasonable persons, they ought [to] or would have intended if they had thought about the question when they made the contract.'[23] Similarly, Lord Singleton in the case of *The Assunzione* stated, 'The court has to determine for the parties what is the proper law which, as just and reasonable persons, they ought to have intended had they thought about the question when they made the contract.'[24] This principle of inferred intention was expressed by Dicey as Rule 127, sub-rule 2, which reads,

> [W]hen the intention of the parties to a contract with regard to the law governing the contract is not expressed in words, their intention is to be inferred from the terms and nature of the contract ... and such inferred intention determines the proper law of the contract.[25]

There are difficulties with this approach. For instance, the persons making the contract may not have been reasonable. As E. J. Cohn observed, this assumes that 'nobody had the right to be what, many years after the event, may appear to be unreasonable to outside observers'.[26] It is therefore easy, and perhaps erroneous, to impute rationality where none actually existed, and to impute intention where the parties may never have had any intentions at all. The view of Lord Denning, MR is that the proper law, 'is not dependent on the intention of the parties. They never thought about it. They had no intentions

---

[22] Cited in Castel, op. cit., p. 810–17.

[23] Cited in Morris, op. cit.

[24] The facts of the case are cited in Morris and North, *Cases and Materials*, op. cit., pp. 439–41. For commentary, see Graveson, op. cit., pp. 290–1; Castel, op. cit., pp. 815–16.

[25] Dicey, op. cit.

[26] E. J. Cohn, 'The objectivist practice on the proper law of contract', *International and Comparative Law Quarterly*, vol. 6, 1957, p. 884.

upon it.'[27] Carter stated that the subjective approach embodies 'a fiction in cases in which no actual intention can realistically, or perhaps even plausibly, be inferred'.[28] Similarly, North and Fawcett argued that 'it is scarcely possible to be content with the aphorism that the proper law is the law intended by the parties'. They continue:

> The whole notion of inferring an *actual* intent is based, at best, upon making assumptions which may or may not be correct, and, at worst, upon a form of dishonesty. It would be better to apply a purely objective test in all cases where there is no express choice of law clause.[29]

The objective method, or the 'localization theory', of determining the proper law of the contract attempts to establish the factors that lead to a calculated determination of the law of the 'closest connection', or the 'centre of gravity' to which naturally the contract is pulled. As described by Graveson, the objectivist theory isolates the proper law as that indicated by 'the most important' of the connecting factors,[30] which Maniruzzaman termed the 'principle of the most significant relationship'.[31]

Lord Simonds, in the lead case *Bonython v. The Commonwealth of Australia* articulated that the contract should be the one with which the transaction has its 'closest and most real connexion'.[32] This was repeated by Denning, LJ, in *Boissevain v. Weil* when he said that the proper law 'depends not so much on the ... intention of the parties', but 'on the place with which [the contract] has the most substantial connection'.[33] Dicey explained this in Rule 127, sub-rule 3, as:

> When the intention of the parties to a contract with regard to the law governing it is not expressed and cannot be inferred from the circumstances, the contract is governed by the system of law with which the transaction has its closest and most real connection.[34]

---

27 North and Fawcett, op. cit., p. 462.

28 Carter, op. cit., p. 8.

29 North and Fawcett, op. cit., p. 461.

30 Graveson, op. cit., p. 291.

31 Maniruzzaman, 'Conflict of laws issues in international arbitration: practice and trends', *Arbitration International*, vol. 9, no. 4, pp. 371–403, at p. 377.

32 *Bonython v. Commonwealth of Australia*, in Morris and North, op. cit., pp. 457–9. For commentary, see Castel, op. cit., pp. 814–15; Graveson, op. cit., p. 88.

33 Cited in Castel, op. cit., p. 814–18.

34 Dicey, op. cit.

The 'converging' or 'connecting' factors that assist in making the determination were enumerated by Clive Schmitthoff as:

> the place where the contract has been concluded, the place where the contract is to be performed, the language and terminology employed by the parties, the form of the documents made with respect to the transaction, the personality of the parties, the subject-matter of the contract, a submission to arbitration, the situation of the funds which are liable for discharge ... a connection with a preceding transaction, the effect attributed to the transaction by a particular legal system.[35]

The advantage of the objective method is supposedly its detachment, which is said to lend greater predictability to determining the proper law. However, this method raises practical difficulties. The complexity of some contracts may render an objective evaluation exceedingly difficult. For instance, the *lex loci solutionis*, the place of performance, can be very difficult to determine in an international finance agreement, if the lenders are of multiple nationalities and the repayment of the funds could take place in any of a multitude of branches of a multinational bank.[36] Similarly, the place of contracting, the *lex loci contractus*, can be ambiguous in a case connected to both English and German law, for instance, where the posting or receipt of a letter of acceptance, respectively, determine the validity of a contract. Similarly, the *lex domicilii* presents difficulties, for under the French and German systems a corporation is the subject of the law where its administrative centre is situated, whereas English law regards the corporation to be governed by the law of the country in which it is incorporated.[37] According to Morris, such considerations 'reduce the force of the predictability argument almost to the vanishing point'.[38]

There are also epistemological questions. For Morris, the conflict of laws is a 'science'[39] for determining the proper law of a contract. It is doubtful that Morris had in mind any reference to a particular epistemology in the social sciences, but the criticisms of any attempt to liken judgement in the selection of criteria to a 'science' are of

---

[35] Schmitthoff, *The English Conflict of Laws*, op. cit., pp. 110–11.

[36] Zouhair A. Kronfol, 'The proper law of international loans', *Journal of World Trade Law*, vol. 10, p. 131. See also Wood, op. cit.

[37] This is discussed in F. A. Mann, 'The proper law in the conflict of laws', *International and Comparative Law Quarterly*, vol. 36, 1987, esp. pp. 437–9.

[38] Morris, op. cit., p. 267.

[39] Morris and North, op. cit., p. 259.

relevance here none the less.[40] E. J. Cohn criticized the objective method as 'an easy path [which] leads from [a] theoretic objectivism to a practical subjectivism'.[41] According to North and Fawcett, what is 'most important' is determined by a process whereby all the factors are 'carefully weighed in the balance'.[42] Yet, as Maniruzzaman argued, 'while applying the test the arbitrator aims at the substantive law pointed to by the preponderant number of, *or what he considers the most important,* connecting factors'.[43] Thus, the purportedly 'objective' determination of which of the various connecting factors is more important in itself requires a subjective evaluation.

In practice, these methods are used complementarily. Maniruzzaman concluded that the English practice 'can be considered to satisfy both subjectivist and objectivist tests of conflicts of laws'.[44] Dicey implied that there is a progression in logic from the subjective to the objective method in Rule 145, Sub-rule 3:

> When the intention of the parties to a contract with regard to the law governing it is not expressed and cannot be inferred from the circumstances, the contract is governed by the system of law with which the transaction has its closest and most real connection.[45]

The English practice may not even be to follow this strict order that Dicey suggests, but rather to meld the two in an attempt to ascertain the proper law. Indeed, as Patrick Ross Williams noted, this results in 'the implied choice/closest connection distinction being merged into a presumed intention test'.[46] This has the merits of flexibility, for the law that is most relevant or useful to a particular case can be applied. A good example of this is the *Amin Rasheed Shipping Corpn v. Kuwait Insurance Co.*, where the standard Lloyds insurance forms provided a

---

40 See in particular E. Nagel, *The Structure of Science: Problems in the Logic of Scientific Explanation*, London: Routledge & Kegan Paul, 1979; Karl Popper, *The Logic of Scientific Discovery*, London: RK Press, 1968, esp. his section on objective knowledge, p. 319; and Popper, *The Poverty of Historicism*, London: Routledge & Kegan Paul, 1972, esp. pp. 1–10.

41 Cohn, op. cit., p. 374.

42 North and Fawcett, op. cit., p. 461.

43 Maniruzzaman, 'Conflict of laws issues in international arbitration', op. cit., p. 380. Emphasis added.

44 Ibid., p. 402.

45 Dicey, op. cit., p. 796.

46 Patrick Ross Williams, 'The EEC Convention on the law applicable to contractual obligations', *International and Comparative Law Quarterly*, vol. 35, 1986, pp. 1–31, at p. 13.

connection with English law, which was in the interests of justice to the case because Kuwaiti law was undeveloped in the areas at issue.[47]

However, the conflict of laws rules, taken as a whole, do not always lend predictability to an international commercial transaction. Heightened interdependence among the international commercial community, the increased complexity of contracts, and the number of different legal systems involved have rendered international business so complex as to impart to it a special character, one that is not easily amenable to the choice of municipal laws. The international trade system is indeed globalized, in the sense that the volume of commerce has increased faster than output every year since 1947 (with the exception of two years in the early 1980s), and the annual value of international trade is currently US$5 trillion annually.[48] It is also the most globalized system of the international economy in terms of its geographic spread.[49] Municipal law may serve well in a domestic context but does not perform optimally to the needs of, for instance, a multilateral commercial agreement with numerous embedded contracts. As De Ly has noted, 'It may not only be difficult, but arbitrary to localise some international business transactions in one jurisdiction.'[50]

This is particularly true if the system with which the transaction has its closest connection is undeveloped in the particular aspect of commerce of concern in the contract. This is also true in the case of contracts between private persons and states, the latter of which has the capacity to exercise the power of eminent domain to change the laws, as sometimes has been done arbitrarily. The stability, predictability and confidence which underpin international commerce would be jeopardized if parties suspected suboptimal results from a dispute. For these reasons, the 'traditional' conflicts of laws approach has been deemed by many scholars to be inappropriate to evolving, and increasingly globalized commerce.

Thus, a theory of 'transnational law', also referred to as 'anational law', 'supranational law', 'truly international law', 'international customs and usages', or a *Lex Mercatoria*, began to be articulated.

---

[47] The facts and discussion of the case can be found in North and Fawcett, op. cit., pp. 451–65.

[48] World Trade Organization, 'Ruggiero calls for trading system to be kept in line with globalisation process', press release, Press/43, 22 February 1996.

[49] See Paul Hirst and Grahame Thompson, *Globalisation in Question*, Cambridge: Polity Press, 1996.

[50] Filip De Ly, *International Business Law and Lex Mercatoria*, London: North-Holland, 1992, p. 58.

Beginning in the 1950s,[51] scholars began to challenge the 'traditional' approach to private international commercial law, referring to it as an 'unwarranted hegemony of municipal law'.[52]

THE *LEX MERCATORIA*

The 'theory' of the *Lex Mercatoria* is not a coherent set of ideas. Two distinct approaches to the subject are discernible from the literature. The 'autonomist' approach conceives of an anational, autonomous, self-generating system of laws articulated by the international commercial community to regulate its activities. Its practices, usages and customs, supplemented by the general principles of law recognized by commercial nations form a – not yet fully developed – normative order that exists independent of any national system of law. On the other hand, the 'positivist' position views the *Lex Mercatoria* as having transnational origins, but only by virtue of states giving effect to conventions and uniform laws by ratification into municipal codes, and by trade usages that are articulated by international agencies.

Proponents of the autonomous view argue that the *Lex Mercatoria* dates from the Rolls of Oleron in the twelfth century, the Consolato del Mare, and the Maritime Code of Wisby[53] which governed international commerce before the consolidation of the states system. In the pre-national stage in Europe, the 'law merchant' consisted of a 'body of truly international customary rules governing the cosmopolitan community of international merchants'[54] on the high seas and in

---

[51] Arguably the first was Lambert, writing '*Sources du droit comparé ou supranational, législation uniforme et jurisprudence comparative*' in the 1920s. However, most scholars credit Jessup's, *Transnational Law*, 1956, as beginning the debate. Given the exigencies of space here, it is not possible to provide a comprehensive genealogy of the evolution of the theory. However, this is done with exceptional clarity by De Ly, op. cit., esp. Chapters 4 and 5.

[52] Thomas E. Carbonneau, 'The remaking of arbitration: design and destiny', in Carbonneau (ed.), *Lex Mercatoria and Arbitration*, Dobbs Ferry, New York: Transnational Juris Publications, Inc., 1990, p. 7.

[53] See Trakman, 'The evolution of the law merchant: our commercial heritage', *Journal of Maritime Law of Commerce*, vol. 153, 1981, pp. 179–96; B. M. Cremades and S. L. Plehn, 'The new Lex Mercatoria and the harmonisation of the laws of international commercial transactions', *Boston University International Law Journal*, 1984, p. 317.

[54] Schmitthoff, 'International business law: a new law merchant', *Current Law and Social Problems*, vol. 129, 1961 (reprinted in Chia-Jui Ceng (ed.), *Clive M. Schmitthoff's*

the conduct of fairs. The Carta Mercatoria (1303), and the Statute of the Staples (1353) assured the application of the *Lex Mercatoria* (as opposed to feudal law) in the Court of Piepowder, the equivalent of modern permanent arbitral tribunals. The notary public also contributed to the harmonization of commercial practice by creating model contracts which were observed by the commercial community at large.

As states consolidated national systems of law from about 1600 to 1640, the King's Bench and Courts of Common Pleas in England replaced the merchant courts, and under Chief Justice Mansfield, the law merchant was absorbed into common law that became applicable to all subjects. Proponents of the autonomist view argue that there is now a reversion to the principle of a truly international commercial law. As Clive Schmitthoff stated, '[W]e are beginning to rediscover the international character of commercial law ... the general trend of commercial law everywhere is to move away from the restrictions of national law to a universal, international conception of the law of international trade.'[55] Others, such as Goldman, argue that commerce never has been confined to territorial boundaries, and that the principles of law harken back to the *ius gentium* of Roman law.[56]

According to the autonomist view, international commerce has a 'sui generis character that warrants a special, separate regime of governance'.[57] This autonomous order is seen to rest on three pillars: the everyday practices of the international business community, the codified usages in international conventions, and the general principles of law.[58] The autonomous order is 'spontaneous', because it rests upon the will of the parties who create rules best suited to their particular needs. Such rules include mainly international customs, usages and contract terms which are used with frequency by the international

---

contd.
Select Essays on International Trade, London: Martinus Nijhoff Publishers, 1988, pp. 20–37, at p. 20); and Schmitthoff, 'The unification of the law of international trade', *Journal of Business Law*, 1968, pp. 105–19 (reprinted in Chia-Jui Ceng, ibid., pp. 105–19). For a more detailed exposition of the medieval mercantile law, see Harold J. Berman and Colin Kaufman, 'The law of international commercial transactions (*Lex Mercatoria*)', *Harvard International Law Journal*, vol. 19, no. 1, 1978, pp. 221–77.

[55] Schmitthoff, 'International business law: a new law merchant', op. cit., p. 27.

[56] See Goldman, 'The applicable law: general principles of law – the Lex Mercatoria', in J. Lew (ed.), *Contemporary Problems in International Arbitration*, Dordrecht: Martinus Nijhoff, 1987.

[57] Carbonneau, op. cit., p. 14.

[58] See Goldman, op. cit.

business community. For the autonomist perspective, the fact that traders repeatedly act in the same ways and subsequently feel bound by such precedents of behaviour is evidence of an autonomous legal order specific to that community (i.e. a Grotian regime, in International Relations parlance).

Codified usages and international conventions are seen as the formal part of the *Lex Mercatoria* because they are legitimated and can be enforced. Supplemented by universal principles of law, this order is seen to form substantive transnational rules. Distilled from a vast literature, these general principles have been enumerated by Lord Justice Mustill as (in abridged form):[59]

1. *Pacta sunt servanda* (contracts should be enforced according to their terms).
2. *Rebus sic stantibus* (substantially changed circumstances can entail a revision of contract terms).
3. *Abus de droit* (unfair and unconscionable contracts should not be enforced).
4. *Culpa in contrahendo.*
5. Good faith.
6. Bribes render a contract void or unenforceable.
7. A state may not evade its obligations by denying its own capacity to make an agreement to arbitrate.
8. The controlling interest of a group of companies is regarded as contracting on behalf of all members.
9. Parties should negotiate in good faith if unforeseen circumstances arise.
10. 'Gold clause' agreements are valid and enforceable.
11. One party may be released from its obligations if there is a fundamental breach by the other.
12. No party can be allowed by its own act to bring about a non-performance of a condition precedent to its own obligation.
13. A tribunal is bound by the characterization of the contract ascribed to it by the parties.
14. Damages for breach of contract are limited to the foreseeable consequences of the breach.
15. A party which has suffered a breach of contract must mitigate its losses.

---

[59] The Rt. Hon. Lord Justice Mustill, 'The new *Lex Mercatoria*: the first twenty-five years', in Maarten Bos and Ian Brownlie, *Liber Amicorum for the Rt. Hon. Lord Wilberforce*, Oxford: Clarendon Press, 1987, pp. 149–83, at pp. 174–7.

16. Damages for non-delivery are calculated by reference to the market price of the goods and the price at which the buyer has purchased equivalent goods in replacement.
17. A party must act promptly to enforce its rights, lest it lose them by waiver.
18. A debtor may set off his own cross-claim to diminish his liability to a creditor.
19. Contracts should be construed according to *ut res magis valeat quam pereat*.
20. Failure to respond to a letter is regarded as evidence of assent to its terms.

The sources for these principles, compiled from various sources, are: public international law; uniform laws and conventions; trade usages and customs, including standard form contracts; general principles of law common to commercial states, which are discovered through a comparative approach; the rules of international organizations; and the reports of international commercial arbitral awards.[60]

The other conception of the *Lex Mercatoria* is the positivist one, for which Clive M. Schmitthoff is the principal advocate.[61] He argued that the origins of the *Lex Mercatoria* lie in the medieval 'law merchant', but in principle only; the modern *Lex Mercatoria* is a 'new law merchant', which is the third stage of an historical process that blends features of the previous two. Interestingly for present purposes, this 'third stage' represents the harmonization of the laws of many states, with various

---

[60] This list is compiled from: Emmanuel Gaillard (ed.), *Transnational Rules in International Commercial Arbitration*, Paris: Institute of International Business Law and Practice, International Chamber of Commerce, 1993, pp. 67–8; Ugo Dreatta, Ralph B. Lake, and Ved. P. Nanda, *Breach and Adaptation of International Contracts: An Introduction to the Lex Mercatoria*, London: Butterworths, 1992, esp. p. 13; Ole Lando, 'The Lex Mercatoria in international commercial arbitration', *International and Comparative Law Quarterly*, vol. 34, 1985, pp. 747–68, esp. pp. 748–52; and Mustill, op. cit.

[61] Schmitthoff, 'International business law: a new law merchant', op. cit., pp. 34–6; Schmitthoff, 'The law of international trade, its growth and operation', in Schmitthoff (ed.), *The Sources of International Trade With Special Reference to East-West Trade*, London: Stevens & Sons Ltd., 1964, pp. 3–38 (reprinted in Chia-Jui Ceng, op. cit., pp. 137–69, at p. 148); Schmitthoff, 'the new sources of the law of international trade', *International Social Sciences Journal*, vol. XV, no. 2 (reprinted in Chia-Jui Ceng, op. cit., pp. 131–6); and Schmitthoff, 'The unification of international trade', *The Unification of the Law of International Trade*, Handelshögskolans Skrifter 1964–1965, Gothenburg School of Economics and Business Administration Publication, 1964, pp. 5–28 (reprinted in Chia-Jui Ceng, op. cit., pp. 170–87).

legal traditions and cultures, akin to the transnational character of law when the international trade system was the most 'liberal', i.e., prior to the consolidation of states and the mercantile system of economy. The feature retained from the 'modern' period is that the *Lex Mercatoria* is given expression, and coercive force, *because* it is codified in national laws.

For Schmitthoff, the *Lex Mercatoria* is derived from principles that are so universally recognized as to make them independent of any particular legal system, and from conventions reached under international law. Examples of such principles are *pacta sunt servanda,* and party autonomy to choose the law applicable to their contract (subject to legality and mandatory public law rules). Examples of conventions are numerous, and include in particular those international conventions and uniform laws formulated by UNCITRAL[62] and Unidroit.[63]

Another source is international custom and the standard form of contract, which, Schmitthoff contended, create law unto themselves. Schmitthoff attributed great importance to international custom, as these were functional, in his words, 'formulated by international agencies'. Among these are the International Chamber of Commerce (ICC), which has elaborated INCOTERMS (1990); the Uniform Customs and Practice for Documentary Credits (UCP, 1983); ICC Rules for Conciliation and Arbitration (1988); Uniform Rules for a Combined Transport Document (1975); and Uniform Rules of Conduct for Interchange of Trade Data by Teletransmission (1988). There are also customs incorporated into standard contracts, as issued by international commodity traders, such as the London Corn Trade Association, the International Air Transport Association (uniform air way bills), and the Lloyds Marine Insurance Policy. Indeed, many of these private international associations were working on harmonization long before the establishment of the modern intergovernmental agencies, such as the Hamburg Bourse for Corn Traders (1868), the Bremen Cotton Bourse (1872), the Silk Association of America (1873), and the London Corn Trade Association (1877). Taken together,

---

[62] The work of UNCITRAL is discussed below. See generally Gerold Hermann, 'The contribution of UNCITRAL to the development of international trade law', in Norbert Horn and Clive M. Schmitthoff (eds), *The Transnational Law of International Commercial Transactions,* London: Kluwer, 1982.

[63] On which, see Bonell, 'The unidroit initiative for the progressive codification of international trade law', *International and Comparative Law Quarterly,* vol. 27, 1987, pp. 413–37; and Rudolf Dolzer, 'International agencies for the formulation of transnational economic law', in Horn and Schmitthoff (eds), ibid.

Schmitthoff contended that the proliferation of transnational standardized terms and customs 'render it redundant to refer to any legal system'. He continued, 'The proper law of the contract is determined by ascertaining the free will of the parties ... the parties ... can generally make their own law and *this need not be a system of national law*.'[64]

The third aspect of commercial practice defining the *Lex Mercatoria* is the growing popularity of international commercial arbitration, which gives parties the freedom to choose the forum to hear their disputes, such as the London Court of Arbitration (LCA), the International Chamber of Commerce in Paris (ICC), or the World Bank's International Centre for the Settlement of Investment Disputes (ICSID). These fora increasingly have deliberated contracts on the basis of the *Lex Mercatoria*, as will be elaborated below.

Schmitthoff's approach concentrates on the unification and harmonization of international trade law,[65] and is very firmly based on national jurisdiction, for it only gains the force of law if it is recognized by a state. Although the sources of the *Lex Mercatoria* are truly international, Schmitthoff stresses that it owes its existence, in one way or another, to the state. International conventions – 'deliberate' law creation – are given effect by their acceptance by states and depend on their transposition into municipal law (either multilaterally, in the case of conventions, or unilaterally, as with model laws). Agencies such as UNCITRAL, the ICC, Unidroit, the Hague Convention on Private International Law and the International Maritime Committee articulate these, and parties give them effect by inserting them into their contract.[66] However, these must be recognized by the courts of states in considering cases and in making awards. Even where an international commercial tribunal decides a case, the parties still must seek enforcement of the award through the courts of states.

Thus, for Schmitthoff the *Lex Mercatoria* owes its existence to the stability accorded to it by sovereign states. He argued that parties 'cannot provide for every detail, but can in practice make the proper

---

[64] Schmitthoff, 'The unification of international trade', op. cit., p. 32. Emphasis added.

[65] Schmitthoff, 'Export law – then and now', *'Export', Journal of the Institute of Export*, vol. 48, no. 9, 1985, pp. 34–5. (reprinted in Chia-Jui Ceng (ed.), op. cit., pp. 123–7, at p. 123).

[66] Schmitthoff, 'The unification or harmonisation of law by means of standard contracts and general conditions', *International Comparative Law Quarterly*, vol. 17, 1968, p. 551 (reprinted in Chia-Jui Ceng, op. cit., pp. 188–205).

law dormant'.[67] In other words, the parties to a contract can suppress national law in favour of transnationally accepted rules. Thus, Schmitthoff continued, it is 'wrong to attribute the character of ... supranational law to international trade law. It acquires its autonomous character by leave and licence of all national sovereigns. Ultimately, it is founded on national law.'[68] Thus, Schmitthoff defines the *Lex Mercatoria* as the harmonization of municipal trade laws.

CRITICISMS OF THE *LEX MERCATORIA*

The autonomist position on the *Lex Mercatoria* has been faulted for its imprecision, particularly over its sources and component principles, and its overzealous claim of universality. The positivist view has been dismissed by autonomists as essentially a dry description of functional harmonization. It is not criticized empirically, since its approach is descriptive.

For present purposes, it is precisely the functional harmonization of trade law that is of concern to this discussion. The conventions concerning international commercial arbitration, the institutional rules of arbitral tribunals, the rules for *ad hoc* arbitration, and particularly the enactments in numerous municipal legislations to recognize awards based on the *Lex Mercatoria* and to give them effect have enabled these cosmopolitan principles to ride on the coercive apparatuses of states. The positivist conception is a description of a harmonization process which is a product of a phenomenon which, at the structural level of the international economy, is drawing the practice of international commerce to a closer normative consensus, and drawing the law of states closer along with it. Before explaining this in more detail, the following briefly will consider the criticisms of the autonomist position of the *Lex Mercatoria*.

The greatest criticism is that what the autonomists are describing can hardly be termed 'law', if 'law' is equated with the command of a sovereign enforced by the threat of coercive sanction in the case of non-compliance.[69] A standard form of contract can hardly create an

---

[67] Schmitthoff, 'The unification of the law of international trade', op. cit., p. 182.
[68] Schmitthoff, 'The law of international trade', *Commercial Law in a Changing Economic Climate*, 2nd edn, 1981, pp. 18–31 (reprinted in Chia-Jui Ceng, op. cit., pp. 219–30).
[69] Keith Highet, 'The enigma of the Lex Mercatoria', in Carbonneau, op. cit., p. 106.

independent legal system if its terms cannot be backed by coercive force. Contracts create enforceable rights, but do not create law. After an exhaustive survey of the German, Swiss, Italian, Austrian, Dutch, French, and Belgian legal systems, De Ly concluded that international custom and trade usages have a normative value only and are not recognized as formal sources of law.[70]

There is support for alternative conceptions of law, meaning a stable normative system where individuals feel morally bound to observe certain rules of behaviour. To claim that law is a coercive order risks overstating the extent to which a civil society is based upon a series of commands backed by threats. As H. L. A. Hart has pointed out with respect to law in general,[71] Hans Kelsen with regard to international law,[72] and Friedrich Kratchowil in his discussion on the power of norms,[73] the effectiveness of law must not be equated with the effectiveness of the legal sanction. Rational individuals, aware of their long-term self-interest, may observe the norms of their society due to their demand for reciprocity without the need for a continual threat of sanction. For example, one honours one's commitments in good faith in the expectation that others will reciprocate, in the words of Robert Keohane, 'even if there is no convincing evidence to that effect'.[74] This is, in essence, the substance of international law; though it is not coercive because of ultimate state sovereignty, it is nevertheless 'law'.

It is doubtful whether this debate can reach a satisfactory conclusion, and it is certainly one that could easily overrun the confines of this chapter. Suffice to say that there are alternative, and equally valid, conceptions of 'law' within which the *Lex Mercatoria* may be classified.

Nevertheless, the status of public international law as a component of the autonomous *Lex Mercatoria* is unsettled. There is, of course, the traditional view that only states are subjects of public international law. On the other hand, there is the view that the provisions of the

---

[70] De Ly, op. cit., p. 134.

[71] H. L. A. Hart, *The Concept of Law*, London: Oxford University Press, 1961.

[72] Hans Kelsen, *General Theory of Law and the State*, (translated by Anders Wedberg), New York: Russell & Russell, 1961; Kelsen, *The Pure Theory of Law*, (translated by Max Knight), Berkeley: University of California Press, 1970.

[73] Friedrich V. Kratchowil, *Rules, Norms, and Decisions: On the Conditions of Practical and Legal Reasoning in International Relations and Domestic Affairs*, Cambridge: Cambridge University Press, 1989.

[74] R. Keohane, 'Reciprocity in international relations', in Keohane (ed.), *International Institutions and State Power*, Boulder: Westview, 1989, pp. 146–7.

Vienna Convention on the Law of Treaties (1969) reflect common practices and therefore are suitable to international contracts.[75] Supporters of the latter view point to the concept of 'internationalized' contracts which has been applied to, for example, the *Texaco v. Libya* arbitration. The rationale for this is that foreign investors would not submit a long-term contract to the vagaries of the law of the host state, while the host state would not submit to the laws of another state. Therefore, there emerged an 'international law of contracts'.[76] Proponents argue that the concession agreements of the 1940s and 1950s make reference to vague internationalized choices of law which demonstrates that 'the parties are groping after some legal system which is not the territorial law of either party'.[77]

Moreover, Article 42 of the ICSID Convention does permit an arbitrator to apply the laws of the host state as well as general principles of international law to a dispute where the parties have not made an express choice of law. And, as Lord McNair has argued, public international law derives its source from general principles of law (i.e., consistent with Article 38(1)c of the Statute of the International Court of Justice). In his words: 'The legal system appropriate to the type of contract under consideration is not public international law but shares with public international law a common source of recruitment and inspiration, namely, the general principles of law recognised by civilised nations.'[78]

Having said that, the extent to which 'general principles of law common to commercial nations' is a reliable source also has been questioned. Schlosser raised the point that although different systems of law have provisions for, for instance, a case where defective goods are delivered, some provide that damages should be paid, while others simply permit the buyer to cancel the contract.[79] Thus, while laws are indeed common to commercial states at some level of abstraction, there are numerous differences in the detail. In this connection, Lord Mustill asked, 'What principles of trade law, apart from those which are so general as to be useless, are common to the legal systems of the

---

[75] Dreatta, Lake and Nanda, op. cit., pp. 13–14.

[76] *Texaco Overseas Petroleum and California Asiatic Oil Company v. The Government of the Libyan Arab Republic*, 53 *ILR* 1979. This concept has been rejected by Sonorajah, *The Pursuit of Nationalised Property*, Dordrecht: Martinus Nijhoff, 1986.

[77] Ibid., p. 10.

[78] Lord McNair, 'The general principles of law recognised by civilised nations', *British Yearbook of International Law*, vol. 33, 1957, pp. 1–19, at p. 6.

[79] In Gaillard, op. cit., p. 29.

members of such a community?'[80] The principle of *pacata sunt servanda*, for example, can be taken as given. For a piece of paper to be a contract there must be an *a priori* assumption that a contract is something that should be performed. Precisely how it should be performed, what interpretations are to be given to its clauses, and what are the respective rights and obligations of parties are the issues that are determined by law. Commercial law is a device for conflict avoidance and management. To state that contracts must be performed is to state the obvious, without giving any guidance as to how disputes are to be resolved. A similar point can be made of 'good faith', and so on.

Thus, to state that 'general principles' constitute a self-contained system of law is tantamount to suggesting that because buildings are constructed in all states of the world, the universal use of sand, limestone and pebbles constitutes an 'autonomous building order'. Of course, this is not the case, since bricks can be moulded in different shapes and sizes, some are engineered in a more technologically advanced manner to withstand higher stress tolerances, and architecture is influenced by geography, climate, culture, and so on. It is this imprecision that renders the components of the autonomist *Lex Mercatoria* more properly termed 'stepping stones' to real rules of law, rather than law themselves.[81]

As regard customs and usages, it has been argued that,

> If the custom of international commercial transactions were sufficiently well understood throughout the world, there would be no need for national legislation embodying it; and if national legislation were sufficiently uniform throughout the world, there would be no need for international codification.[82]

The legal status of INCOTERMS is unsettled, although its terms are used widely, since different national systems have different attitudes towards the legal status of such trade usages.[83]

Moreover, it has been suggested that one would be hard-pressed to find any principles of law common to Saudi Arabia and China, for example, to make them meaningful to settling a dispute.[84] In this context, some have advocated a 'micro *Lex Mercatoria*'. As explained

---

80 Mustill, op. cit., p. 156.
81 Highet, op. cit., p. 100.
82 Berman and Kaufman, op. cit., p. 264.
83 De Ly, op. cit., pp. 172–4.
84 Dreatta, Lake and Nanda, op. cit., p. 15.

by Mustill, this involves only the legal systems that are directly concerned with the contract. The drawback of this is there would exist 'constellations of para-laws, Franco-Belgian, Anglo-Dutch, Italo-Hispano-Korean, and so on'.[85] It is conceivable that there could be a series of functional, transnational micro *Lex Mercatoriae* for each area of trade. For instance, the commercial communities of corn traders, while relying on such universal terms as f.o.b. and c.i.f., could supplement these with their own rules that would be distinct from those of, say, rubber traders, and which the businesspersons of both Saudi Arabia and China must observe if they wish to participate effectively within the trading regimes that govern these areas. Yet even then, Mustill pointed out that there is 'no guarantee of homogeneity even within a single trade' and that 'if the parties to a commodity transaction do not wish to bind themselves to, say, the GAFTA Contract Form No. 100, there is no legal or other institution which can compel them to do so'.[86]

Moreover, traders from all states would not necessarily be participants to even these micro *Lex Mercatoriae*, since not all municipal systems permit party autonomy, which is the fundamental 'trunc commun' that permits the *Lex Mercatoria* to come into being. While parties to a contract are generally free to express a choice of law in their contract, proponents of the autonomist view overstate the extent to which the principle is recognized 'universally'. For instance, the Chinese law on economic contracts restricts the choice of law to one that is connected with the contract, and Venezuelan law restricts the choice of law. Moreover, some North African and Arab countries require that any contract performed in their countries be governed by their own national laws and jurisdictions.[87] The choice of Saudi Arabia in the example in the preceding paragraph is (deliberately) erroneous – merchants in Saudi Arabia are required to choose Saudi law. Thus, critics, such as De Ly, have argued that there are varying degrees of 'opposition to the notion of universally conceived principles of

---

[85] Mustill, op. cit., p. 157.

[86] Ibid., p. 159; De Ly, op. cit., pp. 183–92.

[87] Norbert Horn, 'Uniformity and diversity in the law of international commercial contracts', in Norbert Horn and Clive M. Schmitthoff (eds), *The Transnational Law of International Commercial Transactions*, London: Kluwer, 1982, p. 10. Specifically, Horacio A. Grigera Naòn cites Article 804 of the Bolivian Civil Code which mandates that contracts that are to be performed in Bolivia, even if concluded outside the country, are to be governed by Bolivian law. See Naòn, 'The UN Convention on contracts for the international sale of goods', in ibid., pp. 89–124, at p. 98. See also De Ly, op. cit., p. 52.

international business law or a universal and autonomous lex mercatoria'.[88]

HARMONIZATION OF LAW AND COERCIVE FORCE

The debate about the standing of the *Lex Mercatoria* in law continues to rage. For present purposes, the descriptive positivist view of the functional harmonization of municipal laws to give effect to rules with transnational origin is important. The harmonization activities of intergovernmental institutions and international professional organizations have been mentioned. This section examines provisions for the recognition of the *Lex Mercatoria* in the UNCITRAL Arbitration Rules which formed the basis of such important arbitral tribunals as the Iran–US Claims Tribunal. This section also examines several regional arbitration conventions providing for the use of the *Lex Mercatoria* and the recognition in the municipal laws of states arbitral awards based on the *Lex Mercatoria*. The point of this section is to illustrate the widespread acceptance of transnational rules, as illustrated by the harmonization of the laws of states with diverse cultures and legal traditions.

The United Nations Commission on International Trade Law (UNCITRAL) was established by General Assembly Resolution 2205 (XXI) of 17 December 1966, and became fully operative on 1 January 1968.[89] UNCITRAL was the brain-child of Professor Clive M. Schmitthoff, a lifetime advocate of the harmonization of international trade law.[90] The Commission was charged with the mandate to 'further the progressive harmonisation and unification of the law of international trade' through such means as developing international conventions, model laws, and uniform laws; promoting the codification

---

[88] Ibid., p. 53.

[89] G.A. Resolution 2205(XXI), 17 December 1955. Reprinted in *UNCITRAL Yearbook, 1968–1970*, vol. I, Part I. On UNCITRAL, and the other UN agencies working towards the harmonization of international commercial law, see Suy, 'Achievements of the United Nations Commission on international trade law', *International Lawyer*, p. 139.

[90] He was also an honorary professor of law at the University of Kent at Canterbury. Schmitthoff describes his involvement in the creation of UNCITRAL in 'The unification of the law of international trade', *Journal of Business Law* (1968), reprinted in Chia-Jui Ceng (ed.), *Clive M. Schmitthoff's Select Essays on International Trade Law*, London: Martinus Nijhoff Publishers, 1988, pp. 213–15.

of trade terms, customs and practices; and coordinating the activities of the various agencies concerned with international trade.

Among UNCITRAL's notable achievements in the area of uniform laws are the Convention on the Limitation Period in the International Sale of Goods (New York, 1974); the United Nations Convention on the Carriage of Goods by Sea (Hamburg, 1978); the United Nations Convention on Bills of Exchange and Promissory Notes (New York, 1988); and the United Nations Convention on the Liability of Operators of Transport Terminals in International Trade (Vienna, 1991).[91] The wide acceptability of such conventions is important. For instance, the United Nations Convention on Contracts for the International Sale of Goods (Vienna Sales Convention, 1980) has been ratified by over 30 countries of diverse legal traditions.

Also, UNCITRAL has completed numerous model laws, such as the Procurement of Goods and Construction (1993),[92] and the Model Law Incorporating Services Procurement Procedures (1994).[93] UNCITRAL is continuing work on a Uniform Law on Guarantees and Set Rules on Electronic Data Interchange.[94] In the area of international commercial arbitration, UNCITRAL has elaborated a set of Arbitration Rules (1976), Conciliation Rules (1980), and a Model Law on International Commercial Arbitration (1985).

UNCITRAL has taken a truly global, as opposed to merely Western, perspective in the elaboration of international commercial rules. Beginning in the 1950s and especially in the 1960s, some economic organs of the United Nations system were criticized for being Western in orientation and for failing to address the special needs of developing countries. The reaction was to create a number of specialized agencies, such as the UNCTAD or the United Nations Centre for Transnational Corporations under the aegis of ECOSOC, which would emphasize the

---

[91] For a summary, see Gerold Hermann, 'The contribution of UNCITRAL to the development of international trade law', in Norbert Horn and Clive M. Schmitthoff (eds), *The Transnational Law of International Commercial Transactions*, London: Kluwer, 1982.

[92] 'Sixth Committee takes up UNCITRAL report', Forty-eighth General Assembly, GA\L\2774, Sixth Committee, 4 October 1993.

[93] 'United Nations Commission on international trade law concludes twenty-seventh session, 31 May–17 June; adopts model law incorporating services, procurement procedures and guide to its enactment', L\TR\226, 17 June 1994.

[94] 'United Nations Commission on international trade law to hold twenty-seventh session in New York, 31 May–17 June', Background Release, L\TR\225, 31 May 1994.

special needs of developing states, which then constituted the majority of the UN's membership.[95]

UNCITRAL was established 'with particular regard to the interests of developing countries'.[96] Indeed, Article 9 of its constitution states that the Commission 'shall bear in mind the interests of all peoples, and particularly those of developing countries'. However, unlike UNCTAD, UNCITRAL was not established with the aim of reallocating values within the UN system. Rather, UNCITRAL was driven by the desire to formulate rules for the conduct of international trade that would be truly global in character. The membership of the Commission consisted of representatives from the principal economic and legal systems of the world: 9 delegates from Africa, 7 from Asia, 5 from Eastern Europe, 6 from Latin America, and 9 from the industrialized West. The aim was to depoliticize the application of international trade law; the political battles occurred during the drafting stages of common rules so that they would emerge with universal acceptance.[97]

What has resulted from this global approach are conventions that have been ratified by the international community of trading states, and model laws which have been adopted unilaterally by states with diverse commercial cultures. The Arbitration Rules share this wide appeal; in the words of Gerold Herrmann, they have been 'acceptable in the different legal and economic systems' of the world.[98] Indeed, these rules took into consideration various existing conventions[99] and rules[100] relating to international arbitration. As a result, the

---

95 On this, see Robert W. Gregg, 'The politics of international economic cooperation and development', in Lawrence S. Finkelstein (ed.), *Politics in the United Nations System*, London: Duke University Press, 1988, pp. 106–47.

96 Rudolf Dolzer, 'International agencies for the formulation of transnational economic law', in Horn and Schmitthoff, op. cit., p. 64.

97 This was evidenced during the drafting of the UNCITRAL Arbitration Rules. See in particular Isaak I. Dore, *The UNCITRAL Framework for Arbitration in Contemporary Perspective*, Graham Thomas, Martinus Nijhoff, 1993.

98 Herrmann, op. cit., p. 40.

99 The New York Convention on the Recognition and Enforcement of Foreign Arbitral Awards (1958); the Geneva Convention (European Convention on International Commercial Arbitration, 1961); the Washington Convention on the Settlement of Investment Disputes Between States and Nationals of the States (ICSID, 1965); the Council of Europe Convention Providing a Uniform Law on Arbitration (1966); and the Moscow Convention of 1972 on the Settlement by Arbitration of Disputes Arising out of Economic, Scientific and Technical Cooperation.

100 The Economic Commission for Europe Rules (1966); the Economic Commission for Asia and the Far East Rules (1966); the Uniform Rules of Procedure for Arbitration in the Arbitration Courts of Council for Mutual Economic Assistance Countries

UNCITRAL rules have been adopted as the institutional rules of such diverse tribunals as the Inter-American Commercial Arbitration Commission (IACAC) and the Regional Arbitration Centres under the Asian-African Legal Consultative Committee (AALCC). Other permanent arbitral tribunals, such as the London Court of Arbitration and the American Arbitration Association, have amended their institutional rules to accommodate parties wishing to make use of the UNCITRAL Rules.

The UNCITRAL Arbitration Rules have been articulated in such a manner as to render them useful to various legal systems, traditions and commercial cultures, because they are flexible on the question of the applicable law. Perhaps nowhere is this acceptability of the UNCITRAL Arbitration Rules better illustrated than in their application by the Iran–US Claims Tribunal.[101] Not only was this an arbitration between two hostile parties (the arbitrators appointed by the parties were reputed to have come to blows in the foyer of the Peace Palace),[102] but between two parties of radically different legal

---

contd.
(1974); the International Chamber of Commerce Rules (1975); the Rules of the American Arbitration Association (AAA); the International Arbitration Association (IAA); and the Rules of the Foreign Trade Arbitration Commission at the USSR Chamber of Commerce.

[101] The Iran–US Claims Tribunal was established on 19 January 1981 following the nationalization of a number of US companies in Iran following the 1979 revolution, which resulted in 3,839 claims against Iran. See generally, Charles N. Brower, 'Current developments in the law of expropriation and compensation: a preliminary survey of awards of the Iran–United States claims tribunal', *International Lawyer*, vol. 21, 1987, pp. 639–69; David D. Caron, 'The nature of the Iran–United States claims tribunal and the evolving structure of international dispute resolution', *American Journal of International Law*, vol. 84, 1990, pp. 104–56; Rahmatullah Khan, *The Iran–United States Claims Tribunal: Controversies, Cases and Contribution*, Dordrecht: Martinus Nijhoff, 1990; Allahyar Mouri, *The International Law of Expropriation as Reflected in the Work of the Iran–U.S. Claims Tribunal*, Dordrecht: Martinus Nijhoff, 1994; Davis R. Robinson, 'Recent developments at the Iran–United States claims tribunal', *International Lawyer*, vol. 17, 1983, pp. 661–7; and Erik Suy, 'Settling US claims against Iran through arbitration', *American Journal of International and Comparative Law*, vol. 29, 1981, pp. 523–47.

[102] There were reports of unconventional diplomatic practice by 'two attacking Iranian Arbitrators', Judges Kashani and Shafeiei, who physically assaulted the Dutch arbitrator chosen by the United States, Judge Mangard, and threw him out of the building. Reported by a US Agent, reproduced in Stewart Abercrombie Baker and Mark David Davis, 'Establishment of an arbitral tribunal under the UNCITRAL rules: the experience of the Iran–United States claims tribunal', *International Lawyer*, vol. 23, 1989, pp. 81–135, at pp. 114–15.

systems. That states with such diametrically opposed world-views as a post-revolutionary anti-Western Iran, and the liberal, capitalist, common-law-inspired hegemon of the free world United States could agree to a set of rules to settle their disputes is testament to their global appeal.

The UNCITRAL Arbitration Rules were adopted by the Iran–US Claims Tribunal with some modifications (they were designed to be flexible). Article V of the Claims Settlement Declaration mandated the Tribunal to employ aspects of the *Lex Mercatoria* under Article 33(1) of the UNCITRAL Rules. The Tribunal was free to select its own choice of law rules, and was mandated to 'decide all cases on the basis of respect for law ... taking into account relevant usages of trade, contract provisions and changed circumstances'. Notably, the primacy normally accorded to the law chosen by the parties has been changed to the law that the Tribunal deems to be applicable, and the application of a municipal law, however determined, is placed on the same level as general principles of law, the provisions of the contract to hand, and relevant trade usages.

The Tribunal tried, in the words of Avanessian, 'as much as possible, to avoid a positive choice of law', preferring to rely upon contract provisions and general principles of law. As the Tribunal stated in *CMI International, Inc*, it did 'not believe ... that it is rigidly tied to the law of the contract [as its] search for justice and equity, even in cases where arguably relevant national laws might be designed to further other and doubtless quite legitimate goals'.[103] As Judge Bellet stated:

> it would have been extremely awkward for these arbitrators to have resorted to the classic rules of conflict of law, forcing the arbitrators to choose between Iranian law and American law. With tensions running high, it was worth avoiding such choices, particularly in cases where the parties alleged political or economic coercion in the execution of certain contracts. In this way claimants and their opponents were practically always in agreement not to invoke any rigid conflict of law rules.[104]

There have been cases where the Tribunal has applied widely recognized trade usages,[105] and has relied on the provisions of the

---

[103] Quoted in Aida Avanessian, *The Iran-US Claims Tribunal in Action*, London: Graham & Trotman/Martinus Nijhoff, 1993, p. 248.

[104] Cited in Grant Hanessian, 'General principles of law in the Iran–US Claims Tribunal', *Columbia Journal of Transnational Law*, vol. 27, 1989, pp. 309–52, at p. 314.

[105] Such as *Carolina Brass, Inc. v. Arya Shipping Lines*. See Avanessian, op. cit., p. 260.

contract without making reference to any municipal law.[106] According to Crook, the majority of cases have been decided on the basis of the parties' contracts, without making any reference to an applicable law, particularly in claims for payment, issues of performance, and in interpreting the validity of the contract.[107]

The Tribunal also employed 'general principles' common to the legal systems of Iran and the United States in cases concerned with contract formation, interpretation, performance, breach, termination, unjust enrichment, negotiable instruments, bailment, liability for unjustified attachment, third party beneficiaries, and partnerships.[108] And it has resorted to such principles of law as *pacta sunt servanda, rebus sic stantibus* and *force majeure*, equity, and the obligation to perform duties with 'due diligence'.[109] It has been suggested that the invocation of 'general principles of law' has been in the context of the *Lex Mercatoria*. According to Hanessian, '[t]he Tribunal's "general principles of law" also draw upon the international "law merchant" or lex mercatoria'.[110] Carbonneau agreed that the Tribunal might 'augur well for the possible elaboration ... of normative commercial legal principles having a transnational legal dimension'.[111]

Thus, transnationally accepted rules, customs and principles provided a basis for reconciling the parties from two different legal systems in the interests of fairness (and acceptability) to both parties. According to Avanessian,

> Article V, by giving the Tribunal authority to decide according to the principles of international and commercial law, trade usages and

---

[106] For instance, *Bendix Corp. v. Iran, Iran National Airlines Co. v. United States, Sola Tiles, Inc. v. Iran.* See Jacomijn J. van Hof, *Commentary on the UNCITRAL Arbitration Rules: The Application by the Iran–U.S. Claims Tribunal*, Deventer: Kluwer, 1991, pp. 244–6.

[107] John R. Crook, 'Applicable law in international arbitration: the Iran–US claims tribunal experience', *American Journal of International Law*, vol. 83, 1989, pp. 278–311, at pp. 288–292.

[108] To name a few: *Mobil Oil v. Iran, Watkins-Johnson Company v. Iran, Anaconda-Iran, Inc. v. Iran.* See Avanessian, op. cit., p. 259; van Hof, op. cit., pp. 239–41 and 256–70; and Hanessian, op. cit., pp. 330–2.

[109] See especially S. A. Baker and M. D. Davis, *The UNCITRAL Arbitration Rules in Practice: The Experience of the Iran–United States Claims Tribunal*, Deventer, Boston: Kluwer Law and Taxation Publishers, 1992, pp. 175–81; Also, van Hof, op. cit., pp. 227–72; Hanessian, op. cit., pp. 318–20; and Crook, pp. 292–7.

[110] Hanessian, op. cit., p. 312.

[111] Carbonneau, 'The elaboration of substantive legal norms and arbitral adjucation: the case of the Iran–United States claims tribunal', quoted in Crook, op. cit., p. 292.

> provisions of the contract, has, in effect, given the Tribunal maximum discretion in applying any non-national rules that it may deem appropriate in the particular case.[112]

Van Hof observed, 'The cases discussed show that when applying private international law rules, the Tribunal usually refers to general principles of private international law or sometimes an "anti-choice" or cumulative method without reference to any particular choice of law system.'[113]

It is interesting to note that the Iran–US Claims Tribunal has also clarified many general principles of law, such as *rebus sic stantibus* – of which the Tribunal stated that the concept 'has in its basic form been incorporated into so many legal systems that it may be regarded as a general principle of law' – thus further contributing to the elaboration of the *Lex Mercatoria*.[114] Indeed, De Ly noted that 'general principles of law may have a *structural* function within a legal system where they may provide tools for its development, particularly in relation to filling its gaps'.[115]

There appears to be a trend more widely in the arbitration rules of numerous institutionalized arbitral tribunals, and in the rules for *ad hoc* arbitration, to take into account the *Lex Mercatoria* on several levels. Other international conventions and national legislations relating to international commercial arbitration are increasingly giving recognition to the *Lex Mercatoria*. For instance, in the absence of an expressed choice of law by the parties, arbitrators are permitted to take into account aspects of the *Lex Mercatoria* under such diverse arbitration conventions as Article VII(1) of the European Convention on International Commercial Arbitration (1961), Article 13.5 of the ICC Rules, and Article 28(2) of the ICC Model Law.

Article VII of the European Convention on International Commercial Arbitration (1961) provides that if the parties fail to choose a substantive law, 'the arbitrators shall apply the proper law under the rule of conflict that the arbitrators deem applicable'. However, it further provides that 'the arbitrators shall take account of the terms of the contract and trade usages' whether or not the parties have chosen

---

[112] Avanessian, op. cit., p. 242.

[113] Van Hof, op. cit., p. 231.

[114] The *Questech* decision, in *Iran-US C.T.R*, 122–123; quoted in Emmanuel Gaillard, *Transnational Rules in International Commercial Arbitration*, Paris: Institute of International Business Law and Practice, International Chamber of Commerce, 1993, p.111.

[115] De Ly, op. cit., p. 194. Emphasis in original.

an applicable law.[116] And a 1992 Resolution on Transnational Rules Adopted at the 65th International Association Conference in Cairo stated that:

> The fact that an international arbitrator has based an award on transnational rules (general principles of law, principles common to several jurisdictions, international law, usages of trade, etc.) rather than the law of a particular state should not in itself affect the validity of the award; 1) where the parties have agreed that the arbitrator may apply transnational rules; 2) where the parties have remained silent concerning the applicable law.[117]

The *Lex Mercatoria* is explicitly recognized (and the trend towards 'fully fledged' delocalization is further illustrated) in the Inter-American Convention on the Law Applicable to International Contracts (Mexico, 1994).[118] The previous Inter-American Convention on International Commercial Arbitration (1975) contained some remnants of the historical aversion of Latin American states even to permitting party autonomy in choosing the proper law of their contract. However, the 1994 Convention accords usages and conventions a prominent place in the absence of an express choice of law by the parties. Article 7(1) gives the arbitrators the discretion to take into account 'the parties' behaviour and ... the clauses of the contract'. Article 9 similarly enables the enforcement of 'general principles'. It states that the arbitrator '... shall also take into account the general principles of international commercial law recognised by international organisations'. Article 10 is most explicit. It reads:

> In addition to the provisions in the foregoing articles, the guidelines, customs, and principles of international commercial law as well as commercial usage and practices generally accepted shall apply in order to discharge the requirement of justice and equity in the particular case.

The particular significance of this Convention is that states with both common law and civil law traditions in Latin America, which had been hostile even to the autonomy of parties to chose an applicable law, have adopted a Convention that is at the forefront of developments in accepting the *Lex Mercatoria*.

---

[116] This is reproduced in Indira Carr and Richard Kidner, *Statutes and Conventions on International Trade Law*, London: Cavendish Publishing Ltd., 1993, p. 310.

[117] Cited in Gaillard, op. cit., p. 36.

[118] See Friedrich K. Juenger, 'The Inter-American Convention on the Law Applicable to International Contracts: Some Highlights and Comparisons', *American Journal of Comparative Law*, vol. 42, no. 2, 1994, pp. 381–93.

The *Lex Mercatoria* is also gaining coercive force, in the sense that states are recognizing arbitral awards that are based on it. In effect, transnationally inspired principles, norms, usages and customs are riding on the coercive apparatuses of the state.

The 'old' view of arbitration is the 'localization' theory. This holds that an arbitrator should apply the substantive law of the seat of arbitration. This was widely accepted in the 1940s and 1950s.[119] However, there have been trends towards 'delocalization', whereby an arbitrator can determine a case according to any law, the ultimate conclusion of which is the application of the *Lex Mercatoria*. There are various permutations of delocalized arbitration. Carlo Croff has suggested four.[120] In the order of detachment from municipal laws, these are where the arbitrator, sitting outside of the state of closest connection with the contract: 1) makes use of the conflict of laws rules of the state which would have had jurisdiction over a particular case; 2) makes use of a cumulative, or comparative, conflicts of laws system which looks at all the systems which may be connected with the dispute; 3) employs an international conflict of laws rules or general principles of international law; and 4) proceeds directly to the applicable law without any consideration of conflicts of laws.[121]

Even in 'fully delocalized' arbitrations, which are neither connected to the forum of arbitration nor which apply any national law (i.e., in favour of the *Lex Mercatoria*), the award is not independent of national legal system, since it must be recognized as valid in the jurisdiction where the party seeks to have it enforced.[122] Highet is quite right to point out that all arbitral awards must be enforced somewhere. He stated, 'A stateless contract only looks like a contract ... As soon as the aggrieved party goes to a court to seek an injunction to force the other party to perform or to go to arbitration, the tribute of alleged

---

[119] See A. M. F. Maniruzzaman, 'Conflict of laws issues in international arbitration', op. cit.

[120] See Croff, 'The applicable law in an international commercial arbitration: is it still a conflict of laws problem?', *International Lawyer*, vol. 16, 1982, pp. 613–45.

[121] It should be noted that the issue of delocalization remains unsettled, as for instance, F. A. Mann, holding to the traditional conflicts of laws view, has argued that the arbitrator has to make reference to a 'particular system of law'. See Mann, 'England rejects "delocalised" contracts and arbitration', op. cit.

[122] See Jan Paulsson, 'Delocalisation of international commercial arbitration: when and why it matters', *International Commercial Law Quarterly*, vol. 32, 1983, pp. 53–61, esp. p. 57.

statelessness disappears.'[123] In this connection, the *Lex Mercatoria* is 'borrowing' the coercive apparatuses of states, as the latter are increasingly recognizing it as a legitimate basis for arbitral awards. It is being given recognition and enforceability through international conventions and national legislation.

The New York Convention on the Recognition and Enforcement of Foreign Arbitral Awards (1958) emphasizes municipal laws in dealing with the capacity of contracting parties, the validity of the arbitral award, and the procedural law to be applied to the conduct of the arbitration. However, there is nothing in Article V, dealing with the grounds for the refusal of the enforcement of the award, about the fact that the award is based on the *Lex Mercatoria*.[124] For Carlo Croff, this means that the award must be enforced 'whether the arbitrator applies an international conflict of laws rule, or settles the dispute directly through the lex mercatoria'.[125]

National laws give force to the *Lex Mercatoria*. For instance, The Netherlands amended its rules to harmonize with the Iran–US Claims Tribunal. The Hague was the seat of arbitration. The Tribunal registered its awards in the courts of The Netherlands, as required by the law of that state.[126] To give effect to awards based on transnational rules, the Netherlands Arbitration Act (1986), Article 1054, states that 'in all cases the arbitral tribunal shall take into account any applicable trade usages'.[127]

Similarly, under the French Arbitration Decree of 14 May 1981, Article 1496 of the French Civil Code was amended to release arbitrators from any obligation to refer to any national law in handing down an award for it to be considered valid in France. They may apply any law that is applicable, and the French courts reviewing the award are not entitled to interfere with the decision of the arbitrator to apply transnational rules, so long as this choice is consistent with the choice of the parties and does not contravene any mandatory public law provisions. According to Jean-Pierre Ancel, this 'represents the outline of a system which applies "truly international" rules and principles,

---

123 Highet, op. cit.

124 The Convention is reproduced in Carr and Kidner, op. cit., esp. p. 304.

125 Croff, op. cit.

126 Baker and Davis, op. cit., p. 9.

127 Cited in Alan Redfern and Martin Hunter, *International Commercial Arbitration*, 2nd edn, London: Sweet and Maxwell, 1991, p. 120.

since they are not part of the French legal system, no more than they are a part of any national legal system'.[128]

In addition, the Canadian Arbitration Law was modified in 1985 to permit arbitrators the flexibility to make use of the *Lex Mercatoria*.[129] And, whereas the Vienna Court of Appeal and the English Court of Appeal had set aside arbitral awards that were based on the *Lex Mercatoria*, each of these was overturned by the Austrian Supreme Court, and the Court of Appeal, respectively, since in both cases the application of the *Lex Mercatoria* was stipulated by the parties and the awards did not violate any relevant public policy.[130]

CONCLUSION

Scholarly debate over the *Lex Mercatoria* in international law circles has turned on the question of whether transnationally articulated rules, widely accepted practice, and the standardization of customs by international organizations and professional associations are truly 'law', defined as the will of a legislator backed by legitimate sanction. It is quite proper that the debate should be so focused in that discipline, unless its relatively unsophisticated appreciation of the level of analysis problem in the social sciences and methodology more widely is to be lamented by those outside of it. Because of the different perspectives on what constitutes 'law', there is difficulty in reconciling the approach of the positivists with that of the autonomists for whom anything goes. In the absence of criteria for evaluation and selection, everything stays. Thus, there is a recipe for stagnation in the theory, notwithstanding the apparent growth in the practical application of the *Lex Mercatoria*.

In reviewing the acceptability of the *Lex Mercatoria*, the foregoing discussion has concentrated on the manner in which transnational – or anational – law is being given coercive force in the laws of states. Interestingly, the 'third stage' of international commercial law is reverting to its roots as a functional, cosmopolitan expression of codes for behaviour, while riding on the 'modern' stage of law by virtue of

---

[128] Jean-Pierre Ancel, 'French judicial attitudes towards international arbitration', *Arbitration International*, vol. 9, no. 2, 1993, pp. 121–9, at p. 127; Lando, op. cit., p. 756.

[129] Dreatta, Lake and Nanda, op. cit., p. 16.

[130] Redfern and Hunter, op. cit., pp. 118–20; also Lando, op. cit., p. 757.

the fact that it is being recognized in the municipal laws of states and enforced by their coercive apparatuses. If international commercial law is entering postmodernity by embracing the best of cosmopolitanism while retaining the force of the Westphalian system, this surely is to be welcomed.

For many international lawyers, the positivist approach to the *Lex Mercatoria* is an unexciting 'state of the art' snapshot of the culmination of fifty years of harmonization and unification activities in international commercial law and practice. It is fortunate that the frames of reference in International Relations are wider, for this is precisely what is important here. Surely the fact that the bankers' associations in 175 states accepted the 1974 edition of the UCP is significant, even if the 'legal' status of such trade usages is open to question.[131] Surely it is important that the ICC documents, such as INCOTERMS which stipulate the meaning of such common terms as c.i.f. and f.o.b., have been accepted by commercial states, even if the debate in the discipline of law has focused narrowly on the fact that there is no codifying 'authority' in the cosmopolitan community of merchants.

Rather than engage in what is essentially a semantic discussion of what constitutes law – one could have the same discussion about whether bilateral investment treaties, the Resolutions of the UN General Assembly, or even international law are properly called 'law' – it is surely important to recognize the autonomist conception of the *Lex Mercatoria* as a component of a growing international normative practice. For International Relations, surely the fact that the practice of states to recognize this consensus among a cosmopolitan commercial community is also important. This growing consensus is not self-contained; it lays the foundation for the harmonization of the laws of states. Whether this, in turn, is a product of a larger harmonizing tendency arising out of the globalization of liberal capital is perhaps the most important question. It is on this question that this book concludes.

---

[131] De Ly, op. cit., pp. 175–83.

CHAPTER 8

CONCLUSION
Re-establishing Protective Jurisdiction in the Era of Globalization – Empire of Law?

This book began by questioning the strong thesis of globalization that states are 'hollowing out', and in particular that states no longer are able to respond effectively to transnational risks that frustrate the application of public policy in many areas. Rather than accept the criteria, which at times are fanciful at best, on which many have thrown in the towel on behalf of the state, this book reframed the question of a loss of control by asking how states are responding to challenges of globalization in specific areas. It investigated areas taken to be paradigmatic by many in the globalization school: international finance, money laundering, and the Internet. The analysis found that the states of the transatlantic community, to which the discussion was limited, are responding by 'domesticating' control of transnational risks by bringing them under municipal law, and as a corollary to this, by harmonizing municipal systems of law, thus leading to a convergence of systems of municipal law among distinct sovereign states.

The aspects of globalization investigated in this book have been more or less state-driven processes. This was seen, for example, in the shift in international finance from a government-managed system under Bretton Woods to a more diffuse market-led system after the early 1970s, and in the efforts of the US government and the European Commission to develop privately operated high-speed computer-mediated communication networks. The deregulation and liberalization of these areas have been one aspect of these states' policies, and the risks that have resulted from this deregulation emanated from the private realm, in other words, from private individuals. These private individuals, or transnational civil society actors, have frustrated other aspects of governments' public policy, such as ensuring safety and soundness of the financial system and protecting frameworks that promote the creativity necessary for the flourishing of the information society. What this book has argued is that re-regulation has occurred at the level of municipal law, because this is the level at which private individuals operate. The prevailing ideology of liberalism that led to deregulation and privatization has also led to the strategy of controlling civil society actors at the level of municipal law.

It was shown that the process of domestication, which was defined as the passage of municipal law to rein in undesirable aspects of globalization, has several elements. The first is to nationalize authority over the actors who present risks and to localize control of transnational civil society actors, for instance by placing the onus on banks to police the international financial system for money laundering and by attempting to place liability on system operators to police the Internet for copyright infringements. This has had, as a corollary, the privatization of the functions of governance.

It has also been shown that harmonization of municipal laws has been a corollary to domestication. It was shown that with the increased systemic and contagion risks in the globalized international financial system, the evolving norm across the Atlantic has been to balance the availability of private credit with safety and soundness, particularly since these states maintain government-sponsored safety nets for depositors and retain the role of lender of last resort. The Basle Committee's Minimum Standards, and particularly the national legislation adopted in conformity with them, are attempts to ensure stability through municipal law in international finance that has been deregulated at the public level. Similarly, it was shown that the deregulation of capital movements has enabled transnational criminals to launder money under the cover of background noise in the interbank payments networks. This has been met by a privatization of the function of policing the cleanliness of deposits through the enactment of municipal legislation by requiring banks, under pain of criminal charges, to report suspicious transactions to the authorities.

Finally, it was shown that both the US government and the European Commission are actively promoting the development of the Internet – the National Information Society and the European Information Society, respectively – as a medium for the rapid transmission of textual information, for a host of social and economic reasons. One of the main challenges in this endeavour has been, and remains, to adapt existing systems of copyrights to a mode of delivery that potentially can permit the infringement of rights on an unprecedented scale. The benefits of the Internet possibly will not be realized unless there is confidence in such systems of legal protection. It was shown that the approach favoured by both the US government and the European Commission has been to adapt existing legislation to the new digital environment, and that the issues that have been considered, and the approaches taken to date to draft new legislation, have been very similar.

Are the domestication of risk and the harmonization of law in these areas a sufficient basis on which to reject the strong thesis of globalization that states are 'hollowing out' and losing power in the era of globalization? The answer is a qualified negative, for two reasons relating to the efficacy of the strategy of harmonization and to the foreclosure of policy options.

The efficacy of harmonization of law in a limited geographical area is suspect, as was shown. For harmonization to be a truly effective strategy to mitigate risks from transnational civil society requires that all states adopt the same laws, and indeed also to be equally committed and able to enforce them. Without a truly global response, there will remain the problem of havens for inadequately supervised banks, money laundering and copyright infringement. But for the laws of all states to become the same requires the assimilation of a host of social, economic, political, administrative and cultural prerequisites. For economic reasons, some states wish to offer foreign banks an environment that is less strictly regulated, and some states do not question the source or cleanliness of badly needed capital. For both economic and cultural reasons, some states do not have the same attitudes towards granting protection to intellectual property. Not all states would define the same things as a crime from which is derived 'dirty' money. This is without mentioning that states have different legal traditions and developmental experiences, and to some states the thought of legislating away all problems may be seen as a uniquely Western response that derives from certain national traditions and administrative abilities, and indeed, of a liberal heritage that prioritizes the separation of public and private and the rule of law. The main impediment to the spread globally of harmonized systems of municipal law is that systems of law *follow* normative-social structures of ethical communities and administrative centres; law does not create them.

The second qualification in the answer to whether the strong thesis of globalization can be rejected relates to the foreclosure of policy options. Why have the states of the transatlantic community pursued the strategy of domestication and harmonization of municipal laws as opposed to any other strategy in a range of possible options? For instance, states could have pursued a binding international treaty, or they could have chosen to extraterritorialize the application of their municipal laws. However, the former most likely would require a similarity of ends, i.e., vague statements of purpose, as opposed to a similarity of means (assimilation of laws). It is unlikely that states would agree in a treaty the exact provisions of the municipal laws to be enacted because of the difficulty of then reversing, changing, or amending the laws, as this would require the negotiation of a new treaty. Moreover, it is unlikely that legislators, particularly in the United States, would not challenge on constitutional grounds the executive branch forcing the adoption of specific laws through an international treaty and thereby circumscribing the legislative process. While the extraterritorialization of municipal laws does occur in some instances, for instance concerning terrorism or US antitrust legislation, the international system would become a complex, and indeed a conflict-prone place if each state were to appropriate for itself the right to enforce a range of its own laws on the territory of another.[1] While extraterritoriality potentially could extend internationally the application of law to the extent that transnational civil society actors are active internationally, the extraterritorialization of a whole range of municipal laws would undermine the conceptions of territoriality that accompany the Westphalian system, meaning notions of sovereign states as juridical entities that are bounded territorially.

While it could be overstating the case to suggest that states have had no option but to pursue a strategy of domestication and harmonization, it is reasonable to suggest that a range of factors have foreclosed policy options for dealing with the problems of globalization. The problem that has confronted states in the areas investigated here has been how to discipline civil society actors whose transnational reach extends further than the legal jurisdiction of states, and how to reconcile the practices of cosmopolitan communities with the maintenance of a Westphalian system of law backed by coercion, all the while attempting to preserve domestic law-making processes. One can suggest that the foreclosure of options for governance at the level of public policy has been forced by the ideology of neoliberalism, which forces attention on the adaptation of municipal laws and on the privatization of governance.

---

[1] As Malcolm Shaw has pointed out, claims for the extraterritorial application of municipal laws based on the 'effects doctrine' has provoked 'considerable controversy'. See M. N. Shaw, *International Law*, 2nd edn, Cambridge: Grotius Publications Limited, 1986, pp. 367–71.

Indeed, the strategy of domestication and harmonization is an attempt to *preserve* the liberal globalizing economy, and to *preserve* the strictures of the Westphalian system of law backed by coercive force, while arresting the negative impacts on states' public policy of international civil society. However much the laws of states may be brought into harmony, the laws of each state remain enforceable by the coercive apparatuses of each state. Through a strategy of domestication and harmonization, the legislator remains sovereign on his territory, and the sanction is confined territorially.

And, indeed, the fundamental rationality of governance underlying domestication is as it always has been *within* modern states. It has been said that 'law is not possible in a state of nature, only in a civil society'.[2] It goes without saying that there is no international sovereign, but there is an international civil society, if this is defined as organic communities that transcend regulatory spaces. However, these individuals are members of legal communities, and operate in them although perhaps not their own. As Benjamin R. Barber put it bluntly, 'Law for the purposes of nations is the capacity of enforcement; for sovereign nations its essence lies in its sanctions.'[3] The strategy is 'rational' to the extent that 'rational' means, in Michel Foucault's terms, 'a kind of rationality which was intrinsic to the art of government', or to use his neologism 'governmentality'.[4] The rationality of international governance through municipal law can be seen, quite simply, as an extension of the governmentality of organizing a modern state: laws are tactics to govern civil society, a means to an end. What characterizes international governance pursued through private regulations is not so much a shift in the rationality of governance, but the extension transnationally of the logic of Western governmentality: the shift is occurring in the application of laws from purely domestic civil society actors to transnationally mobile civil society actors.

Thus, to summarize, it is not sufficient for the strong thesis of globalization to proclaim that the emperor has no clothes and to

---

[2] Hans Rees, describing Immanuel Kant's philosophy of law, in *Kant's Political Writings*, Cambridge: Cambridge University Press, 1970, p. 22.

[3] Benjamin R. Barber, 'Global democracy or global law: which comes first?', *Indiana Journal of Global Legal Studies*, vol. 1, no. 1, 1993. Available http://www.law.indiana.edu/glsj/col11/barber.html

[4] I am indebted to Stefan Rossbach for enlightening me on this question. See Michel Foucault, 'Governmentality', in Graham Burchell, Colin Gordon and Peter Miller (eds), *The Foucault Effect: Studies in Governmentality*, London: Harvester Wheatsheaf, 1991, p. 89.

discount the role of the state in adapting to change and deflecting the burden of adjustment onto private actors, particularly when the burden of adjustment on private actors is borne out of the state's policy to deregulate and liberalize in the first place.[5] Globalization – in more concrete terms, the activities of private individuals deregulated at the public level – is not some superior force that once unleashed by states hovers in the ether above the control of state authorities. However, the very neoliberalism that has led to the problem of risk by transnational civil society actors has also foreclosed policy options in dealing with that risk. Highly integrative practices of the liberalised capitalist economy are promoting the codification of laws to govern transnational civil society actors engaged in a given transnational practice, and the laws of states that share a level of interest in mitigating risks are engaging in the project of harmonization of municipal laws. And it is here that an important paradox has been missed by the globalization literature that may well, in the end, reinforce its claim that states have lost sovereignty, or hollowed out, if one defines sovereignty as the maintenance of *distinct* ethical and juridical communities, governed independently according to systems of law that are dictated by *them*, flourishing in *difference*.

GLOBAL SOCIETY AND THE STATE SYSTEM: THE EMPIRE OF LAW

It has been argued that the project of international governance has concentrated on 'high level' governance at the level of states' public policies, whether this be through ambitious plans for world 'government' or through the comparatively conservative means of international law, treaties, organizations and institutions, and regimes. Perhaps the global economy is integrative at the level of national laws to an extent that a renewed contemplation of international 'government' – though at a lower level of analysis – is not misplaced? This question is a large one indeed, and there is not room here to

[5] Indeed, the state should be 'brought back in' to the analysis of globalization, and one area in which scholars of International Relations may do so is in further investigation of the harmonization of municipal laws, just as the state has been 'brought back in' to other analyses of state adaptation. Linda Weiss, *The Myth of the Powerless State: Governing the Economy in a Global Era*, Cambridge: Polity Press, 1998.

investigate it fully. However, some implications of this study that can inform such a project can be sketched out.

The first implication is that transnationally assimilated systems of *municipal* law have become mechanisms of *international* governance. Even though this governance is not global, assimilated systems of municipal law are creating a system of super-territorial governance backed by the coercive apparatuses of individual states. An important consequence that follows from this is that the effect of the whole of this process of domestication and harmonization could be greater than the sum of its parts. In other words, assimilated systems of municipal law could be creating a system of super-territorial governance, particular to a given practice of civil society, backed by the coercive apparatuses of individual states.

The second implication of this study to be investigated is where this process is leading. Having said that the harmonization of municipal law is designed to reinforce the state system of compartmentalized jurisdictions, the nature of the states system in terms of difference in legal–administrative spaces is changing profoundly. The implication of the existence of a group of transnationally mobile persons united by cosmopolitan practices, yet subject to the assimilated systems of municipal laws in distinct sovereign states, could represent an intersection between modern and post-modern systems of social organization.[6] The regulation of transnational communities of civil society actors engaged in particular practices governed by more or less undifferentiated laws administered by different state authorities can be conceived as no less than an Empire of Law. It is the marriage of a transnational rationality of governance with transnationally uniform and integrative practices that gives rise to transnationally assimilated systems of law enforced by distinct public authorities. This Empire is partly modern, that being the enactment of positive law and its enforceability within territorially differentiated authority jurisdictions. But it is also half post-modern, or, indeed, pre-modern: it is a transnational assimilation of laws that is going into the future backwards – back to a universal law.

As such, the investigation could draw on the experience of the past, for it would not be the first time in history that systems of law have

---

[6] On postmodern aspects of governance, see John Gerrard Ruggie, 'Territoriality and beyond: problematizing modernity in international relations', *International Organization*, vol. 47, no. 1, 1993, pp. 139–74.

transcended distinct political–administrative spaces.[7] The legal foundations of capitalism themselves evolved precisely out of the customary practice of individuals, as the examination of private international trade law showed. In a wider survey of the evolution of agrarian economies into market systems John R. Commons argued that the codification of such basic laws as contract followed commercial practice. Commons concluded that, 'from the time of the Norman Conquest to the Twentieth Century ... each stage [of social organization] proceeds by the evolution of customs and the formulation of customs into working rules by a government'.[8]

Similarly, J. B. Condliffe observed that the evolution of legal systems followed the activities of the private commercial community. However, Condliffe went further than Commons to argue that not only did systems of law evolve in reaction to the practices of individuals, so did political systems. Following a survey of the history of commerce from the Dark Ages he concluded that, 'Throughout recorded history new forms of trading have disturbed the established political order. Through all the groupings and regroupings of peoples, the shifts in power and the development of political ideas, the trader has woven and rewoven his web of international economic integration.'[9] In other words, commerce played a significant role in determining forms of governance in the pre-national era. For instance, after the Dark Ages, '[most of] the experiments in government in the

---

[7] Roman jurists recognized *jus civile*, 'the enactments or the customary law of a particular state, what would now be called positive municipal law'. But they also recognized a universal law based on principles 'that were inherently reasonable and right without reference to their occurrence in any system of law'. This law transcended different communities, and constituted a 'higher law than the enactments of any particular state'. (George H. Sabine, *A History of Political Theory*, 3rd edn, London: Holt, Rinehart and Winston, 1964, pp. 168–9). The *jus gentium* and *jus naturale*, which derived from Natural Law of the Stoics and Cicero. These conceived of law as having such universal character as to govern all individuals, since everyone shares at a very basic level the capacity for rational thought irrespective of where in the Holy Roman Empire they happened to be situated, and irrespective of which language they spoke and which customs and traditions they happened to practise by virtue of the circumstance of their birth. Traces of this natural law basis of Roman law still underlie legal reasoning in modern states (i.e., the concept of 'reasonableness' in common law'). See J. L. Brierly, *The Law of Nations: An Introduction to the International Law of Peace*, 6th edn, Oxford: Oxford University Press, 1963, p. 24.

[8] John R. Commons, *The Legal Foundations of Capitalism*, Winconsin: Wisconsin University Press, 1957, p. 313.

[9] J. B. Condliffe, *The Commerce of Nations*, London: George Allen & Unwin Ltd., 1951, p. 832.

troubled centuries between the collapse of the Roman administrative structure and the consolidation of national governments ... were an outgrowth of foreign trade'.[10] He continued,

> The revival of trade went parallel with, if it did not precede, the revival of ordered government. It would be wrong to believe that trade awaited the restoration of law and order. Indeed the merchants who began the process of transforming European feudal society into the commercial, democratic, international trading world of our day were merchant adventurers in the crudest sense. Unless we realise this fact, we cannot understand the continuous struggles between them and the church in its efforts to apply the doctrines of the Canon Law.[11]

The codification of systems of law in the national context followed the activities of the private commercial community. The codification of such basic provisions as contract law in different states is, of course, due not only to a shared rationality of governing and shared experiences of consolidating public authorities, but also, at the same time, to the exigencies of having to play by 'the rules of the game' according to an accepted practice. As Berman and Kaufman have noted of the *Lex Mercatoria*, the 'general similarities of contract practice and contract law are due in part to common commercial needs shared by all who participate in international trade transactions'.[12] In other words, the exigencies of a universal practice – buying and selling – have mandated similar behaviour, since the act of trading is an integrative practice for its participants.

Therefore, in systems of political organization other than the sovereign states system municipal law has transcended different administrative political–authority spaces. It would be dangerous at this juncture to draw too much of a parallel between the pre-Westphalian system and the harmonization of modern municipal laws in the era of

---

[10] Ibid., p. 42.

[11] Ibid., p. 23. It is curious that, while all of the conclusions of his study point to the fact that governance has always been linked to systems of municipal law developed to regulate private actors in the economy, Condliffe concluded that the progress in governing the international economy would be in 'building up' in international organizations. While he appreciated the early signs of globalization – 'the application of new scientific discoveries to transport and communications bring the peoples of the world into closer contact' – and that 'these activities cross borders', he focused on the public policy of governments in international institutions as the focus of authority and as 'the embryonic organs of world government'. Ibid., p. 843.

[12] Harold J. Berman and Colin Kaufman, 'The law of international commercial transactions (Lex Mercatoria)', *Harvard International Law Journal*, vol. 19, no. 1, 1978, p. 222.

globalization, because the character of the transcendent law in the former was natural law (*Jus gentium*), while that in the latter is positive municipal law (*Jus civile*). However, at some level, both epochs have in common the coexistence of independent authorities at a political (namely, administrative) level with transcendent law operating at the level of civil society actors. Cicero (143–106 BC) is quoted as saying that business practices were 'in great measure, not the law of a single country, but of the commercial world', and Grotius, that, 'Between contracting parties there is a closer society than the common society of mankind.'[13] It was not until the Middle Ages (e.g., the seventh to ninth centuries) that the concept of law became more communitarian in orientation, embedded within particular communities and applicable to persons by virtue of their membership in that community. Yet, up to the Carta Mercatoria (1303) and the Statute of the Staples (1353), cosmopolitan laws akin to the *jus gentium* (*Lex Mercatoria*) applicable to the cosmopolitan commercial community coexisted with a communitarian civil law, barbarian codes out of which grew the concept that law is tied to a territory (the King's law) and differentiated by virtue of *ordre public*. As Colin Gordon remarked, the 'harmonization of administrative "clarity" with commercial "certainty" smoothed the convergence of the state's interests with those of nascent capitalism',[14] and as the investigation of private international trade law has shown, high degrees of interaction into this basic structure of the international economy has led to high degrees of assimilation of the laws of distinct states, including those with very differentiated legal, administrative and political traditions.

Perhaps, if the process of globalization integrates economies further, the municipal laws of states will follow to a greater degree. As Harrison and Mungall note, 'increasing levels of economic specialisation, world-shrinking communication ... suggest both an awareness and actuality of interdependence are expanding phenomena. In such circumstances, the scope for harmonization will increase.'[15] Stephen Zamora agrees: 'In a world in which there are increasing contacts between citizens of different countries, the trend towards harmonization

---

[13] Hugo Grotius, quoted in Martin Wight, *Systems of States*, London: Leicester University Press, 1977, p. 127.

[14] Colin Gordon, 'The soul of the citizen: Max Weber and Michel Foucault on rationality and government', in S. Lash and S. Whimster (eds), *Max Weber, Rationality and Modernity*, London: Allen &Unwin, 1987, p. 301.

[15] R. J. Harrison and Stuart Mungall, in A. J. R. Groom and Paul Taylor (eds), *Frameworks for International Cooperation*, London: Pinter Publishers, 1990, p. 65.

and accommodation of legal differences is likely to continue.'[16] Perhaps the global economy is integrative at the level of national laws to the extent that a renewed philosophical investigation of 'world government', though on very different terms than in the past, is not misplaced.

And there is a range of cosmopolitan philosophy on which to draw. Neither international society, nor the progress of the international capitalist economy are by any stretch of the imagination 'new',[17] and accompanying both of these concepts has long been a realization of socially integrative tendencies.[18] Marx, and neo-Marxists, have long understood the transnationalization of social authority structures that derive from the transnationalization of capital. Karl Marx and Friedrich Engels argued that the spread of capitalism 'compels all nations, on pain of extinction, to adopt the bourgeois mode of production; it compels them to introduce what we call civilization into their midst, i.e., to become bourgeois themselves. In one word, it creates a world after its own image.'[19] Neo-Marxist studies, and those using neo-Gramscian conceptions of power, have built upon, and refined this idea.[20] International lawyers also have recognized that the spread of capital, in terms of multinational corporations, has led to a convergence of legal systems.[21] International Relations should marry its strengths in the study of sociological processes of world society and its strengths in international governance with its heritage of cosmopolitan philosophy to engage more fully the question of where 'low level' international governance could be leading. This will require greater interaction with

---

16 Stephen Zamora, 'NAFTA and the harmonization of domestic legal systems: the side effects of free trade', *Arizona Journal of International and Comparative Law*, vol. 12, Fall 1995, pp. 401–27.

17 'International society' here refers to the English School conception. See Hedley Bull, *The Anarchical Society: A Study of Order in World Politics*, London: Macmillan, 1977; Martin Wight, op. cit.; and James Mayall, 'International society and international theory', in Michael Donelan (ed.), *The Reason of States*, London: Allen & Unwin, 1978. On the not-so-newness of globalization, see Hirst and Thompson, *Globalisation in Question*, Cambridge: Polity Press, 1996.

18 See, for instance, Immanuel Wallerstein, *The Modern World-System: Capitalist Agriculture and the Origins of the European World-Economy in the Sixteenth Century*, New York and London: Academic Press, 1974.

19 Karl Marx and Friedrich Engels, *The Communist Manifesto*, in Robert C. Tucker (ed.), *The Marx-Engels Reader*, New York: W. W. Norton, 1972, pp. 338–9.

20 See in particular Robert W. Cox, *Power, Production and World Order: Social Forces in the Making of History*, New York: Columbia University Press, 1987.

21 See Wolfgang Wiegand, 'The reception of American law in Europe', *American Journal of International Law*, vol. 39, 1991, pp. 236–46.

law and international law, and reuniting International Relations with its sister discipline.

Certainly the pursuit of the question of international governance arising out of assimilated systems of law will invigorate cosmopolitans and worry conservatives. For there could indeed be a dark side to this kind of international order. Prompted by fears of a loss of sovereign control, and designed to reassert sovereignty, harmonization of municipal laws, ironically, could be undermining the very sovereignty that states are seeking to reassert. With transnationally assimilated legal structures comes the spectre of 'a tyranny of sameness',[22] a possible end to the traditional methods of lawmaking that calls into question democratic accountability and legitimacy, and a possible end to difference. Harrison and Mungall observed that as harmonization spreads, 'valid alternatives open to national actors are perceived to be progressively closed'.[23]

Indeed, what happens to the Westphalian system if harmonization continues to be a corollary to domestication? By states system is generally meant 'several states that are so connected as to seem to constitute one body but whose members retain sovereignty'.[24] By Westphalian system is meant a system of more or less self-contained legal communities, whose politically independent (sovereign) authorities articulate laws (including rules, norms, and administrative procedures) that are consistent with the traditions, values, culture, and social mores of the community. However, the globalized economy increasingly presents states with challenges and opportunities that are the same (depending on their level of integration into its various systems), and the evidence presented here shows that the legal frameworks of states are becoming increasingly the same as well. Otherwise sovereign and independent at a political level, the laws of states are converging on an administrative level.

Therefore, it seems reasonable to ask, what does continued sovereignty at the political level really mean when the laws that states use to exercise sovereignty in disciplining civil society actors are increasingly the same? With the emergence of transnationally assimilated systems of law, states retain administrative authority, but

---

[22] This wonderful phrase is not mine, it is David Held's. See Held, *Models of Democracy*, 2nd edn, Cambridge: Polity Press, 1996.

[23] Harrison and Mungall, op. cit., p. 66.

[24] Martin Wight, quoting Pufendorf, in *System of States*, London: Leicester University Press, 1977, at p. 21.

is that authority becoming little more than the administration of a transnationally assimilated law to discipline the transnational practices of civil society actors? Clearly not, since the authority of states, and the tactics at their disposal, extend well beyond their municipal legal frameworks. However, the narrower question must be engaged; what does continued sovereignty *within* the practices investigated here, and perhaps others, really mean when the laws that states use to exercise sovereignty in disciplining civil society actors in those practices are increasingly the same? At a superficial level, the arguments both that sovereignty is eroded and strengthened by harmonization parallel those raised in the context of the European Union. One side of the argument speaks of a 'democratic deficit' because laws are framed outside the context of national inputs and only 'residual sovereignty' remaining in Member States in areas not subject to harmonization.[25] It has been shown that accompanying domestication and harmonization is a dynamic of 'harmonization creep', that is, that ancillary aspects of national laws and traditions follow from the initial harmonization undertaken to come to terms with a particular problem. The experience of the EU, an advanced stage of integration, has shown that complex markets require a host of related areas also to be harmonized. Similarly, to control money laundering, the United States and the European Union have harmonized their national legislation dealing with the definition and control of money laundering, and this has required a 'deeper' harmonization relating to bank secrecy, the civil liability of banks, the traditions of the banker–customer relationship, and indeed, the very definition of a 'crime' that would precipitate dirty money entering the banking system. The difficulties of other states adopting the same standards was illustrated through an examination of the changed laws of Switzerland. The dynamics of a liberal capitalist economy may of itself promote such harmonization creep without necessarily having to accompany a politically constructive process of integration. Thus, there is an intrusive dynamic into laws and traditions more firmly rooted in political and administrative cultures and traditions.

The other side of the debate about sovereignty points out that member states are better able to grapple problems in unison more effectively than they could by acting alone.[26] However, it was shown

---

[25] 'The "democratic deficit" between London and Brussels may not be as large as the PM would have us think', *The Guardian*, 6 November 1990, p. 21.

[26] Robert Keohane and Stanley Hoffman, *The New European Community: Decision Making and Institutional Change*, Colorado: Westview, 1991.

that for domestication and harmonization truly to be effective would require all states to harmonize their laws according to an agreed standard. So long as some states free-ride off the efforts of others to stop money laundering for the purposes of attracting capital irrespective of its origin, hot and dirty money will continue to enter the international financial system. Similarly, so long as some states do not supervise international banks prudently, systemic risks and contagion risks will continue to inhere in a private financial system. But there are pressures for 'harmonization spread'. Several of these pressures were discussed, ranging from diplomatic coercion to market incentives to prompt a greater number of states to adopt similar provisions in their national laws to those that have already done so. For instance, it was shown that there are incentives built into the legislation adopted by the United States and the European Union in banking to force other states to adopt similar measures. The US and EU are large markets for banking services, and notwithstanding their concomitant desire to liberalize financial services, such as through the WTO, their domestic legislation permits them to lock out banks incorporated in jurisdictions which do not exercise prudential supervision. The sheer force of market incentives could force banks to incorporate elsewhere to gain access to their markets. It was also shown that the United States in particular has been exerting diplomatic pressure on states to adopt more coercive laws against money laundering.

It is from this coercion, perhaps, that the greatest challenge to state sovereignty comes. It was shown that the United States is pressuring 'rogue' states to adopt systems of municipal legislation similar to its own. For instance, it was shown that as more states crack down on money laundering, the United States has issued lists of priority countries to target (the Department of State's International Narcotic Control Strategy Report) with diplomatic coercion. Moreover, as the principles promulgated as the basis for an international regime against money laundering, now still in its infancy, gain more normative force, the United States and others could have recourse to greater normative pressures to use to force others to join the club of states which take a 'respectable and civilized' approach to controlling money laundering.

Is the United States, by pressuring other states to adopt similar municipal legislation, behaving as a 'postmodern hegemon'? Traditional conceptions of US hegemony concentrate on the activities of the US to pressure states through a variety of coercion and inducements in international institutions following the Second World War to cooperate at the level of public policy in framing policy according to certain principles.[27] The term 'postmodern hegemony' is to distinguish the US project of coordinating public policy from a directed assimilation of states' municipal legislation. This coercion risks challenging the states system as one of differentiated legal systems where laws are derived from the customs, attitudes, values and traditions of the people within each state. While at a superficial level, those interested in questions of governance and order could find this refreshing, communitarians, as well as cosmopolitans, following Kant, very well could lament any change in the dynamics of law-making that intrude on 'the greatest possible human freedom in accordance with laws which ensure that the freedom of each can coexist with the freedom of all others'.[28]

To conclude, while it may be fashionable, and overstating the case, for some scholars to point to the dangers of the 'hollowed-out' state being incapable of exercising authority effectively in a globalized international system, perhaps the real danger lies in the symphony for which present harmonization efforts are now only just beginning to write the score; it could be a symphony for the devil of a new kind of Leviathan, an Empire of law built of postmodern hegemony, an end to difference. If transnationally assimilated laws guarantee freedom for individuals, balance rights, protect government-designed social safety nets, and stop criminals, why worry? However, if the impetus to further harmonization comes as a coercive diplomatic overture, and the source of the laws of a community no longer derive from the custom, values, attitudes, and culture of that community, there is a case for sounding a distant early warning, or we just might find a world government by stealth after all, and it will not be federal in design.

---

[27] I have engaged the theory of hegemonic stability elsewhere. See *Making Rules in the Uruguay Round of the GATT: A Study of International Leadership*, Aldershot: Dartmouth, 1995.

[28] See Kant, 'The metaphysics of morals', Part C, in Rees, op. cit., p. 23, and p. 133.

SELECT BIBLIOGRAPHY

Abbott, Frederick M. (1993) 'Regional integration mechanisms in the law of the United States: starting over', *Indiana Journal of Global Legal Studies*, vol. 1, no. 1. Available at www.law.indiana.edu/glsj/vol11/abbott.html.

Ad Hoc Alliance for a Digital Future (1996) 'Industry coalition warns of WIPO threat to information society', press release, 28 November 1996. Available at www.dfc.org/docs/adhocpr.htm.

Ahvenainen, Jorma (1986) 'Telegraphs, trade and policy: the role of the international telegraph in the years 1870–1914', in Wolfram Fischer, R. Marvin McInnis, and Jurgen Schneider (eds), *The Emergence of a World Economy, 1500–1914*, Part II: 1850–1914. Papers of the IX International Conference of Economic History, in Komission bei Frank Steiner Verlag Weisbaden GmbH.

Alford, Duncan E. (1992) 'Basle Committee Minimum Standards: international regulatory response to the failure of BCCI', *George Washington Journal of International Law and Economics*, vol. 26, 241–91.

——(1994) 'Anti-money laundering regulations: a burden on financial institutions', *North Carolina Journal of International Law and Commercial Regulation*, vol. 19, 865–98.

Aman, Alfred C. Jr. (1993) 'Indiana Journal of Global Legal Studies: an introduction', *Indiana Journal of Global Legal Studies*, vol. 1, no. 1. Available: http://www.law.indiana.edu/glsj/vol11/aman.html.

American Library Association (1996) 'America's libraries call for caution as international copyright negotiations for the digital age commence', press release, 29 November 1996. Available at www.dfc.org/dfc/docs/libpr.htm.

Ancel, Jean-Pierre (1993) 'French judicial attitudes towards international arbitration', *Arbitration International*, vol. 9, no. 2, pp. 121–9.

Andreotta, Ralph J. (1995) 'The National Information Infrastructure: its implications, opportunities, and challenges', *Wake Forest Law Review*, vol. 30, Spring, pp. 221–40.

Arora, Anu (1993) *Electronic Banking and the Law*, 2nd edn, London: Banking Technology Ltd.

Ashworth, William (1981) *A Short History of the International Economy Since 1850*, 3rd edn, London: Longman.

Avanessian, Aida (1993) *The Iran-US Claims Tribunal in Action*, London/Dordrecht/Boston: Graham & Trotman/Martinus Nijhoff.

Axford, Barrie (1995) *The Global System: Economics, Politics and Culture*, Cambridge: Polity Press.

Bainbridge, David I. (1995) *Cases and Materials in Intellectual Property Law*, London: Pitman.

Baker, Stewart Abercrombie and Davis, Mark David (1989) 'Establishment of an arbitral tribunal under the UNCITRAL rules: the experience of the Iran–United States claims tribunal', *International Lawyer*, vol. 23, pp. 81–135.

——(1992) *The UNCITRAL Arbitration Rules in Practice: The Experience of the Iran-United States Claims Tribunal*, Deventer, Boston: Kluwer Law and Taxation Publishers.

Bank for International Settlements (1983) 'Revised Basle Concordat on principles for the supervision of banks' foreign establishments', in *International Legal Materials*, vol. 22. Available at www.bis.org.

——(1992a) 'Committee on banking regulation and supervisory practices, Basle Concordat on principles for the supervision of banks' foreign establishments', in International Monetary Fund, *International Capital Markets: Recent Developments and Short-Term Prospects*, Occasional Paper no. 7. Available at www.bis.org.

——(1991) 'International convergence of capital measurement and capital standards, *International Legal Materials*, vol. 30. Available at www.bis.org.

——(1992b) 'Minimum standards for the supervision of banking groups and their cross-border establishments'. Available at www.bis.org.

Barber, Benjamin R. (1993) 'Global democracy or global law: which comes first?', *Indiana Journal of Global Legal Studies*, vol. 1, no. 1. Available at www.law.indiana.edu/glsj/vol11/barber.html.

Barlow, J.P. (1994) 'The economy of ideas: a framework for rethinking patents and copyrights in the digital age', *Wired*, vol. 2, no. 3.

Bartelson, Jens (1995) *A Genealogy of Sovereignty*, Cambridge: Cambridge University Press.

Bencivenga, Dominic (1997) 'Corporate update: global copyright pacts – treaties address works transmitted on Internet', *New York Law Journal*, 9 January 1997. Available at www.ljx.com/internet/0109wipo.html.

Berman, Harold J. and Kaufman, Colin (1978) 'The law of international commercial transactions (*Lex Mercatoria*)', *Harvard International Law Journal*, vol. 19, no. 1, pp. 221–77.

Bhagwati, Jagdish and Patrick, Hugh T. (eds) (1991) *Aggressive Unilateralism: America's 301 Trade Policy and the World Trading System*, Ann Arbor: University of Michigan Press.

Bond, Monica (1994) 'Money laundering', *Accountants Digest*, no. 324, September.

Bonell (1987) 'The Unidroit initiative for the progressive codification of international trade law', *International and Comparative Law Quarterly*, vol. 27.

Born, Karl Erich (1977) *International Banking in the 19th and 20th Centuries*, Warwickshire: Berg Publishers Ltd.

Bos, Maarten and Brownlie, Ian (eds) (1987) *Liber Amicorum for the Rt. Hon. Lord Wilberforce*, Oxford: Clarendon Press.

Boutros-Ghali, Boutros (1996) 'Global leadership after the cold war', *Foreign Affairs*, March/April, pp. 86–98.

Bradley, Caroline (1991) '1992: the case of financial services', *Journal of International Law and Business*, vol. 12.

Brett, E. A. (1983) *International Money and Capitalist Crisis*, London: Heinemann.

Brierly, J. L. (1963) *The Law of Nations: An Introduction to the International Law of Peace*, 6th edn, Oxford: Oxford University Press.

Broadbent, Edward (1998) 'The rise and fall of economic and social rights: thoughts on justice and stability in the North Atlantic world', *Global Society: Journal of Interdisciplinary International Relations*, vol. 12, no. 2, January, pp. 15–31.

Broadhead, Lee-Anne (1996) 'Commissioning consent: globalization and global governance', *International Journal*, LI, vol. 4, Autumn, pp. 651–88.

Brower, Charles N. (1987) 'Current developments in the law of expropriation and compensation: a preliminary survey of awards of the Iran–United States claims tribunal', *International Lawyer*, vol. 21, pp. 639–69.

Brown, Chris (1996) 'Back to normal? Some reflections on sovereignty and self-determination after the cold war', *Global Society: Journal of Interdisciplinary International Relations*, vol. 10, no. 1, pp. 11–23.

Buchanan, James (1968) *The Demand and Supply of Public Goods*, Chicago: Rand McNally & Company.

Bull, Hedley (1977) *The Anarchical Society: A Study of Order in World Politics*, London: Macmillan.

Burk, Dan (1993) 'Patents in cyberspace: territoriality and infringement on global computer networks', *Tulane Law Review*, vol. 68, no. 1, pp. 2–67.

Burton, John (1972) *World Society*, Cambridge: Cambridge University Press.

Byrne, John G. (1995) 'Changes on the frontier of intellectual property law: an overview of the changes required by GATT', *Dusquesne Law Review*, vol. 34, Fall, pp. 121–36.

Canadian Banker (1992) 'Three for free trade: North American Free Trade Agreement', vol. 99, no. 2.

Canova, Timothy A. (1995) 'The transformation of US banking and finance: from regulated competition to free-market receivership', *Brooklyn Law Review*, vol. 60, 1295–1354.

Carbonneau, Thomas E. (ed.) (1990) *Lex Mercatoria and Arbitration*, New York: Transnational Juris Publications, Inc., Dobbs Ferry.

Caron, David D. (1990) 'The nature of the Iran–United States claims tribunal and the evolving structure of international dispute resolution', *American Journal of International Law*, vol. 84, 1990, pp. 104–56.

Carr, E. H. (1939) *The Twenty Years' Crisis*, London: Macmillan.

Carr, Indira and Kidner, Richard (1993) *Statutes and Conventions on International Trade Law*, London: Cavendish Publishing Ltd.

Carter, P. B. (1986) 'Contracts in English private international law', *British Yearbook of International Law*, vol. 57.

Castel, J. G. (1968) *Conflict of Laws: Cases, Notes, and Materials*, 2nd edn, Toronto: Butterworths.

Cate, Fred H. (1994) 'Global information policymaking and domestic law', *Indiana Journal of Global Legal Studies*, vol. 1, no. 2. Available: www.law.indiana.edu/glsj/vol1/cate.html.

Cerny, Phil (ed.) (1993) *Finance and World Politics*, Aldershot: Edward Elgar.

Chair's Conclusions of the G7 Ministerial Conference on the Information Society (1994), Brussels, 25–26 February 1995. Document dated 7 November 1994 obtained from Larry Irving, Assistant Secretary of Commerce for Communications and Information.

Chan, Stephen and Wiener, Jarrod (eds) (1998) *Twentieth Century International History: A Reader*, London: I.B. Tauris.

Cheng, Chia-Jui (ed.) (1988) *Clive M. Schmitthoff's Select Essays on International Trade*, London: Martinus Nijhoff Publishers.

Cheshire, Geoffrey Chevalier (1965) *Private International Law*, London: Butterworths.

Chorley, Lord and Smart, P. E. (1977) *Leading Cases in the Law of Banking* (4th edn), London: Sweet & Maxwell.

Clark, Grenville and Sohn, Louis B. (1966) *World Peace Through World Law: Two Alternative Plans*, Cambridge, MA: Harvard University Press.

Clarke, Michael (1995) 'How will the money laundering regulations work?', *Journal of Financial Regulation and Compliance*, vol. 31, no. 1, pp. 36–42.

Claude, Innis L. Jr. (1956) *Swords into Ploughshares: The Problems and Progress of International Organization*, 3rd edn, New York: Random House.

Codding, George A. Jr. (1990) 'World federalism: the conceptual setting', in A. J. R. Groom and Paul Taylor, *Frameworks for International Cooperation*, London: Pinter, pp. 217–33.

Cohen, Saul S. (1995) 'Financial services regulation: a mid-decade review: colloquium: the challenges of derivatives', *Fordham Law Review*, vol. 63, pp. 1993–2012.

Cohn, E. J. (1957) 'The objectivist practice on the proper law of contract', *International and Comparative Law Quarterly*, vol. 6, 1994–2029.

Colas, Alejandro (1997) 'The promises of international civil society', *Global Society: Journal of Interdisciplinary International Relations*, vol. 11, no. 3, 261–78.

Commission of the European Communities (1985) *The Completion of the Internal Market: White Paper of the Commission to the Attention of the European Council*. COM(85) 310 final, Office for Official Publications of the European Communities, Brussels, 14 June 1985.

——(1988) *Copyright and the New Technologies, Green Paper on Copyright and the Challenge of Technology: Problems in Copyright Calling for Immediate Action*, COM(88) 172 final, Brussels: Office for Official Publications of the European Communities, 17 June 1988. Available: www.echo.lu.

——(1989) *Second Council Directive on the Coordination of the Laws, Regulations and Administrative Provisions Relating to the Taking-up and Pursuit of the Business of Credit Institutions and Amending Directive 77/780/EEC, 89/646/ EEC, Official Journal of the European Communities*, no. 1, 386, Brussels.

——(1991a) *Proposal for a Council Decision Setting Up a Programme for an*

Information Services Market, COM(570) final, Brussels: Office for Official Publications of the European Communities, 23 January 1991. Available at www.echo.lu/programmes/en/DELTA_2.html.

——(1991b) *Council Directive 91/250/EEC of 14 May 1991 on the Legal Protection of Computer Programmes*, Brussels: Office for Official Publications of the European Communities. Available at www.echo.lu.

——(1991c) *Directive on the Prevention of the Use of the Financial System for the Purposes of Money Laundering*. Council Directive 91/308, *Official Journal of the European Communities*, L166, Brussels, 1991.

——(1991d) *Working Programme of the Commission in the Field of Copyright and Neighbouring Rights: Follow-up to the Green Paper*. COM(90) 584 final, Brussels: Office for Official Publications of the European Communities, 17 January 1991.

——(1992a) 'Council Directive 92/30 of 6 April 1992 on the Supervision of Credit Institutions on a Consolidated Basis', *Official Journal of the European Communities*, L110, Brussels, 1992.

——(1992b) 'Second Council Directive 92/30 of 6 April 1992 on the Supervision of Credit Institutions on a Consolidated Basis', *Official Journal of the European Communities*, L110, Brussels, 1992.

——(1993a) *Council Directive 93/83/EEC of 27 September 1993 on the Coordination of Certain Rules Concerning Copyright and Rights Related to Copyright Applicable to Satellite Broadcasting and Cable Retransmission*, Brussels: Office for Official Publications of the European Communities. Available at www.echo.lu.

——(1993b) *Council Directive 93/98/EEC of 29 October 1993 to Harmonise the Term of Protection of Copyright and Certain Related Rights*, Brussels: Office for Official Publications of the European Communities. Available at www.echo.lu.

——(1993bc) *Proposal for a Council Decision on Inter-Administration Telematic Networks for Statistics Relating to the Trading of Goods Between Member States*. COM(93) 73 final. Brussels: Office for Official Publications of the European Communities. Available at www.echo.lu.

——(1994a) *Proposal for a Council Decision on a Specific Programme of Research, Technological Development and Demonstration in the Areas of Advanced Communications Technologies and Services (1994–1998)*. COM(94) 68 final, Brussels: Office for Official Publications of the European Communities.

——(1994b) *Europe and the Information Society: The Way Forward: An Action Plan*, COM(94)347, Brussels: Office for Official Publications of the European Communities. Available at www.echo.lu.

——(1994c) *Europe and the Global Information Society: Recommendations of the High Level Group on the Information Society to the Corfu European Council*, Brussels: Office for Official Publications of the European Communities, 26 May 1994. Available at www.echo.lu.

——(1994d) *Directorate General XIII, Information Market Observatory, The Internet and the European Information Industry*, IMO Working Paper 94/3, September 1994.

——(1994e) Europe's Way to the Information Society: An Action Plan, Communication from the Commission. COM(94) 347 final, Brussels: Office for Official Publications of the European Communities, 19 July 1994.

——(1995) *Copyrights and Related Rights in the Information Society*, COM(95) 382 final, 19 July 1995, Brussels: Office for Official Publications of the European Communities. Available at www.echo.lu.

——(1996a) *Directive 96/9/EC of the European Parliament and of the Council of 11 March 1996 on the Legal Protection of Databases*, Brussels: Office for Official Publications of the European Communities. Available at www.echo.lu.

——(1996b) *Follow-up to the Green Paper on Copyright and Related Rights in the Information Society*, COM(96) 586 final, Brussels: Office for Official Publications of the European Communities, 20 November 1996.

Commons, John R. (1957) *The Legal Foundations of Capitalism*, Wisconsin: Wisconsin University Press.

Comstock, M.B. (1994) 'GATT and GATS: a public morals attack on money laundering', *Journal of International Law and Business*, vol. 15, Fall 1994, pp. 139–77.

Condliffe, John (1951) *The Commerce of Nations*, London: George Allen & Unwin Ltd.

Cornish, W. R. (1989) *Intellectual Property: Patents, Copyright, Trade Marks and Allied Rights*, 2nd edn, London: Sweet & Maxwell.

Corti, Count (1928) *The Rise of the House of Rothschild* (translated from the German by Brian and Beatrix Lunn), London: Victor Gollancz Ltd.

Cousins, Norman (1961) *In Place of Folly*, New York: Harper.

Cowhey, Peter F. (1990) 'The international telecommunications regime: the political roots of regimes for high technology', *International Organization*, vol. 44, Spring.

Cox, Robert W. (ed.) (1969) *International Organisation: World Politics*, London: Macmillan.

——(1987) *Power, Production and World Order: Social Forces in the Making of History*, New York: Columbia University Press.

Cranston, Ross (1995) 'Bankers' duty of confidentiality: English law', paper presented to the Cambridge International Symposium on Economic Crime, 11 September 1995.

Cremades, B. M. and Plehn, S. L. (1984) 'The next Lex Mercatoria and the harmonization of the laws of international commercial transactions', *Boston University International Law Journal*, p. 317.

Cresswell, Blair, Hill and Wood (1995) *Encyclopaedia of Banking Law*, London: Butterworths.

Croff, Carlo (1982) 'The applicable law in an international commercial arbitration: is it still a conflict of laws problem?', *International Lawyer*, vol. 16, pp. 613–45.

Crook, John R. (1989) 'Applicable law in international arbitration: the Iran–US claims tribunal experience', *American Journal of International Law*, vol. 83, pp. 278–311.

Cutler, Claire (1995) 'Global capitalism and liberal myths: dispute settlement in private international trade relations', *Millennium: Journal of International Studies*, vol. 24, no. 3, pp. 377–97.

Dale, Richard (1992) *International Banking Deregulation: The Great Banking Experiment*, Oxford: Blackwell.

Danjee, Rajan and Boisson de Chazournes, Lawrence (1998) 'Trade Related Aspects of Intellectual Property Rights (TRIPS): objectives, approaches and basic principles of the GATT intellectual property conventions', *Journal of World Trade*, vol. 24, no. 5, 6–15.

Dante (1916) *De Monarchia*, E. Moore (ed.), London: Clarendon Press.

Das, Dilip K. (ed.) (1993) *International Finance: Contemporary Issues*, London: Routledge.

de Hevesy, Paul (1966) *The Unification of the World: Proposals of a Diplomatist*, London: Pergamon Press.

Delbruck, Jost (1993) 'Globalization of law, politics and markets – implications for domestic law: a European perspective', *Indiana Journal of Global Legal Studies*, vol. 1, no.1. Available at www.law.indiana.edu/glsj/vol1/delbruck.html.

De Ly, Filip (1992) *International Business Law and Lex Mercatoria*, London: North-Holland.

Demiray, A. David (1994) 'Intellectual property and the external power of the European Community', *Michigan Journal of International Law*, vol. 16, Fall, pp. 187–237.

Desai (1989) 'India and the Uruguay Round', *Journal of World Trade Law*, vol. 33.

Deutsch, Karl W. (1954) *Political Community and the North Atlantic Area*, New York: Doubleday.

'Digimarc Corp. announces new copyright protection technology: irremovable signatures protect creative property in the digital age', *Business Wire*, 28 June 1995.

Digital Future Coalition (1998) 'Real world problems created by H.R. 2281, as reported to the Judiciary Committee', 3 June 1998. Available at www.ari.net/dfc/issues/wipo/realwrd/ realwrd.html.

Dillon, Thomas J. Jr. (1995) 'The World Trade Organization: a new legal order for world trade?', *Michigan Journal of International Law*, vol. 16, Winter 1995, pp. 349–401.

Dore, Isaak I. (1993) *The UNCITRAL Framework for Arbitration in Contemporary Perspective*, Dordrecht: Graham Thomas, Martinus Nijhoff.

Drake, William J. and Kalypso, Nicolaidis (1992) 'Ideas, interests, and institutionalization: 'Trade in Services and the Uruguay Round', *International Organization*, vol. 46, no. 1, pp. 37–100.

Dreatta, Ugo, Lake, Ralph B. and Nanda, Ved. P. (1992) *Breach and Adaptation of International Contracts: An Introduction to the Lex Mercatoria*, London: Butterworths.

'Drug barons laundered millions through HK banks', *Reuters Report*, 30 October 1995.

Dutton, H. I. (1984) *The Patent System and Inventive Activity During the Industrial Revolution*, Manchester: Manchester University Press.
Economist Intelligence Unit, *EIU Country Forecasts*, London.
EIU (1995) 'Financing foreign operations: Switzerland', *Economics Intelligence Unit*, 1 October 1995.
'EU-US: Commission plans renewal of transatlantic relations', *European Information Service: European Report*, 29 June 1995.
Executive Office of the President (1993a) 'The National Information Infrastructure: agenda for action', Office of the Vice President, Accompanying Report of the National Performance Review, September 1993. Available at gopher.wiretap.spies.
——(1993b) 'Reengineering through information technology, part II', Office of the Vice President, Accompanying Report of the National Performance Review, September 1993. Available: gopher.wiretap.spies.
——(1993c) 'Technology for America's growth: a new direction to build economic strength', Washington, DC: US Government Printing Office.
Falk, Richard (1995) 'Liberalism at the global level: the last of the independent commissions', *Millennium: Journal of International Studies*, vol. 24, no. 3, pp. 563–76.
Featherstone, Mike (ed.) (1991) *Global Culture: Nationalism, Globalisation and the World System*, London: Macmillan.
Federal Coordinating Council for Science, Engineering and Technology, High Performance Computing and Communications (1993) *Toward a National Information Infrastructure*, Washington, DC: Office of Science and Technology Policy.
Felsenfeld, Carl (1986) 'Electronic banking and its effects on interstate branching restrictions – an analytic approach', *Fordham Law Review*, vol. 54, May.
Finkelstein, Lawrence S. (ed.) (1988) *Politics in the United Nations System*, London: Duke University Press.
Finney, R. (1993) 'UK money laundering law after the reports of 1993', *Butterworths Journal of International Banking and Finance Law*, December, pp. 530–7.
Footer, Mary E. (1993) 'GATT and the multilateral regulation of banking services', *International Lawyer*, vol. 27.
Foucault, Michel (1991) 'Governmentality', in Burchell, Graham, Gordon, Colin and Miller, Peter (eds), *The Foucault Effect: Studies in Governmentality*, London: Harvester Wheatsheaf.
'Fraudbusters press for more powers', *The Times*, 6 November 1995.
'Funny money: catching the money launderers', *Law Casebook 1996*, p. 28.
Gaillard, Emmanuel (ed.) (1993) *Transnational Rules in International Commercial Arbitration*, Paris: Institute of International Business Law and Practice, International Chamber of Commerce.
Galkin, William (1995) 'Jumping the gun on Sysop liability', *The Computer Law Report*, no. 13, 6 November 1995. Distributed by Galkin@aol.com.
Gardner, Richard N. (1980) *Sterling-Dollar Diplomacy in Current Perspective:*

The Origins and the Prospects of Our International Economic Order, New York: Columbia University Press.

'GATT: intellectual property: who should own it?', *Inter Press Service*, 23 November 1990. Available at www.wto.org.

Geller, Paul Edward (1995) 'Intellectual property in the global marketplace: impact of TRIPS dispute settlements?', *International Lawyer*, vol. 29.

General Agreement on Tariffs and Trade (1993a) Decision on Financial Services, Final Act Embodying the Results of the Uruguay Round, MTN/FA, 15 December 1993 (UR-93-0246). Available at www.wto.org.

——(1993b) Understanding on Rules and Procedures Governing the Settlement of Disputes, Uruguay Round Final Act, Art.3.1, GATT MTN/FA III, 15 December 1993 (UR-93-0246). Available at www.wto.org.

——(1994) Agreement on Trade-Related Aspects of Intellectual Property Rights, Including Trade in Counterfeit Goods (Annex III) GATT MTN/FAIIAIC (1994). Available at www.wto.org.

——(1996) 'Ruggiero calls for trading system to be kept in line with globalisation process', press release, Press/43, 22 February 1996.

Georgini, Jenevra (1994) 'Through seamless webs and forking paths: safeguarding authors' rights in hypertext', *Brooklyn Law Review*, vol. 60, Fall 1994, pp. 1175–227.

Gibson, L. Todd (1995) 'The Foreign Bank Supervision Enhancement Act of 1991: short run consequences en route to the long term goal', *Case Western Reserve Journal of International Law*, vol. 27, 1995, 119–43.

Giddens, Anthony (1998) *The Consequences of Modernity*, Stanford: Stanford University Press.

Gill, Stephen (1990) *American Hegemony and the Trilateral Commission*, Cambridge: Cambridge University Press.

——(1993) (ed.) *Gramsci, Historical Materialism and International Relations*, Cambridge: Cambridge University Press.

——(1995) 'Globalisation, market civilisation, and disciplinary neoliberalism', *Millennium: Journal of International Studies*, vol. 24, no. 3, pp. 399–423.

——and David Law (1988) *The Global Political Economy: Perspectives, Problems, and Policies*, Hertfordshire: Harvester Wheatsheaf.

——(1989) 'Global hegemony and the structural power of capital', *International Studies Quarterly*, vol. 33, no. 4, pp. 475–99.

Gilpin, Robert (1981) *War and Change in World Politics*, Cambridge: Cambridge University Press.

'Global cooperation crucial in fight against fraud', *The Reuter European Business Report*, 8 November 1995.

Gordon, Colin (1987) 'The soul of the citizen: Max Weber and Michel Foucault on rationality and government', in S. Lash and S. Whimster (eds), *Max Weber, Rationality and Modernity*, London: Allen & Unwin.

Gottlieb, Gideon (1993) *Nation Against State*, New York: Council on Foreign Relations.

Gotts, Ilene Knable and Rutenberg, Alan D. (1995) 'Navigating the global information superhighway: a bumpy road lies ahead', *Harvard Journal of Law and Technology*, vol. 8, Spring.

'Government; central banks, markets, foreign exchange; economic news', *AFP-Extel News*, 13 November 1995.

Gowland, David (1990) *The Regulation of Financial Markets in the 1990s*, Aldershot: Edward Elgar.

Graveson, R. H. (1997) *Comparative Conflict of Laws: Selected Essays*, vol. I, Oxford: North-Holland Publishing.

Groom, A. J. R. (1988) 'The advent of international organisation', in Paul Taylor and A. J. R. Groom (eds), *International Institutions at Work*, London: Pinter Publishers, pp. 3–19.

Groom, A. J. R. and Heraclides, Alexis (1985) 'Integration and disintegration', in Margot Light and A. J. R. Groom (eds) *International Relations: A Handbook of Current Theory*, London: Pinter Publishers.

Grotius, Hugo (1957) *Prolegomena to the Law of War and Peace* (1625), New York: Bobbs-Merill.

Haas, Ernst (1964) *Beyond the Nation State*, Stanford: Stanford University Press.

Halbert, Debora 'Computer technology and legal discourse: the potential for modern communication technology to challenge legal discourses of authorship and property', *Murdoch University Electronic Journal of Law*, vol. 1, no. 2. Available: www.murdoch.edu/elaw/issues/v1n2/halbert.txt.

Halliday, Fred (1993) 'International society as homogeneity: Burke, Marx, Fukuyama', *Millennium: Journal of International Studies*, vol. 21, no. 3, pp. 435–61.

Hanessian, Grant (1989) 'General principles of law in the Iran–US claims tribunal', *Columbia Journal of Transnational Law*, vol. 27, pp. 309–52.

Hardy, Trotter I. (1994) 'The proper legal regime for "Cyberspace"', *University of Pittsburgh Law Review*, vol. 55, Summer, pp. 993–1054.

Harrison, R. J. and Mungall, Stuart (1990) 'Harmonization', in A. J. R. Groom and Paul Taylor (eds), *Frameworks for International Co-operation*, London: Pinter Publishers.

Hart, H. L. A. (1961) *The Concept of Law*, London: Oxford University Press.

Hearing of the House Banking and Financial Services Committee: Organized Crime and Banking (1996) Chaired by Representative Jim Leach, *Federal News Wire*, 28 February 1996.

Helleiner, Eric (1992) 'States and the future of global finance', *Review of International Studies*, vol. 18, no. 1, 1992.

——(1995) 'Explaining the globalisation of financial markets: bringing states back in', *Review of International Political Economy*, vol. 2, no. 2, Spring 1995.

Higgott, Richard (1997) 'De Facto and de jure regionalism: the double discourse of regionalism in the Asia Pacific', *Global Society: Journal of Interdisciplinary International Relations*, vol. 11, no. 2, 1997.

Hirst, Paul and Thompson, Grahame (1996) *Globalisation in Question*, Cambridge: Polity Press.

Hobsbawm, E. J. (1969) *Industry and Empire*, London: Penguin.

Honnold, John (1982) *Uniform Law for International Sales Under the 1980 United Nations Convention*, London: Kluwer.

Horn, Norbert and Schmitthoff, Clive M. (eds) (1982) *The Transnational Law of International Commercial Transactions*, London: Kluwer.

Hughes, Sarah Jane (1992) 'Policing money laundering through funds transfers: a critique of the regulation under the Bank Secrecy Act', *Indiana Law Journal*, vol. 67, Winter 1992.

Hull, Cordell (1948) *The Memoirs of Cordell Hull*, vol. I, London: Hodder & Stoughton.

'Intellectual piracy captures the attention of the President and Congress', *National Journal*, 22 February 1986, pp. 443–5.

'International banking: coping with the ups and downs', *The Economist*, Survey, 27 April 1996.

'International drug-smuggling ring smashed', *Deutsche Presse-Agentur*, 10 November 1995.

International Monetary Fund (1996) 'Much is at stake for G-7 in today's globalised world', *IMF Survey*, July 15 1996.

Jackson, Robert (1994) *Quasi States: Sovereignty, International Relations and the Third World*, Cambridge: Cambridge University Press.

Jaffey, A. J. E. (1974) 'Essential validity of contracts in the English conflict of laws', *International and Commercial Law Quarterly*, vol. 23, pp. 1–29.

James, Alan (1986) *Sovereign Statehood: The Basis of International Society*, London: Allen & Unwin.

Juenger, Friedrich K. (1994) 'The inter-American convention on the law applicable to international contracts: some highlights and comparisons', *American Journal of Comparative Law*, vol. 42, no. 2, pp. 381–93.

Kelsen, Hans (1961) *General Theory of Law and the State* (translated by Anders Wedberg), New York: Russell & Russell.

——(1970) *The Pure Theory of Law* (translated by Max Knight), Berkeley: University of California Press.

Kennedy, Matthew (1995) 'Services join the GATT: an analysis of the General Agreement on Trade in Services', *International Trade Law and Regulation*, vol. 1, no. 2, March/April, pp. 11–20.

Kenwood, A. G. and Lougheed, A. L. (1983) *The Growth of the International Economy, 1820–1980: An Introductory Text*, London: George Allen & Unwin.

Keohane, Robert (ed.) (1989) *International Institutions and State Power*, Boulder: Westview.

——and Hoffman, Stanley (1991) *The New European Community: Decision Making and Institutional Change*, Colorado: Westview.

——and Nye, Joseph (1977) *Power and Interdependence: World Politics in Transition*, Boston: Little, Brown.

Khan, Rahmatullah (1990) *The Iran-United States Claims Tribunal: Controversies, Cases and Contribution*, Dordrecht, Boston, London: Martinus Nijhoff.

Kindelberger, Charles (1969) *American Business Abroad*, New Haven: Yale University Press.

——(1973) *The World in Depression, 1929–1939*, London: Allen Lane & Penguin Press.

——(1984) *A Financial History of Western Europe*, London: Allen and Unwin.

——(1995) 'The rise of free trade in Europe', in Jeffrey Frieden and David A. Lake (eds) *International Political Economy: Perspectives on Power and Wealth*, London: Routledge.

Krasner, Stephen D. (ed.) (1983) *International Regimes*, Ithaca, New York: Cornell University Press.

——(1994) 'International political economy: abiding discord', *Review of International Political Economy*, vol. 1, no. 1, Spring, 13–20.

Kratchowil, Friedrich V. (1989) *Rules, Norms, and Decisions: On the Conditions of Practical and Legal Reasoning in International Relations and Domestic Affairs*, Cambridge: Cambridge University Press.

Laiffer, Daniel M. (1992) 'Putting the super back in the supervision of international banking, post-BCCI', *Fordham Law Review*, vol. 60, 1992.

Lando, Ole (1985) 'The Lex Mercatoria in international commercial arbitration', *International and Comparative Law Quarterly*, vol. 34, pp. 747–68.

Leaffer, Marchall A. (1991) 'Protecting United States intellectual property abroad: toward a new multilateralism', *Iowa Law Review*, vol. 76, January 1991.

Leahy, Senator Patrick J. (1992) 'New laws for new technologies: current issues facing the subcommittee on technology and the law', *Harvard Journal of Law and Technology*, vol. 5, no. 1, Spring, pp. 1–23.

Lees, Francis A. (1974) *International Banking and Finance*, Basingstoke: Macmillan.

Lemley, Mark A. (1995) 'Intellectual property and shrinkwrap licenses', *Southern California Law Review*, vol. 68, July, pp. 1239–94.

Lew, J. (ed.) (1987) *Contemporary Problems in International Arbitration*, Dordrecht: Martinus Nijhoff.

Linn, R. J., 'Copyright and information services in the context of the national research and education network'. Available: gopher.wiretap.spies.com.

Lipschutz, Ronnie D. (1992) 'Reconstructing world politics: the emergence of global civil society', *Millennium: Journal of International Studies*, vol. 1, no. 3, pp. 389–420.

Loundy, David J. 'E-law 2.0: computer information systems law and the system operator liability revisited', *Murdoch University Electronic Journal of Law*, vol. 1, no. 3. Available at www.murdoch.edu.au/elaw/issues/v1n3/loundy.txt.

MacDonald, Scott B. (1993) 'Money laundering and the Asia/Pacific region', *Butterworths Journal of International Banking and Finance Law*, June, pp. 271–4.

Mangone, Gerard, J. (1951) *The Idea and Practice of World Government*, New York: Columbia University Press.

Maniruzzaman, A. F. M. (1990) 'International arbitrator and mandatory public law rules in the context of state contracts: an overview', *Journal of International Arbitration*, vol. 7, no. 3, pp. 53–64.

——(1991) 'Conflict of laws issues in international arbitration: practice and trends', *Arbitration International*, vol. 9, no. 4, pp. 371–403.

Mann, F. A. (1984) 'England rejects "delocalised" contracts and arbitration', *International Commercial Law Quarterly*, vol. 33, pp. 172–98.

——(1987) 'The proper law in the conflict of laws', *International and Comparative Law Quarterly*, vol. 36, 437–53.

Marcel, Mario and Palma, Gabriel (1987) *The Debt Crisis: The Third World and British Banks*, Fabian Research Series no. 350, London: Fabian Society.

Marshall, Don D. (1996a) 'Understanding late-twentieth-century capitalism: reassessing the globalisation theme', *Government and Opposition*, vol. 31, no. 2.

——(1996b) 'Tax havens in the commonwealth Caribbean: a merchant capital-global finance connection', *Global Society: Journal of Interdisciplinary International Relations*, vol. 10, no. 3.

Marx, Karl and Engels, Friedrich (1972) 'The Communist Manifesto', in Robert C. Tucker (ed.) *The Marx-Engels Reader*, New York: W. W. Norton.

Mascus, Keith E. 'Normative concerns in the international protection of intellectual property rights', *World Economy*, vol. 13, pp. 387–8.

Mayall, James (1978) 'International society and international theory', in Michael Donelan (ed.) *The Reason of States*, London: Allen & Unwin.

McCormack, Gerard (1995) 'Money laundering and banking secrecy', *The Company Lawyer*, vol. 16, no. 1, pp. 6–10.

McGrew, Anthony (1998) 'The globalisation debate: putting the advanced capitalist state in its place', *Global Society: Journal of Interdisciplinary International Relations*, vol. 13, no. 3, September.

McInerney III, Thomas F. (1994) 'Towards the next phase in international banking regulation', *DePaul Business Law Journal*, vol. 7, Fall 1994.

McNair, Lord (1957) 'The general principles of law recognised by civilised nations', *British Yearbook of International Law*, vol. 33, pp. 1–19.

Megrah, Maurice and Ryder, F. R. (1972) *Paget's Law of Banking*, 8th edn, London: Butterworths, p. 167.

Meyer, Charles J. (1995) 'National and international copyright liability for electronic system operators', *Indiana Journal of Global Legal Issues*, vol. 2, no. 2. Available: www.law.indiana.edu/glsj/vol2/no2/meyer.html.

Millman, Gregory J. (1995) *Around the World on a Trillion Dollars a Day: How Rebel Currency Traders Destroy Banks and Defy Governments*, London: Bantam Press.

Millspaugh, Peter E. (1992) 'Global securities trading: the question of a watchdog', *George Washington Journal of International Law and Economics*, vol. 26, 355–77.

Mitrany, David (1966) *A Working Peace System*, Chicago: Quadrangle Books.

'Money laundering manual will surface in December', *The Regulatory Compliance Watch* (American Banker-Bond Buyer), 13 November 1995, vol. 5, no. 43, p. 12.

Morgenthau, Hans (1985) *Politics Among Nations: The Struggle for Power and Peace*, 6th edn, New York: Alfred Knopf.

Morris, J. H. C. (1984) *The Conflict of Laws*, 3rd edn, London: Stevens & Sons.

Morris, J. H. C. and North, P.M. (1984) *Cases and Materials on Private International Law*, London: Butterworths.

Mortman, Scott E. (1992) 'Putting starch in European efforts to combat money laundering', *Fordham Law Review*, vol. 60, 429–66.

Mouri, Allahyar (1994) *The International Law of Expropriation as Reflected in the Work of the Iran–U.S. Claims Tribunal*, Dordrecht: Martinus Nijhoff Publishers.

Murphy, Craig N. (1994) *International Organization and Industrial Change Since 1850*, Cambridge: Polity Press.

Nagel, E. (1979) *The Structure of Science: Problems in the Logic of Scientific Explanation*, London: Routledge & Kegan Paul.

Nash, Marian (1995) 'US–UK treaty on mutual legal assistance in criminal matters', *The American Journal of International Law*, July 1995, vol. 89, pp. 589–96.

National Information Infrastructure Task Force, Working Group on Intellectual Property Rights (1994) *Intellectual Property and the National Information Infrastructure: A Preliminary Draft of the Report of the Working Group on Intellectual Property Rights*, Washington, DC: Government Printing Office.

'New tricks to learn: survey of international banking', *The Economist*, 10 April 1993.

'New US foreign policy concept evolving', *Reuters Newswire*, 23 October 1995.

Nimmer, David (1995) 'The end of copyright', *Vanderbilt Law Review*, vol. 48, 1385–1419.

North, Peter (1990) *Private International Law Problems in Common Law Jurisdictions*, London: Martinus Nijhoff.

North, Peter and Fawcett, J. J. (1987) *Cheshire & North's Private International Law*, 11th edn, London: Butterworths.

Norton, Joseph Jude (1989) 'The work of the Basle Supervisors Committee on bank capital adequacy and the July 1988 Report on "International Convergence of Capital Measurements and Capital Standards"', *International Lawyer*, vol. 23, 1989, 245–63.

Norton, Joseph Jude, Cheng, Chia-Jui and Fletcher (eds) (1994) *International Banking Regulation and Supervision: Change and Transformation in the 1990s*, Dordrecht: Martinus Nijhoff.

O'Brien, Richard (1992) *Global Financial Deregulation: The End of Geography*, London: Pinter.

Ohmae, Kenichi (1990) *The Borderless World: Power and Strategy in the Interlinked Economy*, London: Collins.

——(1995) *The End of the Nation-State*, London: HarperCollins.

Organisation for Economic Cooperation and Development, Committee for Information, Computer and Communications Policy (1997) 'Global information infrastructure – global information society (GII-GIS): policy requirements', OECD/GD(97)139, Paris, 22 August 1997. Available: www.oecd.org/dsti/iccp/gii-gis.html.

Padoa-Schioppa, Tommaso and Saccomanni, Fabrizio (1994) 'Managing a market-led global financial system', in Peter B. Kenen (ed.) *Managing the World Economy: Fifty Years After Bretton Woods*, Washington, DC: Institute for International Economics.

Paulsson, Jan (1983) 'Delocalisation of international commercial arbitration: when and why it matters', *International Commercial Law Quarterly*, vol. 32, pp. 53–61.

Pearse, Richard (1994) 'Library open-distribution systems and copyright infringement in Canada and the United States', *Law Library Journal*, vol. 86, Summer, pp. 399–443.

Penrose, Edith Tilton (1951) *The Economics of the International Patent System*, Baltimore: Johns Hopkins Press.

Perritt, Henry H. Jr. (1994) 'President Clinton's National Information Infrastructure Initiative: community regained?', *IIT Chicago-Kent Law Review*, vol. 69, pp. 991–1013.

Peters, Rebecca G. (1990) 'Money laundering and its current status in Switzerland: new disincentives for financial tourism', *Journal of International Law and Business*, vol. 11, Spring pp. 104–39.

Pierson, Christopher (1998) 'Globalisation and the changing governance of welfare states: superannuation reform in Australia', *Global Society: Journal of Interdisciplinary International Relations*, vol. 12, no. 2, January, pp. 31–49.

Pisciotta, Aileen A. and Barker, James H. (1992) 'Current issues in electronic data interchange: telecommunications regulatory implications for international EDI transactions', *Journal of International Law and Business*, vol. 13, Spring/Summer, 71–116.

Polanyi, Karl (1986) *The Great Transformation*, London: Beacon Press.

Popper, Karl (1968) *The Logic of Scientific Discovery*, London: RK Press.

——(1972) *The Poverty of Historicism*, London: Routledge and Kegan Paul.

Post, Gaines (1964) *Studies in Medieval Legal Thought*, Princeton: Princeton University Press.

Puchala, Donald J. (1981) 'Integration theory and the study of international relations', in Richard L. Merritt and Bruce M. Russett (eds), *From National Development to Global Community: Essays in Honor of Karl W. Deutsch*, London: George Allen and Unwin.

Pufendorf, Samuel (1717) *The Law of Nature and of Nations* (1672), London: R. Sare.

Razzano, F.C. (1994) 'American money laundering statutes: the case for a worldwide system of banking compliance programs', *Detroit College of Law Journal of International Law and Practice*, vol. 3, pp. 277–307.

'Ready for prime time?', *Time International*, 26 December 1994–2 January 1995.

Redfern, Alan and Hunter, Martin (1991) *International Commercial Arbitration*, 2nd edn, London: Sweet and Maxwell.

Reeday, T. G. (1980) *The Law Relating to Banking*, 4th edn., London: Butterworths.

Rees, Hans (1970 [1988]) *Kant's Political Writings*, Cambridge: Cambridge University Press.

Reichman, J. H. (1995a) 'Charting the collapse of the patent-copyright dichotomy: premises for a restructured international intellectual property system', *Cardozo Arts and Entertainment Law Journal*, vol. 13, no. 2. Available at www.yu1.yu.edu/cs1/journals/aelj/articles/13-2/reichman.html.

——(1995b) 'Universal minimum standards of intellectual property protection under the TRIPS component of the WTO Agreement', *International Lawyer*, vol. 29.

Reuter, Paul (1958) *International Institutions*, London: George Allen and Unwin.

Rider, Barry (1993) 'The financial world at risk: the dangers of organized crime, money laundering and corruption', *Managerial Auditing Journal*, vol. 8, no. 7, 3–14.

——(1995) 'Taking money launderers to the cleaners'. Unpublished, 1 April 1995.

——(1997) 'Editorial', *Journal of Money Laundering Control*, vol. 1, no. 1, p. 4.

Robertson, Ronald (1992) *Globalisation: Social Theory and Global Change*, London: Sage.

Robinson, Davis R. (1983) 'Recent developments in the Iran–United States claims tribunal', *International Lawyer*, vol. 17, pp. 661–7.

Rodrik; Dani (1997) *Has Globalization Gone Too Far?*, Washington, DC: Institute for International Economics.

Rosenau, James (1995) 'Governance in the twenty-first century', *Global Governance: Review of Multilateral and International Organization*, vol. 1, no. 1, Winter, 13–43.

Rosenberg, Justin (1994) *Empire of Civil Society: A Critique of the Realist Theory of International Relations*, London: Verso.

Rosenbloum, Robert A. (1995) 'The rental rights directive: a step in the right and wrong directions', *Loyola of Los Angeles Entertainment Law Journal*, vol. 15, Summer, pp. 547–74.

Ruggie, John Gerrard (1989) 'International structure and international transformation: space, time and method', in Ernst-Otto Czempiel and James Rosenau (eds) *Global Changes and Theoretical Challenges: Approaches to World Politics for the 1990s*, New York: Lexington Books.

——(1993) 'Territoriality and beyond: problematizing modernity in international relations', *International Organization*, vol. 47, no. 1, Winter, pp. 139–74.

Ruigrok, Winfried (1991) 'Paradigms crisis in international trade theory', *Journal of World Trade*, vol. 25, no. 1.

Rusch, J. J. (1988) 'Hue and cry in the counting-house: some observations on the Bank Secrecy Act', *Catholic University Law Review*, vol. 37, Winter, pp. 465–88.

Russell-Smith, H. F. (1914) *Harrington and His Oceana: A Study of a 17th Century Utopia and its Influence in America*, Cambridge: Cambridge University Press.

Rutledge, G. Philip 'Bank secrecy laws: an American perspective', ms. Unpublished, n.d.

Sabine, George H. (1964) *A History of Political Theory*, 3rd edn, London: Holt, Rinehart and Winston.

Schmitthoff, Clive M. (1990) *Schmitthoff's Export Trade: The Law and Practice of International Trade*, 9th edn, London: Stevens & Sons.

Schwartz, Herman (1994) *States Versus Markets: History, Geography, and the Development of the International Political Economy*, New York: St. Martin's Press.

'Secure electronic VISA purchases begin'. Available: www.visa.com/gci-bin/vėe/vw/news/PRelco042997.htm.

Shapiro, Martin (1993) 'The globalisation of law', *Indiana Journal of Global Legal Studies*, vol. 1, no. 1. Available at www.law.indiana.edu/glsj/vol1/shapiro.html.

Shaw, M. N. (1986) *International Law*, 2nd edn, Cambridge: Grotius Publications Limited.

Sherer, F. M. (1980) *Industrial Market Structure and Economic Performance*, 2nd edn, Chicago: Rand McNally.

Shuman, Frederick (1952) *The Commonwealth of Man*, New York: Alfred Knopf.

Simai, Mihaly (1994) *The Future of Global Governance: Managing Risk and Change in the International System*, Washington, DC: US Institute of Peace.

Singh, Kanwar M. (1991) 'Nowhere to hide: judicial assistance in piercing the veil of Swiss banking secrecy', *Boston University Law Review*, vol. 71, November, pp. 847–61.

Smedresman, Peter S. and Lowenfeld, Andreas F. (1989) 'Eurodollars, multinational banks, and national laws', *New York University Law Review*, vol. 64.

Smith, Adam (1937) *An Inquiry into the Nature and Causes of the Wealth of Nations*, New York: Modern Library.

Sonorajah (1986) *The Pursuit of Nationalised Property*, Dordrecht: Martinus Nijhoff.

Spero, Joan (1985) *The Politics of International Economic Relations*, 3rd edn, New York: St. Martin's Press.

Strange, Susan (1986) *Casino Capitalism*, London: Blackwell.

——(1988) *States and Markets: An Introduction to International Political Economy*, London: Pinter.

Strange, S. and Stopford, John (1991) *Rival States, Rival Firms: Competition for World Market Shares*, Cambridge: Cambridge University Press.

——(1994) 'Wake up, Krasner! The world *has* changed', *Review of International Political Economy*, vol. 1, no. 2, 1994.

——(1996) *Retreat of the State*, Cambridge: Cambridge University Press.

Streit, Clarence K. (1939) *Union Now: Proposal for a Federal Union of the Democracies of the North Atlantic*, London: Jonathan Cape.

Stubbs, Richard and Underhill, Geoffrey (eds) (1994) *Political Economy and the Changing Global Order*, London: Macmillan.

Sumner Maine, Henry (1874) *Ancient Law: Its Connection with the Early History of Society and its Relation to Modern Times*, 5th edn, London: John Murray.

Suy, Erik (1981) 'Settling US claims against Iran through arbitration', *American Journal of International and Comparative Law*, vol. 29, pp. 523–47.

'Swiss experts say Eastern crime money a threat', *The Reuters European Business Report*, 24 October 1995.

Taylor, Russell (1993) *Going for Broke: How Banking Mismanagement in the Eighties Lost £ Thousands of Billions*, London: Simon & Schuster.

Taylor, S. (1995) 'Knowing too much and saying too little, the risks to banks', paper presented to the Cambridge International Symposium on Economic Crime, 11 September 1995.

Toynbee, Arnold J. (1915) *Nationality and the War*, London.

Trakman, B. (1981) 'The Evolution of the law merchant: our commercial heritage', *Journal of Maritime Law of Commerce*, vol. 153, pp. 179–96.

'Transnational crime: a new security threat?', *Strategic Survey, 1994/95*, London: Institute for Strategic Studies, pp. 25–33.

Truell, Peter and Gurwin, Gary (1992) *BCCI: The Inside Story of the World's Most Corrupt Financial Empire*, London: Bloomsbury Publishing.

Underhill, Geoffrey (1991) 'Markets beyond politics? The state and the internationalisation of financial markets', *European Journal of Political Research*, vol. 19, no. 2–3.

United Nations (1989) Convention Against Illicit Traffic in Narcotic Drugs and Psychotropic Substances, UN Doc.E/CONF.82/15 (1988), *International Legal Materials*, vol. 28, p. 493.

——(1955) General Assembly Resolution 2205(XXI), 17 December 1955. Reprinted in *UNCITRAL Yearbook, 1968–1970*, vol. 1, Part 1.

United Nations Commission on International Trade Law (1993) 'Sixth Committee takes up UNCITRAL Report', Forty-eight General Assembly, GA\L\2774, Sixth Committee, 4 October 1993.

——(1994a) 'United Nations Commission on international trade law to hold twenty-seventh session in New York, 31 May–17 June', background release, L\TR\225, 31 May 1994.

——(1994b) 'United Nations Commission on international trade law concludes twenty-seventh session, 31 May–17 June; adopts model law incorporating services, procurement procedures and guide to its enactment', L\TR\226, 17 June 1994.

United States Congress (1930) Trade Act, 1930, 19 USC, S.1526. Washington, DC: Government Printing Office.

——(1978) International Banking Act of 1978, 12 USC, 3101-3108. Washington, DC: Government Printing Office.

——(1983) Caribbean Basin Economy Recovery Act of 1983, 26 USCA, S.6015 (repealed), Washington, DC: Government Printing Office.

——(1984) Trade and Tariff Act of 1984, 19 USCA, S.1654. Washington, DC: Government Printing Office.

——(1986) *Intellectual Property Rights in an Age of Electronic Information*, Office of Technology Assessment, Washington, DC: Government Printing Office.

——(1988) Omnibus Trade and Competitiveness Act of 1988, Pub. L. no. 100–418, 102 Stat. 1107, Washington, DC: Government Printing Office.

——(1991a) Foreign Bank Supervision Enhancement Act of 1991, FBSEA,

Pub. L. no. 101–242, sections 201–215, 105 Stat. 2236–305, Washington, DC: Government Printing Office.
——(1991b) High Performance Computing Act of 1991 (P.L 102–94), Washington, DC: Government Printing Office.
——(1992a) Office of Management and Budget, Information Resources Management Plan of the Federal Government, Washington, DC: Government Printing Office.
——(1992b) North American Free Trade Agreement, 330-817/70635, Washington, DC: Government Printing Office.
——(1993a) High Performance Computing and High Speed Networking Applications Act of 1993, USC H.R. 1757, Washington, DC: Government Printing Office.
——(1993b) Office of Science and Technology Policy, High Performance Computing and Communications: Toward a National Information Infrastructure, Accompanying Report of the National Performance Review to the Federal coordinating Council for Science, Engineering and Technology, Washington, DC: Government Printing Office.
——(1993c) Communications Competitiveness and Infrastructure Modernization Act of 1993, H.R. 1504, Washington, DC: Government Printing Office.
——(1993d) Telecommunications Infrastructure Act of 1993, S.1086, Washington, DC: Government Printing Office.
——(1995) NII Copyright Protection Act of 1995 (H.R.2441 and S.1284), Washington, DC: Government Printing Office. Available at www.thomas.loc.gov.
——(1997a) Digital Era Copyright Enhancement Act, H.R. 3048, 105th.C., 13 November 1997, Washington, DC: Government Printing Office. Available: www.thomas.loc.gov.
——(1997b) WIPO Copyright Treaties Implementation Act, H.R.2281,105th. C., 29 July 1997. Available at www.thomas.loc.gov.
——(1998a) Digital Millennium Copyright Act of 1998, S.2037, 12 May 1998, Washington, DC: Government Printing Office. Available at www.thomas.loc.gov.
——(1998b) On-Line Copyright Liability Limitation Act, H.R.2180,105th.C., 17 July 1997; and H.R.3209, 105th.C., 12 February 1998, Washington, DC: Government Printing Office. Available at www.thomas.loc.gov.
——(1998c) No Electronic Theft (NET) Act, H.R.2265, 105th.C. Erolled Bill sent to the President. Available at www.thomas.loc.gov.
United States Department of Commerce (1995) Information Infrastructure Task Force, Intellectual Property and the National Information Infrastructure: The Report of the Working Group in Intellectual Property Rights, Department of Commerce, Washington, DC: Government Printing Office.
United States International Trade Commission (1993) *Industry and Trade Summary: Commercial Banking*, USITC Publication 2638 (SV-4), Washington, DC, June 1993.

——(1988) *Foreign Protection of Intellectual Property Rights and the Effects on US Industry and Trade*, USITC Publication No. 2065, Washington, DC.

'UN must declare a war on drugs and crime, says Clinton', *The Times*, 23 October 1995.

'USA apparently pushing Thailand to adopt money-laundering law', *BBC Summary of World Broadcasts*, 26 October 1995.

'US intellectual property proposal is unveiled before GATT negotiating group', *International Trade Reporter*, vol. 4, no. 43, 4 November 1987.

Van Hof, Jacomijn J. (1991) *Commentary on the UNCITRAL Arbitration Rules: The Application by the Iran–U.S. Claims Tribunal*, Deventer: Kluwer.

Vignes, Daniel (1990) 'The harmonisation of the national legislation of the EEC', *European Law Review*, pp. 358–74.

Virilio, Paul (1993) *Pure War*, New York: Semiotext(e).

Wagman, Sarah A. (1994) 'Laws separating commercial banking and securities activities as an impediment to free trade in financial services: a comparative study of competitiveness in the international market for financial services', *Michigan Journal of International Law*, vol. 15, 999–1035.

Wagner, Michael J. and Allison, Matthew G. (1997) 'Internet law', *The National Law Journal*, 7 July, p. BO5. Available at www.ljx.com/internet/0707juris.html.

Walker, Gordon R. and Fox, Mark A. (1996) 'Globalisation: an analytical framework', *Indiana Journal of Global Legal Studies*, vol. 3, no. 2. Available: www.law.indiana. edu/glsj/vol3/no2/walker/html.

Walker, R. B. J. (1993) *Inside/Outside: International Relations as Political Theory*, Cambridge: Cambridge University Press.

Walker, William N. (1994) 'Private initiative to thwart the trade in counterfeit goods', *World Economy*, vol. 29, no. 4.

Wallerstein, Immanuel (1974) *The Modern World-System: Capitalist Agriculture and the Origins of the European World-Economy in the Sixteenth Century*, New York and London, Academic Press.

Walter, Andrew (1993) *World Power and World Money: The Role of Hegemony and International Monetary Order*, London: Harvester Wheatsheaf.

Waltz, Kenneth (1979) *Theory of International Politics*, London: Addison-Wesley.

Waters, Malcolm (1995) *Globalisation*, London: Routledge.

Weaver, Ole (1995) 'Securitization and desecuritization', in Ronnie D. Lipschutz (ed.) *On Security*, New York: Columbia University Press, pp. 46–86.

——, Barry Buzan, Morten Kelstrup and Pierre Lemaitre (1993) *Identity, Migration and the New Security Agenda in Europe*, London: Pinter.

Weber, Cynthia (1995) *Simulating Sovereignty: Intervention, the State and Symbolic Exchange*, Cambridge: Cambridge University Press.

Weiss, Linda (1998) *The Myth of the Powerless State: Governing the Economy in a Global Era*, Cambridge: Polity Press.

'Welcome to cyberspace', *Time International*, Spring 1995, p. 7.

Wiegand, Wolfgang (1991) 'The reception of American law in Europe', *American Journal of International Law*, vol. 39.

Wiener, Jarrod (1995) *Making Rules in the Uruguay Round of the GATT: A Study of International Leadership*, Aldershot: Dartmouth.

——(1996) 'Editor's note', *Global Society: Journal of Interdisciplinary International Relations*, vol. 1, no. 1, pp. 7–10.

——(1997) 'Money laundering: transnational criminals, globalisation, and the forces of "redomestication"', *Journal of Money Laundering Control*, vol. 1, no. 1, May, pp. 54–66.

Wight, Martin (1977) *Systems of States*, London: Leicester University Press.

Williams, Andrew J. (forthcoming) *Failed Imagination: New World Orders of the Twentieth Century in Historical Perspective*, Manchester: Manchester University Press.

Williams, Patrick Ross (1986) 'The EEC Convention on the law applicable to contractual obligations', *International and Comparative Law Quarterly*, vol. 35, pp. 1–31.

Windecker, George H. (1993) 'The Eurodollar deposit market: strategies for regulation', *The American University Journal of International Law and Policy*, vol. 9, Fall 1993.

Winter, Harvey J. (1987) 'The role of the United States Government in improving intellectual property protection', *Journal of Law and Technology*, vol. 2, Fall 1987.

'Wiring the world', *Time International*, 17 July 1995.

World Intellectual Property Organization (1986) Berne Convention for the Protection of Literary and Artistic Works, 9 September 1886. Revised by the Paris Convention 24 July 1971. Available at www.wipo.org.

——(1996) WIPO Copyright Treaty, Adopted by the Diplomatic Conference on Certain Copyright and Neighbouring Rights Questions, CRNC/DC/94, Geneva, 23 December 1996.

Wood, Philip (1986) *Law and Practice of International Finance*, London: Sweet & Maxwell.

Yi Wang (1996) 'Most-favoured nation treatment under the General Agreement on Trade in Services – and its application in financial services', *Journal of World Trade*, vol. 30, no. 1, pp. 92–124.

Zagaris, Bruce and MacDonald, Scott B. (1992) 'Money laundering, financial fraud, and technology: the perils of an instantaneous economy', *George Washington Journal of International Law and Economics*, vol. 26, 62–107.

Zamora, Stephen (1994) 'Regulating the global banking network – what role (if any) for the IMF?', *Fordham Law Review*, vol. 62, 1953–73.

——(1995) 'Nafta and the harmonization of domestic legal systems: the side effects of free trade', *Arizona Journal of International and Comparative Law*, vol. 12, no. 1, 401–27.

Zoller, Elizabeth (1995) 'Institutional aspects of international governance', *Indiana Journal of Global Legal Studies*, vol. 3, no. 1. Available: www.law.indiana.edu/glsj/vol3/no1/zoller.html.

INDEX

Ad-Hoc Alliance for a Digital Future 123
Agreement on Measures to Discourage the Importation of Counterfeit Goods 147
Agreement on Trade-Related Aspects of Services *see* General Agreement on Trade in Services
Alford, Duncan 69, 71, 76
Alighieri, Dante 21
Aman, Alfred C. Jr. 29
American Bankers Association 95
American Library Association 123
America Online 113
Amin Rasheed Shipping Copn v. Kuwait Insurance Co. 159
Ancel, Jean-Pierre 181
Annunzio-Wiley Anti-Money Laundering Act of 1992 14, 89
Anti-Drug Abuse Act of 1990 14, 89
Antigua, as off-shore financial centre 64
Asian-African Legal Consultative Committee (AALCC) 175
Assunzione, The 156
Atkin, Lord 153, 156
AT&T 101
Austria, and bank secrecy 144
Austrian Supreme Court 182
Avanessian, Aida 176

Bahamas, as off-shore financial centre 64
Banco Ambrosiano 51, 69
Banco de Occidente 144
Bank Act of 1833 (UK) 57
Bankers' Books Evidence Act of 1879 (UK) 92
Bankers Trust 46
Bankes, L J 91
Bankhaus Herstatt 49, 68
Bank of Credit and Commerce International (BCCI) 2, 51, 71, 73–4, 82, 141
  and money-laundering 87
Bank of England 57
Bank of International Settlements (BIS) 49
Bank Secrecy Act of 1970 89
Barbados, as off-shore financial centre 64
Barber, Benjamin R. 188
Barings Bank 44
Basle Committee on Banking Regulation and Supervisory Practices 11, 41, 67, 68–75, 82, 86, 143,
  Basle Concordat (1975) 50, 68–9, 139
  Capital Adequacy Accord (1988) 51, 71–2
  'Know Your Customer' rule 14, 86, 88, 112, 143
  Minimum Standards for the Supervision of International Banking Groups and their Cross-Border Establishments (1992) 12, 41, 51, 73–75, 135–137, 140–141, 185
  Revised Concordat (1983) 50, 69–71
Bellet, Judge 176
Bentham, Jeremy 106
Berman, Harold J, and Colin Kaufman 192
Bermuda, as off-shore financial centre 64
Berne Convention for the Protection of Literary and Artistic Works 107, 115–117
  'fair-use' doctrine 122–123
Boissevain v. Weil 155
Bolivia, and Debt Crisis 48
Bonython v. The Commonwealth of Australia 157
Born, Karl Erich 54
Boutros-Ghali, Boutros 13
Brazil
  Debt Crisis 48
  intellectual property 148
Bremen Cotton Bourse 165
Bretton Woods 43, 54, 66–7, 139, 184
British Bankers Association Guidance Notes for Banks and Building Societies 96

Brown, Chris 8, 23
Burk, Dan L. 132

Cali drug cartel 87
California Bankers Association v. Schultz 93
Canadian Arbitration Law 182
Canadian Imperial Bank of Commerce (CIBC) 50
Carbonneau, Thomas E. 177
Carr, E. H. 138
Carta Mercatoria 162, 193
Cayman Islands
  and BCCI 73, 141
  and bank secrecy 144
  as off-shore financial centre 64
Cerny, Phil 42
Chubby, Inc. v. Compuserve, Inc. 113
Cicero 193
Citibank 2
  and Debt Crisis 48, 50
Citicorp 47
  and Debt Crisis 49
civil society actors 18, 32, 38, 122, 184–185
Clark, Grenville, and Louis B. Sohn 22
Clearing House Automated Payments System (CHAPS) 4
Clearing House Interbank Payments System (CHIPS) 5, 46
Clinton, William Jefferson 13
CMI International, Inc. 176
Cohn, E. J. 156, 159
Colombia 144, 145
Commons, John R. 191
Companies Act 1948 (UK) 92
Comptroller of the Currency (US) 45
Compuserve 113
Condliffe, J. B. 191–2
conflict of Laws 152–61
  objective method 157–9
  subjective method 156–157
Consolato del Mare 161
Copyright Act 1976 (US) 107
Copyright and Related Rights in the Information Society 1995 (EU) 129
Copyright Clearance Center (CCC) 120
Copyright Designs and Patents Act 1988 (UK) 107, 117
Corrigan, Gerald 49, 136, 140
Costa Rica
  and Debt Crisis 48
Council Directive on Prevention of the Use of the Financial System for the Purposes of Money Laundering 14, 90
Court of Piepowder 162
Courts of Common Pleas in England 162
Cousins, Norman 21
Cox, Robert 27
Criminal Justice Act 1993 (UK) 14, 90, 93, 142
Croff, Carlo 180–1
Crook, John R. 177
Cuba
  and Debt Crisis 48
Currency and Foreign Transaction Reporting Act (CFTA) 89
Cutler, Claire 28

Dale, Richard 63, 65, 72
Debt Crisis 48, 63
de Hevesy, Paul 23
Delors, Jacques 14
De Ly, Filip 160, 171, 178
denationalization 30
  of money 45
Denning, L J 156–7
deregulation 28, 34
derivatives 43–5
Deutsch, Karl 22
Dicey 153, 156–7, 159
Digimark 119
Digital Era Copyright Enhancement Act 1997 (US) 124–5
Digital signatures 16
Diplock, L. J. 92
Directive on the Supervision of Credit Institutions on a Consolidated Basis 1992 (EU) 42, 78–9
disciplinary neoliberalism 19
domestic analogy 22
domestication 12, 34
Donaldson, J 92
Drexel Bank 49, 50
Drug Trafficking Act 1994 (UK) 90, 92
Drug Trafficking Offences Act 1986 (UK) 90

East Asia financial crisis 2
EBSCO Masterfile 120
Eckman v. Midland Bank Ltd. 92
Economist Roubdtable 45
Ecuador 144
electronic fund transfer (EFT) 45
  and money laundering 85
encryption 16

Engels, Friedrich 194
English Court of Appeal 182
'Esprit' 101
eurocurrency 46
euromarket 46–7
  rise of 61–64
European Convention on International Commercial Arbitration 178
European Information Society (EIS) 15, 101
European Union's Directive on the Supervision of Credit Institutions on a Consolidated Basis 11, 138
Europe and the Information Society (Bangemann Report, 1994) 129
Europe's Way to the Information Society: An Action Plan 1994 129
Evans, Justice 46

Federal Bureau of Investigation (FBI) 88
Federal Communications Commission (FCC) 101
Federal Deposit Insurance Company (FDIC) 58
Federal Reserve Board 58, 62, 76–7, 138
  and BCCI 73
Federal Reserve Act of 1937 (US) 62
FedWire 5, 46
Ferussi and Bardi 53
Financial Institutions Reform, Recovery, and Enforcement Act 1989 (US) 93
Finney, R. 97
First World War 24, 55
Follow-up to the Green Paper on Copyright and Related Rights in the Information Society 1996 (EU) 129
Footer, Mary 64
Foreign Bank Supervision Enhancement Act 1992 (FBSEA, US) 11, 41, 76, 135, 138
Foreign Credit Restraint Program 1965 (US) 61
Foreign Investment Program 1965 (US) 61
Foucault, Michel 32, 188
Frank Music Corp v. Compuserve 111
French Arbitration Decree 1981 181
French Civil Code 181
Fukuyama, Francis 18
functionalism 27–28

G7 88, 104
  and Financial Action Task Force on Money Laundering (FAFT) 88, 143
General Agreement on Tariffs and Trade (GATT) 59, 139–40
  Decision on Financial Services 137
  Tokyo round 147
  Uruguay round 136
General Agreement on Trade in Services (GATS) 75, 136–7, 147
Generalised System of Preferences (GSP) 147
Germany 5
Gibson, Todd 135
Gill, Stephen 19
Glass-Steagall Banking Act 1934 (US) 58, 137
global civil society 29
  see also civil society actors
globalization 15, 18, 28, 188–9
  and electronic communication 5–6, 100–3
  and finance 75
  and loss of sovereignty 6–9
  of money 4–5
  of law 30
  and money laundering 5
  and private international governance 28–30
  see also governance, international
Golden Acres Ltd. v. Queensland Estates Ltd. 154
Goldman Sachs 49
Gordon, Colin 193
governance, international 10, 18–39, 185–9.
  see also world government, international organization
Graveson, R. H. 157
Great Depression 57–9, 66
Groom, A. J. R. 23, 24, 34, 35
Grotius, Hugo 193

Hague Conference on Private International Law 151
Hague Convention on Private International Law 166
Hamburg Bourse for Corn Traders 165
Hammersmith and Fulham Borough Council 44
Hanessian, Grant 177
Hardy, I. Trotter 112
harmonization of municipal law 19 34–7, 189–198
  of copyright laws 118–132

of money laundering laws 89–97
of municipal banking laws 76–79
'harmonization creep' 196
'harmonization spread' 16, 197
Harrison, R. J., and Stuart Mungall 37, 193, 195
Hart, H. L. A 168
Helleiner, Eric 42, 61, 65
Heraclides, Alexis 34, 35
Herrmann, Gerold 174
Highet, Keith 180
High Performance Computing Act 1991 (US) 100, 119
Hirst, Paul, and Grahame Thompson 63, 80
Hobsbawm, E. J. 53
homogenization 18
Honduras
and Debt Crisis 48
House Banking and Financial Services Committee on Organised Crime and Banking 85
Hull, Cordell 59
Hutton, Will 63

Impact 101, 114
India
and intellectual property 148
Information Infrastructure Task Force (IITF) 101
intellectual property rights 104–106
and copyright, problems for the Internet 106–114
international protection of 114–118
Intellectual Property Rights Working Group 121
Inter-American Commercial Arbitration Commission (IACAC) 175
Inter-American Convention on International Commercial Arbitration 1975 179
Inter-American Convention on the Law Applicable to International Contracts 1994 179
Interest Equalisation Tax 1964 (US) 61
International Air Transport Association 165
International Bank for Reconstruction and Development (IBRD, World Bank) 59
international banks 41
regulation and supervision of 11–2, 42–81
International Banking Act 1978 (IBA, US) 76
International-Banking Facilities (IBFs) 64
International Chamber of Commerce (ICC) 151, 165–6
ICC Model Law on International Commercial Arbitration 178
INCOTERMS 151, 165, 170, 183
ICC Rules for Conciliation and Arbitration 178
Uniform Customs and Practice for Documentary Credits 1983 (UCP) 165, 183
Internatinal Court of Justice 169
international currency trading 41
international governance *see* governance
International Institute for the Unification of Private Law (Unidroit) 151, 165, 166
International Law Association 151
International Maritime Committee 166
International Monetary Fund (IMF) 25, 59–61, 139–40
and 'dollar overhang' 60
Special Drawing Rights 61
International Organisation of Securities Commissions 88
International organizations 20, 23–26
International regimes 20
International Relations, discipline of 20, 25–7, 29–30, 194–5
Interpol 88
Iran–US Claims Tribunal 172, 175–8

Jaffey, A. J. E. 154
Japan 5

Kant, Immanuel 21, 22
Kelly, Edward 85
Kelsen, Hans 168
Kenney, Martin S. 96
Keohane, Robert 168
Keynes, John Maynard 24, 48, 60
Kindleberger, Charles 42
Knable Gotts, Ilene and Alan D. Rutenberg 108
Knapp, Judge 46
Krasner, Stephen 51
Kratchowil, Friedrick 168
Krieger, Andy 4

Laiffer, Daniel 87
Lamfalussy, Alexandre 49

Legal Advisory Board of the European Commission (LAB) 128
Lexis Council Connect 112
Lexis/Nexis 120
Lex Mercatoria 17–18, 161–83
  and arbitration 172–82
  autonomist perspective 161–4
  criticisms of 167–72
  positivist perspective 164–7
  and Iran-US Claims Tribunal 175–8
Liberalism 28, 31
Libyan Arab Foreign Bank (LAFB) 46
Libyan Arab Foreign Bank v. Bankers Trust Co. 46
Lipschutz, Ronnie D. 31
Lloyds Marine Insurance Policy 165
London Corn Trade Association 165
London Court of Arbitration (LCA) 166
London Economic Summit of 1931 59
Luxemburg, and BCCI 73, 141

Mangone, Gerard 21
Mansfield, Chief Justice 162
Maniruzzaman, A. F. M. 154, 159
Maritime Code of Wisby 161
Marshall, Don 64
Marshall Plan 60
Marx, Karl 18, 194
Mattingly, Virgil Jr. 77
McInerney III, Thomas F. 74, 135
McNair, Lord 169
Megrah, Maurice and Ryder, F. R. 92
Mexico 144
  and Debt Crisis 48
Meyer, Charles 117
Midland Bank
  and Debt Crisis 48
Millman, Gregory 42
Money laundering 12
  international control of 12–14, 85–89
  harmonization of municipal laws for the control of 89–99
  scope of 84–85
Money Laundering Act of 1986 (US) 14, 89
Money Laundering Suppression Act of 1994 (US) 14, 89, 144
Morgenthau, Hans 22
Morris, J. H. C. 158
Mustill, Lord Justice 163, 169, 171

Nabarro Nathanson 97
National Information Infrastructure (NII) 14, 100, 114, 119–127
National Information Infrastructure Task Force (NIITF) 121
Netherlands Arbitration Act 181
New Scotland Yard 88
New York Convention on the Recognition and Enforcement of Foreign Arbitral Awards (1958) 181
NII Copyright Protection Act of 1995 (US) 121–124
NII Working Group on Intellectual Property Rights 108, 111
Nixon, Richard 61
No Electronic Theft (NET) Act 1997 (US) 124
Nordwolle crisis 58
North American Free Trade Agreement (NAFTA) 138
North and Fawcett 157, 159
Northern Ireland (Emergency Provisions) Act of 1991 (UK) 90

O'Brien, Richard 5
Offshore financial centres (OFCs) 64
Ohmae, Kenichi 7
Omnibus Trade and Competitiveness Act 1988 (US) 147
On-Line Copyright Liability Limitation Act 1997 (US) 124, 126
Organization for Economic Cooperation and Development (OECD) 11, 104, 142
Organization of Petroleum Exporting Countries (OPEC) 62

Padoa-Schioppa, Tommaso, and Fabrizio Saccomanni 45, 50, 80
Panama 145
Parry-Jones v. Law Society 92
Pattison, John 50
Pearse, Richard 119
Peel's Bank Charter Act of 1844 (UK) 57
Permanent Court of International Justice 152
Peru 144, 145
  and Debt Crisis 48
Playboy v. Frena 110–111
private international trade law *see* conflict of laws
privatization 28
privatization of governance 13, 34
Prodigy 113

Proposal for a Directive on Copyright and Related Rights in the Information Society 1997 (EU) 129–131
Public international law 20
Public Lending Rights Act 1979 (UK) 120
Puchala, Donald 27

'Race' 101
Razzano, Frank C. 144
Reagan, Ronald 46
regulatory arbitrage 63
relativism 16
Religious Technology Center v. NETCOM 111
Report of the Review Committee on Banking Services (Jack Report, UK) 92
Ricardo, David 57
Rider, Barry 1, 87, 97, 141
Right to Financial Privacy Act (RFPA, UK) 93
Risks
 and civil society actors 3–6
 and international finance 42–51
Rolls of Oleron 161
Roosevelt, Theodore 58, 59
Rosenau, James 26
Rothschilds 3, 53, 54
Ruggie, John Gerrard 27
Ruigrok, Winfried 138
Rusch, Jonathan 94
Rutledge, G. Philip 93
R. v. International Trustee for the Protection of Bondholders Aktiengesellschaft 153, 156

Schmitthoff, Clive M. 158, 162, 164, 165, 166, 167, 172
Schwartz, Herman 55
Scientific Atlanta 101
Second Banking Directive 1989 (EU) 78
Second World War 24, 25
Securitization (political)
 and civil society actors 3–6
 see also risk
Sega Enterprises Ltd. v. MAPHIA 111
Serbian Loans 152
Serious Fraud Office 88
Shuman, Frederick 21
Silicon Graphics 101
Silk Association of America 165
Simai, Mihaly 25
Simonds, Lord 157
Singleton, Lord 156
Smith, Adam 56
Soros, George 4
Sovereignty 8, 32
Special Drawing Rights 61
Statute of Anne of 1710 (UK) 105
Statute of Monopolies 1623 (UK) 105
Statute of the Staples (UK) 162, 193
Strange, Susan 1, 7, 51
Streit, Clarence 21, 22
'Super 301' 147
Swiss Banking Act 146
Swiss Federal Banking Commission 144
Swiss National Bank 144
Swiss Penal Code 144
Switzerland
 and bank secrecy 144–6

Texaco Overseas Petroleum and California Asiatic Oil Company v. The Government of the Libyan Arab Republic 169
Thailand
 and bank secrecy 144
The Netherlands 16
 and Iran-US Claims Tribunal 181
Time-Warner 101
Tournier v. National Provincial and Union Bank of England 91
Trade-Related Aspects of Intellectual Property Rights (TRIPS) *see* World Trade Organization
Treaty of Rome 36

UNCITRAL Arbitration Rules 172, 174–6
Unfair Contract Terms Act 1977 (UK) 155
Uniform Customs and Practice for Documentary Credits (UCP, 1983) 165, 183
Uniform Rules for a Combined Transport Document (1975) 165
Uniform Rules of Conduct for Interchange of Trade Data by Teletransmission (1988) 165
United Nations (UN) 24, 82
United Nations Centre for International Trade Law (UNCITRAL) 151, 165, 166, 172–5
United Nations Centre for Transnational Corporations (UNCTC) 173
United Nations Conference on Trade and Development (UNCTAD) 147, 174

United Nations International Conference on Drug Abuse and Illicit Trafficking 85–6
United Nations (Vienna) Convention Against Illicit Traffic in Narcotic Drugs and Psychotropic Substances 86, 90
United States Treasury Financial Crimes Enforcement Network 95
United States v. Bank of New England 94
United States v. LaMacchia 108
Upjohn, J. 154
US Congress Office of Technology Assessment 6
US-Switzerland Treaty on Mutual Assistance 145
US Trade Act 1984 147
US–UK Treaty on Mutual Assistance in Criminal Matters 145
US v. Miller 93

Van Hof, Jacomin 178
Venezuela 144, 145
Vienna Convention on the Law of Treaties (1969) 169
Vienna Court of Appeal 182
Virilio, Paul 6
Vita Food Products Inc. v. Unus Shipping Co. 153

Wallerstein, Immanuel 5
Walter, Andrew 42, 45, 72
Waters, Malcolm 7
Wells Fargo Asia Ltd. v. Citibank 46
WestLaw 120
White, Harry Dexter 24, 59
Williams, Patrick Ross 159
Wilson, Woodrow 24
Windecker, Harry 47
WIPO Copyright Treaties Implementation Act 1997 (US) 124–5, 131
WIPO Copyright Treaty of 1996 115–7, 123
World Bank's International Centre for the Settlement of Investment Disputes (ICSID) 166, 169
World federalists 21, 22
World government 20, 21–3
World Intellectual Property Organisation (WIPO) 15, 115
World Trade Organisation 75, 136, 139, 149, 197
  Trade-Related Aspects of Intellectual Property Rights (TRIPS) 148–149
Wright, Lord 153, 154, 156
Wriston, Walter 49

Yeutter, Clayton 148
Yntema, Hessel E. 155

Zagaris, Bruce, and Scott B. MacDonald 84, 140
Zamora, Stephen 67, 72, 193

Made in the USA
Monee, IL
13 September 2026

62975581R00133